Cyberpunk Women, F
and Science Fict

Cyberpunk Women, Feminism and Science Fiction

A Critical Study

CARLEN LAVIGNE

McFarland & Company, Inc., Publishers

Jefferson, North Carolina, and London

LIBRARY OF CONGRESS CATALOGUING-IN-PUBLICATION DATA

Lavigne, Carlen, 1976–
    Cyberpunk women, feminism and science fiction :
a critical study / Carlen Lavigne.
        p.   cm.
    Includes bibliographical references and index.

    ISBN 978-0-7864-6653-5
    softcover : acid free paper ∞

    1. Science fiction — History and criticism.   2. Cyberpunk
culture.   3. Women in literature.   4. Science fiction — Women
authors — History and criticism.   5. Women authors —
Interviews.   6. Feminism and literature.   7. Literature and
technology.   8. Postmodernism (Literature).   I. Title.
PN3433.6.L38 2013
809.3'8762—dc23   2012049444

BRITISH LIBRARY CATALOGUING DATA ARE AVAILABLE

On the cover: cyber woman (Hemera/Thinkstock); background
(Photodisc/Thinkstock)

Manufactured in the United States of America

*McFarland & Company, Inc., Publishers
    Box 611, Jefferson, North Carolina 28640
        www.mcfarlandpub.com*

Acknowledgments

I owe thanks to a multitude, without whom this project would never have been realized. Will Straw and Ned Schantz at McGill University have granted me years of sage advice. Veronica Hollinger provided insightful and detailed comments on a draft of this work. Priscilla (Percy) Walton has been a constant source of guidance and goodwill. I am indebted to two anonymous peer reviewers whose feedback was a gracious mix of critical and supportive.

Thank you as well to the friendly authors who took the time to answer my questions: Edith Forbes, Kathleen Ann Goonan, Lisa Mason, Lyda Morehouse, and Melissa Scott.

At Red Deer College, I am grateful for funding from the RDC professional development committee, and for the organizational and moral support provided by Kathy Pallister, Jane MacNeil, and Torben Andersen. I have talked science fiction with Nancy Batty and commiserated with Stéphane Perreault. Heather Marcovitch alternately encourages and endures my shenanigans; both approaches speak to her stellar character.

Erica Pereira and Gwen Larouche Milks have been proofreaders or cheerleaders, as needed, at various stages of this manuscript; I appreciate every minute. I am grateful as well for the continued tolerance of José Pou, Andrea and Dave Principe, Mike Prince, Matt Webber, Andrea Fox, Diana Knapton, Teresa Campbell, and all the other friends and colleagues who make life worthwhile.

I have also spent so much time working from the couches at Red Deer's Café Vero that I promised to thank the kind baristas: Melanie, Jessica, Mackenzie and Jenny. (They know me mainly as "Nonfat Mocha with Dark Roast.")

My nieces, Elsa and Mila, are too young to be thanked, but I hope that when they get older they will like seeing their names in this book.

Finally, I would be nowhere without the staunch support of my parents, Jim and Elizabeth Lavigne. Not only has their faith in me been unshakeable, and their encouragement unflagging, they once packed up my entire apartment so that I would be able to finish my Ph.D. on time. I haven't forgotten.

Table of Contents

Preface

The science fiction subgenre known as cyberpunk was exemplified by mirrored sunglasses, black leather, and computer head chips; its most celebrated author, William Gibson, is famed both for his Hugo Award–winning novel *Neuromancer* (1984) and for first coining the term "cyberspace" — a word that infiltrates our every discussion of today's Internet. Marked by noir-style narratives, techno-dystopian futures, and the sleek computerized aesthetic of the digital age, 1980s cyberpunk was credited with revolutionizing science fiction and having a real impact on the development of the "real world" technologies and software programs that were subsequently created by its tech-savvy fans.

But cyberpunk was also criticized for being misogynist and classist; its virtual realities and digital escapism represented a white, middle-class, heterosexual and very male perspective. It wasn't until after the genre was declared dead, and academic and media attention had moved elsewhere, that women really began writing within its boundaries. These critically neglected feminist works — novels and stories by authors such as Melissa Scott, Marge Piercy, Lyda Morehouse, Laura Mixon, Edith Forbes, Kathleen Ann Goonan, Lisa Mason, Sage Walker, Raphael Carter and Amy Thomson — are interrogated within this study. This book complements the many other academic works that have focused either on cyberpunk or on women's science fiction; it attempts to conflate these two fields, thus filling an important gap by examining women's cyberpunk and cyberfiction as a distinct textual wave.

Women's cyberpunk is positioned herein as part of a larger cultural discussion of feminist issues. Accessibility was a key concern; I have tried to provide key definitions and other background information that will be of use to students and non-academic readers. At the same time, I have provided detailed readings of some lesser-known science fiction texts; as these works have only infrequently been studied, I hope my examinations will also be useful to more advanced scholars in the field. My research traces the origins of the cyberpunk genre, reviews critical reactions, and outlines the ways in which women's cyberpunk advances specifically feminist points of view. Novels are examined within their cultural contexts; their content is compared to broader controversies within contemporary feminism, and their themes are revealed as reflections of feminist discourse at the turn of the twenty-first century. Chapters cover such diverse topics as globalization, virtual reality, cyborg culture, environmentalism, religion, motherhood, and queer rights. First-hand interviews are also performed with feminist cyberpunk authors, in order to examine both their experiences with fans and their motivations for writing. This book treats feminist cyberpunk as a unique vehicle for examining contemporary women's issues, and analyzes feminist science fiction as a complex source of political ideas.

Introduction

In the twenty-first century, cyberpunk has become a cliché. "Hacker" is a mainstream term; virtual realities are a common experience. Anyone who has played a recent video game knows what it's like to take the form of an avatar and conquer unknown digital territory; anyone who has picked up a newspaper (or, more likely, surfed a news website) knows that wars are being waged in cyberspace (and what cyberspace is). We have no need to imagine what would happen if rogue hackers took arms against governments or corporations; the 2010 WikiLeaks scandal made both scenarios real. Thousands of pages of leaked U.S. government secrets were posted online; international diplomatic relations were in an uproar; the White House leveraged all its influence to shut WikiLeaks down; and the site's content was shunted frantically from one server to the next as its supporters waged cyberattacks against MasterCard, Visa, Swiss banks, Sarah Palin, Amazon, and other presumed opponents (Satter and Lawless; Swaine; MacAskill and Halliday). We all know the web is important — and dangerous. The Internet has become something we cannot live without, but viruses, identity thieves, stalkers, and phishers concern even the most casual user.

But in the early 1980s, these scenarios were still firmly in the realm of science fiction; "cyberspace" was still a term in the mind of author William Gibson, while Neal Stephenson had yet to popularize the notion of "avatars." Films like *Blade Runner* (1982), *The Terminator* (1984), and *The Running Man* (1987) were just beginning to explore the dystopian techno-aesthetic that would later be regurgitated and revitalized by 1999's *The Matrix.* Authors like Gibson, Bruce Sterling, Pat Cadigan, Vernor Vinge, Rudy Rucker, and Greg Bear published novels that both created and popularized the idea of the lone hacker hero, his (almost always male) body rife with implants, his mind "jacked in" to a new digital web where anything was possible. Known as "cyberpunk," this newly created science fiction subgenre reflected both man's existential crisis in the information age, and his wary excitement at the possibilities of a new computerized world; it was both lauded as the quintessential example of postmodern narrative and derided as a vehicle for adolescent male power fantasies. In the 1980s and early 1990s, it caused a flurry of debate regarding issues of technology, postmodernism and identity, and it was at least partly responsible for revitalizing academic interest in science fiction.

Cyberpunk is also an excellent site for a study based in gender. Its first wave, written primarily in the 1980s, was almost exclusively the domain of male writers such as Gibson, Sterling, and Rucker. The 1990s subsequently produced a broad range of works by women such as Marge Piercy, Lisa Mason, Melissa Scott and Lyda Morehouse — women whose work was similarly defined by the digital age, while also focusing on more "feminine" issues such as gender, motherhood, ecology, religion and community. Throughout this book, terms such as "women's cyberpunk" and "feminist cyberpunk" are used interchangeably to indicate a subgenre within a subgenre, a portion of science fiction identifiable both as early cyberpunk's descendant, and as a series of works created within its own feminist paradigm. It is impossible to situate women's cyberpunk as a single, definitively monolithic discourse; my explorations also reveal that these works are richly diverse, and reflect complex tensions in contemporary feminism. Nor is it my position that all women authors are feminist authors; rather, I argue that feminist themes within women's cyberpunk may also spring naturally from common social experiences related to woman's place in Western society. In his study of women's science fiction, Brooks Landon focuses on "writers and works that, while not necessarily 'feminist' in any rigorous sense, have opposed or modified the genre's heavily masculinist tendencies" (*Science Fiction* 125); my approach is much the same. Women authors are writing from marginalized social positions, and this inescapably marks their work. While early cyberpunk is predominantly acknowledged as white male, heterosexual, and middle-class in its scope, and mainly appreciated for its postmodern treatment of contemporary technology and identity issues, women's cyberpunk delves into more varied questions. By reconfiguring the conventions of a genre often criticized as misogynist, women have re-created cyberpunk as a medium for feminist political voices; their works may be read as acts of participation in contemporary feminist discourse. By analyzing women's cyberpunk and cyberfiction in relation to science fiction, technology, and women's issues in the latter part of the 20th century, I intend to demonstrate how a subgenre of science fiction may be read as part of a broader social dialogue, and as a forum in which writers have approached feminist topics with a rich degree of imagination.

In its original conception, this was meant to be a study of cyberpunk's influence on today's Internet technologies and cultures; during the course of my research, several things became obvious that redirected my focus. With the exception of Pat Cadigan, the original cyberpunk authors were almost uniformly white, middle-class men; it did not take long for me to begin wondering about women's voices, and whether they might have had any similar impact on new technologies, or whether cyberpunk could provide a forum for women, too, to present philosophies regarding globalization and postmodern identity. What became obvious in reading cyberpunk works from the 1990s was that women writers had significantly altered the genre in order to accommodate feminist ideas — and that the same themes were cropping up again and again. Much as the original cyberpunk works were a loose cluster of novels connected by their similar approaches to issues of alienation and postmodern identity, these next-generation works were a diverse array of texts that nevertheless managed to share similar approaches to issues such as environmentalism, reproduction, and family — in addition to putting new spins on old cyberpunk themes.

Of course, the question of "generations" in cyberpunk can be difficult; as Landon, again, has said, "discussion of waves or swings must remind us of the futility of attempting a static description of science fiction in the twentieth century" (*Science Fiction* 154). My own investigation, primarily contrasting masculinist novels from *True Names* (1981) to *Snow Crash* (1992) with feminist works from *Arachne* (1990) to *Messiah Node* (2003), treats the feminist wave of cyberpunk and cyberfiction as a second generation to the cyberpunk movement — an analysis that is distinct from some other worthy arguments. Thomas Foster is already talking about third generations (*Souls* 86), and Landon has defined *Snow Crash* as a second-generation novel that wears its "cyberpunk ancestry" proudly (*Science Fiction* 154). My approach dovetails more with those of Karen Cadora and E.L. McCallum — Cadora, who in 1995 first defined "feminist cyberpunk" as the first wave's successor, and McCallum, who compares Cadigan's work to *Neuromancer, Islands in the Net,* and *Snow Crash* in the same breath (369). The boundaries of cyberpunk are blurry at best, but the next several chapters should clarify my argument, including *Snow Crash*'s placement as a novel that both exemplifies the major traits of the cyberpunk genre and hints at the feminist ideas that were already springing to life within other texts.

Additionally, the precise criteria used to define cyberpunk have a direct impact on whether or not one can interpret the genre as feminist (Merrick 191); the works I have included as part of the feminist wave range in focus and style from Melissa Scott's *Trouble and Her Friends* to Kathleen Ann Goonan's *Queen City Jazz.* They are admittedly diverse, but no more so than the eclectic mix of short stories found in the cyberpunk anthology *Mirrorshades* (a collection that includes both Greg Bear's "Petra," about a living gargoyle in a postapocalyptic church, and William Gibson's "The Gernsback Continuum," about a twentieth-century photographer who keeps seeing 1920s-era images of "the future"). Any 1990s story that meticulously incorporated every one of cyberpunk's neon, tech-head tropes would be "an instant cliché" (Kelly and Kessel ix); instead, what I define as feminist cyberpunk are women's novels and short stories that show evidence of cyberpunk influence while simultaneously changing the paradigm — works that added a feminist slant to cyberpunk's themes of globalization, capitalism, embodiment and identity, while at the same time dealing with newly voiced concerns such as ecology, feminism, religion and queer rights. These texts have, for the most part, been omitted from studies of the genre; in straying too far from cyberpunk's strict formulas, some have been more commonly defined (and excluded) as "cyberfiction." I feel this is overly limiting; these works extended and modified cyberpunk structures to give feminist twists to old themes, and introduce entirely new ideas. It may be that their dismissal from the movement's main body of work is one of the reasons for their academic neglect.

In short, which works are cyberpunk, and which cyberfiction? Fifty academics may offer fifty different answers. I am less interested in dividing lines than unions. In pursuing examples of cyberpunk's feminist generation, I have sought out speculative, near-future science fiction by women — science fiction that is directly concerned with new technologies and the information age, and takes place within settings clearly influenced by cyberpunk ideas. I have looked for — and found — congruences between these works, which, like the first cyberpunk wave, are loosely affiliated around a series of similar notions. I have also included Raphael Carter's novel *Fortunate Fall,* making Carter — who eschews gender identification — the one exception to my definition of "women's cyberpunk," much in the same way that Joanna Russ included Samuel Delany in her own discussion of feminist science fiction (134). Carter, who is also included in Thomas Foster's analyses of feminist and lesbian science fiction authors (*Souls* xxi), simply fits too well within these discussions to have been excluded, although the unique gender of the author — defined as neither male nor female — must be acknowledged. Obviously my categories are not carved in stone; I set out to look for new ideas and commonalities, with the hope that my thoughts will provide material for further exploration. Cyberpunk from any generation is difficult to pin down, but close examination reveals several definite threads running through what are, on the surface, quite varied writings; in the case of women's cyberpunk, these threads reflect many primary feminist concerns at the turn of the twenty-first century.

The study begins by offering a history and definition of cyberpunk in general, in order to give proper background and context for discussions of the genre's evolution. Ensuing chapters include an analysis of Pat Cadigan's work as it pertains to later feminist novels, and an analysis of women's work both in terms of alterations made to original cyberpunk themes and settings, and in terms of new ideas found only within feminist cyberpunk. Chapters 3 to 9 discuss how women have adapted the original cyberpunk tropes to accommodate themes that match concurrent changes in feminist politics, and the significance of their texts within a larger cultural discussion regarding issues such as women and technology, ecology, and spirituality. I examine how feminist treatments have been given to standard cyberpunk tropes of capitalist globalization, virtual reality, and artificial intelligence, thus placing women's work under the cyberpunk label and illustrating the differences in how the genre was treated by the two waves. Subsequently, I analyze how women have modified cyberpunk's less frequently noted treatments of environmentalism and mythology, and newly introduced themes such as reproductive technologies and queer rights. Finally, the cultural impact of first-wave cyberpunk — its influence on hackers, programmers, and the formation of today's communications technologies — is compared to the impact of women's cyberpunk, which uses similar genre conventions but occupies an entirely different niche, conveying its discussions of contemporary feminist issues to a smaller but more disparate audience.

In his 1991 essay "Inside the Movement," Lewis Shiner wrote: "The novel must face the future. I'm not talking here about a sci-fiberpunk novel that offers escape into techno-macho insensitivity. I'm talking about a novel that presents new paradigms, works against prejudice and limited worldviews" (25). This literature exists, or at least has made a vigorous attempt at existing, in the form of works by women (and Carter). Feminist cyberpunk has been less successful commercially, but more successful in terms of presenting new ideas and challenging the patriarchal status quo. As this study will show, authors such as Marge Piercy, Melissa Scott and Kathleen Ann Goonan have indeed used the cyberpunk mythos to work against prejudice and limited worldviews; they have expanded the genre far beyond its original tenets.

— CHAPTER 1—

The Movement:
Signs and Signifiers

The term "cyberpunk" was originally popularized in a 1985 *Washington Post* article by Gardner Dozois, who borrowed the term from the title of Bruce Bethke's 1983 short story (Dery 75). In Dozois's definition, "cyberpunk" referred to work by authors like William Gibson and Bruce Sterling, who were writing stories about isolated hacker heroes fighting against faceless international megacorporations in a gritty, high-tech near-future. Science fiction publishers embraced the word as a convenient sales tool, and Sterling himself enthusiastically espoused it in 1986 by editing the "cyberpunk reader" *Mirrorshades*. However, Gibson, the crown prince of the cyberpunk movement, has acknowledged that the term "is mainly a marketing strategy—and one that I've come to feel trivializes what I do" (McCaffery interview 279). It is ironic that a genre movement claiming to deride the alienating nature of capitalism was partly defined by the capitalist needs of its publishers; cyberpunk's borders and affiliations have always been indistinct. It is a multi-faceted subgenre of science fiction that has evolved and fragmented since its inception, leading to a host of different definitions. Paul Alkon links it to realism, the Gothic, epic marvels, pulp fiction and film noir (75–76); E.L. McCallum cites it as a continuation of the adventure/travel tale (349); Lewis Shiner traces it back to western pulp heroes (23); and Gary Westfahl and Carol McGuirk both argue that cyberpunk is instead a logical continuation of a lengthy science fiction tradition (Westfahl 88; McGuirk 109). The precise moment of the genre's coalition is equally difficult to pinpoint: Larry McCaffery, for example, traces the works influencing cyberpunk all the way back to Mary Shelley's *Frankenstein*; Sterling gives credit to writers as varied as H.G. Wells and Thomas Pynchon; and a great many critics mention cyberpunk's pastiche of pulp/noir/Western styles.

Certainly the movement's themes as a whole emerged, not as a result of one particular writer — though Gibson is the most famous — but almost simultaneously among the works of several writers, including John Shirley, Vernor Vinge, Lewis Shiner, and Rudy Rucker.[1] Having acknowledged this, the simplest starting point is the publication of Gibson's *Neuromancer* in 1984; although it was not the first cyberpunk work to see print, Gibson's novel garnered significant critical attention and encouraged the crystallization — whether publicist-motivated or otherwise — of cyberpunk as a whole. Marked by a hard-edged narrative style, a technological world set in chrome and neon, and a science fiction future solidly based in the social concerns of the present, *Neuromancer* was the flagship for cyberpunk works published in the 1980s and beyond. Gibson, Sterling and their counterparts fleshed out the genre's pattern and defined what they called "the Movement," an attempt to revitalize what they saw as ailing and outmoded science fiction conventions. Cyberpunk's structures, derivative in nature but unique in final form, produced an exploration of capitalism, technology and the human condition that appealed to science fiction fans and even some mainstream audiences. *Neuromancer* won major science fiction awards (the Hugo, Philip K. Dick Memorial, Nebula, Seiun, and Ditmar awards)[2] and has spawned several editions, a computer game, a graphic novel, an audio book, and continued rumors of film production (Leiren-Young). Cyberpunk author Bruce Sterling argued in his 1986 introduction to *Mirrorshades* that cyberpunk's appeal lay in its reflection of larger social undercurrents:

> Technical culture has gotten out of hand. The advances of the sciences are so deeply radical, so disturbing, upsetting and revolutionary, that they can no longer be contained. They are surging into culture at large; they are invasive; they are everywhere. The traditional power structure, the traditional institutions, have lost control of the pace of change.
>
> And suddenly a new alliance is becoming evident: an integration of technology and the 1980s counterculture. An unholy alliance of the technical world and the world of organized dissent — the underground world of pop culture, visionary fluidity, and street-level anarchy [345].

According to Sterling, cyberpunk's commercial success during the 1980s could be credited to the fact that it both revolutionized science fiction and keenly reflected the voice of the age in which it was written. He was not the only science fiction author to feel that the genre's appeal lay in its address of key contemporary social issues; Pat Cadigan has written, "Popular culture in general is a reflection, warts and all, of what's going on in society. That goes double for science fiction; maybe even triple" (*Ultimate Cyberpunk* x). Timothy Leary was no less effusive, saying of cyberpunk authors:

Every stage of history has produced a name and a heroic legend for the strong, stubborn, creative individual who explores some future frontier, collects and brings back new information, and offers to guide the gene pool to the next stage. Typically, the time-maverick combines bravery with high curiosity, with super-self-esteem. These three talents are considered necessary for those engaged in the profession of genetic guide, a.k.a. philosopher [245].

Not everyone has agreed with this enthusiastic appraisal, however. Paul Alkon suggests that it was the familiarity of cyberpunk's derivations that resounded with the public, stating that Gibson "offers the comfort of pulp literature's happy endings" (76); Kevin Robins feels that the cyberpunk genre offered magical "fantasies of creative mastery" (143) to an audience suffering a postmodern crisis of identity; and author Lewis Shiner, enthusiastic about the genre's beginnings, bemoaned the formulaic literature that later emerged: "The console cowboy is a direct linear descendant of the western pulp heroes. His is an adolescent male fantasy to ride unfettered on the consensual range of the matrix, to shoot it out with the bad guys, and finally to head his chrome horse off into a sunset the color of a dead television channel" (23). According to one argument, then, the genre's revolutionary style and timely themes offered a fresh new science fiction that spoke plainly about technological issues in contemporary society. The counter-position asserts that cyberpunk's liberal borrowing from past successful genres allowed it to succeed through a shallow reliance on the familiar and an appeal to simplistic power fantasies. It is likely that the truth lies somewhere in between: cyberpunk in the 1980s was a new and timely twist on several tried and true formats, both structured by convention and seeking to explore new ideas in a world of globalized communication and personal computing.

Cyberpunk stories are set in a future where globalization and capitalism have led to the rule of multinational conglomerates, while marginalized individuals live in a post-industrial setting defined by cold metal technology, virtual reality, and crime. Unlike some other varieties of science fiction, cyberpunk features no aliens, very few foreign planets, and no intergalactic space battles; few aspects of the cyberpunk environment cannot be, at least theoretically, traced back to our late twentieth-century world. Authors in the genre were among the first to explore a then-strange new world of personal computing, information economy, electronic identity, and global networking; their futuristic settings contain imaginative technological and societal extrapolations, presented in a grittily pragmatic manner that provides a vibrant commentary, not on the future, but rather on the society in which the work was written. Cyberpunk deals with contemporary issues within a narrative structure that allows for dramatic extremes; it possesses an exploratory ability to tease ideas to their theoretical conclusions in a manner that might be difficult to achieve in more realist mainstream fiction. High adventure combines with a critical cultural voice to create a genre paradigm that is both conventionally exciting and potentially insightful.

Tropes: Corporations and Crime

In 1992, breaking down the specifics of cyberpunk, Frances Bonner described the "four Cs" of the genre; two of these were corporations and crime (191). Indeed, early cyberpunk frequently depicts a future ruled by capitalist multinationals, and a post-industrial society in which information serves as the most valuable trading commodity. Bonner aptly notes that cyberpunk elements of corporations and crime are often blended together; any crime in the cyberpunk world tends to be directed against corporations, as the multinationals are often the only remaining law. The corporate/crime syndicates serve as commentaries on the ultimate effects of global capitalism, and are also excellent tools for illustrating the marginalization (and glorification) of the individual protagonist, who for the most part tends to be an outlaw hacker living on the fringes of society. This illustration of marginalized class anger in cyberpunk's "sympathy with the attitudes of a dominated and alienated subculture"—in essence, the "punk" element of the story—may be what first configured the genre as new and exciting, rather than any pretensions toward insights into actual technology and its consequences (Huntington 141). The inevitably corrupt state of the multinational powers is a prevalent part of the cyberpunk setting; the protagonist's crime, perpetrated against vast and faceless corporate entities, is reconfigured as a hero's journey of rebellion.

Cyberpunk is thus closely associated with North American economic and labor concerns of the 1980s; its citizens, devalued as interchangeable and easily replaceable assets within corporate society, are worth exactly as much as the secrets they possess. Gibson's smuggler in "Johnny Mnemonic" (1981, reprinted 1986 in *Burning Chrome*) epitomizes this trend, trading solely in information and transporting sensitive client files inside the cybernetic data system in his head. Terence Whalen, in describing "mirror-shaded writers from a hi-tech counterculture who put a hard dystopian spin on the post-industrial age without ever disputing its ascendance" (76), situates cyberpunk in the context of "Reagan's America" and notes that the genre was both informed and "haunted" by the wider social context of capitalism in the information age: "the suspicion that information is not merely the socially average form of knowledge, but rather the form taken by capital in the signifying environment" (79). Cyberpunk's relation to capitalism and the exchange of information as currency — particularly within the context of globalization, multinationalism, and individual alienation — suggests the potential for speculative truths to be mined from the realm of its unapologetically post-industrial narratives. Nickianne Moody has theorized the rebellion of the outcast hero within uber-capitalist cyberpunk settings as an ideal tool for illustrating societal fears "concerning the social organization of work under the speculative conditions of postindustrial corporate capitalism" (92); in this reading, cyberpunk serves as an expression of uncertainty regarding humanity's place in a new world of electronic labor. Ultimately, the "corporations" and "crime" within cyberpunk are combined, and the result utilized both to promote the individual over the masses, and provide a dramatized commentary on the societal implications of the capitalist economic system.

Tropes: Computers and Corporeality

Bonner's next two cyberpunk "C"s were computers and corporeality (191); these tropes are also frequently combined. Cyberpunk settings are relentlessly technological, often occurring post-environmental disaster; there are very few trees in the world of the mirrorshades, and nature is inescapably marked by machine. As the famous first line of *Neuromancer* states, "The sky above the port was the color of television, tuned to a dead channel." Although most cyberpunk technology is based on modern developments, the precise accuracy of the technological predictions themselves is not as important as the themes these technologies are used to explore; science fiction is thus "less a prediction than a rendering of somebody's possibilities of hope" (Huntington 134). Deborah Lupton has written on the unique cultural meanings surrounding personal computers in contemporary society, observing in 1995 that computers "constitute sites that are redolent with cultural anxieties around the nature of humanity and the self" (108). Cyberpunk from the 1980s onward uses computers and corporeality to explore the same anxieties that Lupton details, reflecting contemporary cultural concerns about technology, the breakdown of community and the alienation of the self.

The genre also uses artificial intelligence and cyborg concepts to explore posthuman possibilities, calling the nature of humanity into question by positing hardware and software characters with their own claims to thought and feeling, and a disconcerting ability to mimic human mannerisms. The virtual Librarian in Neal Stephenson's *Snow Crash* (1992) frequently notes that he (never referred to as "it") is not human, while at the same time exhibiting the same cognitive abilities that he claims not to possess. In *Neuromancer*, artificial intelligences possess citizenship; in Rudy Rucker's *Software* (1982), they stage a revolution of emancipation. More frequently, human characters may be "copied" by computer, such as the Dixie Flatline in *Neuromancer*, or Cobb Anderson in *Software*. This exploration of the Cartesian mind/body dichotomy is a central theme of cyberpunk, and the area where "computers" and "corporeality" begin to blend. Human characters become indistinguishable from machines, or are simply divested of their "meat" as they project themselves into virtual reality worlds; cyberpunk narratives often seek to separate mind from body in a quest for a utopian cyberspace environment that is under the hacker hero's control. Scott Bukatman has explored the implications of cyberspace imagery, stating, "Such ontological and epistemological issues as the nature of the human, the real, experience, sensation, cognition, identity and gender are all placed, if not under erasure, then certainly in question around the discursive object of virtual reality and the postulated existence of perfect, simulated environments" (150). These blends of computers and corporeality in cyberpunk — achieved through depictions of humanity navigating virtual reality environments, or through portrayals of cyborg characters — have attracted much critical attention.

In fact, "cyborg" might be postulated as a fifth "C." Characters whose bodies have been physically modified by technology — either with computer-interface implants, weaponry, or prosthetics — are a notable cyberpunk trope, and lend themselves easily to examinations of identity and human nature. In her 1995 discussion of contemporary cyborg cinema, for example, Samantha Holland states that cyborg film "uses images of the technological body to investigate questions of 'self'-hood, gender, the 'mind-body problem' and the threats posed to such concepts by postmodern technology and AI (artificial intelligence)" (157). Admittedly, questions regarding the nature of consciousness and mental stability, as well as the limits of the body, are not unique to cyberpunk; Francisco Collado Rodriguez has also related them to mythologies of vampires, werewolves, and serial killers. However, he goes on to note that cyborg subjects offer an ideal site from which to pursue these themes; the biotechnological hybridity of cyborg images is both alluring and revolting for audiences confronted with the possibility of a postmodern, posthuman existence that suggests "the instability of the self, a motif that problematizes a previous one: the importance of the individual" (70). If corporations and crime are used to expand on capitalist economics and the marginalization of the individual, computers and corporeality are used to question the individual's basic nature with regard to concepts of "humanity" and structures of identity.

Cyberpunk and Postmodernism

Fredric Jameson has linked cyberpunk to both capitalism and postmodernism; he situates the genre as the potential "supreme literary expression" of either paradigm ("Postmodernism" 157). Cyberpunk has been closely associated with postmodern theory, particularly Jean Baudrillard's arguments regarding simulacra, simulation and hyperreality. In *Simulacra and Simulation,* Baudrillard describes the postmodern "desert of the real," and the sense of social and cultural alienation created by environments in which all perception is mediated by technology and copies cannot reliably be distinguished from (or do not have) originals — a theory easily related to a contemporary Western world in which we cannot tell whether digital photos have been altered, whether news broadcasts are really "live," or whether special effects are computer-generated. Cyberpunk's "virtual realities," in which users can assume any identity and artificial intelligences may masquerade as human subjects, take these digital simulations to extremes; Larry McCaffery explicitly links Baudrillard to cyberpunk, arguing that since technological changes were most responsible for this new postmodern condition, "those artists who have been most in touch with these changes, intuitively as well as intellectually, have relied on themes and aesthetic modes previously associated with [science fiction]" (3). Less effusively, Jenny Wolmark concedes in her study of postmodernism and feminist SF that while she finds cyberpunk to have been less revolutionary than advertised, "it nevertheless appears to represent science fiction's most vigorous response to the kinds of organizational and technological transformations in production and consumption that are characteristic of post-industrial, postmodern societies" (110). If a contemporary Western postmodernism is, in part, the result of new manufacturing and communications technologies, these approaches suggest that the speculative science fiction examining the potential impact of these technologies is surely an important piece of the cultural conversation.

Indeed, Baudrillard's theory of simulacra and simulation — a world of copies without originals, and an increasingly fast-paced society steadily distancing itself from "natural" reality — has continued to fit extraordinarily well with cyberpunk's concepts of virtual reality and the cyberspace matrix. This critical association has held into the twenty-first century; small wonder that Neo, the hacker hero of the 1999 film *The Matrix*, keeps his illegal software disks in a hollowed-out copy of *Simulacra and Simulation*. Nigel Clark cites Marshall McLuhan's "rear-view mirrorism," suggesting that we tend to judge the present by the paradigms or standards of the preceding age, in advancing his theory that cyberpunk's virtual realities and questionable corporealities arise from "the transition from one generation of mediated effects to another" ("Rear-view" 126); cyberpunk may thus span the gap between modern and postmodern, or human and posthuman, existence. Certainly, cyberpunk is notable for its unselfconscious derivativeness; Barnett, citing *The Matrix* as a pastiche of pop culture references and genre conventions, postulates "America's love affair with the postmodern aesthetic" (362), and notes, "Postmodern culture has not only conceded and accepted that tropes are recycled, it celebrates the fact and sings about it" (363). This link between the pastiche of cyberpunk style and postmodern questions of identity and originality positions the genre as a symbolic bridge between old and new technological worlds.

Cyberpunk and the Cultural Zeitgeist

Cyberpunk has additionally proven critically engaging due to its impact on science fiction, and due to what its themes can imply about science fiction's relation to wider cultural contexts. As Sterling claimed in 1986, cyberpunk was a potential game-changer, revamping the stylistics of science fiction even as it borrowed shamelessly from countless other sources. Stephen Brown writes, "The future was beginning to collect like dustballs in the corners and interstices of every home, every office, every street corner. It wasn't the lean, clean linear future of the mainstream science fiction writers, it was messy, disorganized, crowded and clamoring. It needed a new kind of fiction to describe it, dense, complex, jammed-to-the-gills fiction" (176). Cyberpunk was a concerted attempt by fiction writers to address the future facing the citizens of the 1980s — not the hopeful "food pills and flying cars" future projected by the science fiction of the 1920s, or the post-nuclear-holocaust future suggested by the Cold War, but a future based on personal computers and global communications systems.

In Brown's reading, cyberpunk authors "picked up bits and pieces of what was actually coming true, and fed it back to the readers who were already living in Gibson's Sprawl, whether they knew it or not" (177). Likewise, Gibson himself has said, "When I write about technology, I write about how it has *already* affected our lives; I don't extrapolate in the way I was taught an SF writer should" (McCaffery interview 274, original emphasis). Cyberpunk's relation to its origins was immediate and specific — basing its futuristic tech on actual inventions, while at the same time coasting on a scientific vagueness that left plausibility in the realm of the imagination and concentrated on social impact rather than hard schematics.

E.L. McCallum speaks of the genre as a barometer of our relationship to new technologies, stating that cyberpunk replaced science fiction's traditional exploration of the stars with databases and network spaces, availing itself "of innovations in technology, imaginary or actual, in order to play out in fiction the consequences of these innovations" (350). Similarly, P. Chad Barnett argues that cyberpunk is "the most likely source for answers to questions regarding the machine-human dynamic in multinational society" (360). Such statements position cyberpunk as a direct reflection of the human condition in the digital age.

Conversely, and despite its potential for such sociocultural explorations, cyberpunk has also been viewed with suspicion; Kevin Robins interprets fictional concepts of cyberspace as foolishly utopian, depicting man as God and demonstrating a concerted blindness to the difficulties of the modern world. He dismisses cyberpunk fantasies as both asocial and amoral: "The mythology of cyberspace is preferred over its sociology.... We must de-mythologize virtual culture if we are to assess the serious implications it has for our personal and collective lives" (153). In deriding what he sees as the overly — indeed, blindly — optimistic nature of the cyberpunk vision, he exhibits grave reservations as to cyberpunk's impact. Ellen Strain has expressed similar reservations; while she doesn't object to the study of the science-fiction hero as a metaphor for the postmodern condition, she suggests that theories regarding fictional virtual realities have threatened to obscure real-world cyberspaces and their implications (10). Cyberpunk, in other words, may unnecessarily or unfairly romanticize (and thus obscure) the sociocultural impacts of contemporary scientific developments.

Ultimately, of course, it must be acknowledged that cyberpunk failed to live up to the full potential of its revolutionary hype. This is evident within broader studies of science fiction history; Landon asserts that the amount of critical attention granted to cyberpunk has been "disproportionate," suggesting that the genre's "appealing sense of unity" has made it a more attractive research target than less easily categorized (but perhaps more deserving) works (*Science Fiction* 161). In advancing the works of Octavia Butler, Kim Stanley

Robinson, and Orson Scott Card (among others) as being perhaps more worthy of consideration, he notes:

> Born in controversy and hype, cyberpunk mutated into respectability and influence, becoming both more and less than anyone could have imagined: more as an emblem of a cultural convergence that completely outstripped the traditional boundaries of SF and of literature itself, less as a wave within SF that rocked a lot of boats and wrecked its share of coastline but which finally was just a wave, and not, as some expected and others claimed, a whole new kind of ocean [166].

Likewise, Roger Luckhurst has drawn away from the analytical tools of postmodern theory in order to place cyberpunk more securely within the ideological context of the 1980s Star Wars program, the growth of American military technology, and the threat of space militarization, noting "the prominence of the SF megatext in the fantasy life of the American New Right" (202); moreover, he views the genre's frequent use of Japanese iconography as reflecting "another aspect of 1980s hypercapitalism," the mark of an American decade in which the specter of Japanese economic dominance loomed large (207). He, too, relates Gibson in particular to hard-boiled detective fiction, gothic drama, and earlier science fiction (210–211); in such analyses, cyberpunk remains an interesting reflection of its time, but is also a predictable product of socioeconomic factors rather than a prodigious philosophical breakout.

Conclusion

While Bonner's definition (corporations, crime, computers, and corporeality) is necessarily simplistic, it also provides the framework for the main structural components of cyberpunk. Conversely, it might similarly be considered to outline the framework for subsequent publications that Lewis Shiner came to deride as flat "sci-fiberpunk" imitations of the original creative works: "Within science fiction [cyberpunk] evokes a very restricted formula; to wit, novels about monolithic corporations opposed by violent, leather-clad drug users with wetware implants" (17). Shiner asserts that cyberpunk was supposed to be more than black leather and head chips; the Movement, he claims, was about making science fiction modern and real, rock and roll. With such a difficult revolutionary spirit to live up to — the same spirit Bruce Sterling proselytized in his introduction to *Mirrorshades* (1986) — perhaps it's no wonder that the storm of enthusiasm that surrounded cyberpunk was short-lived.

The original literature and academic reactions were "summed up" in anthologies such as *Storming the Reality Studio* (McCaffery, 1991), *Fiction 2000: Cyberpunk and the Future of Narrative* (Slusser and Shippey, 1992), and *Cyberspace/Cyberbodies/Cyberpunk* (Featherstone and Burrows, 1995). Explorations of cyberpunk's implications have since slowed, although they are still ongoing; Graham J. Murphy and Sherryl Vint's *Beyond Cyberpunk: New Critical Perspectives* (2010) demonstrates that some critical interest in the genre has continued well into the twenty-first century.

Much has been made of cyberpunk-as-counterculture — of the rebellion of the individual against mass production and globalization, of the rebellion of science fiction writers against the clean, wondrous future posited in early pulp magazines (and first advocated by Hugo Gernsback in *Amazing Stories* [1926]), and of the rebellion of human against robot or robot against human. Cyberpunk itself tends to be ambiguous with regard to new technologies and their impacts; neither explicitly for nor against such developments, the genre's narratives have been taken as encouragement by technophobes and technophiles alike. It is utopian; it is dystopian; it is postmodern; it is posthuman; it is a reflection of the times; it is a protest against the times. The academic interest surrounding cyberpunk marks its importance to disciplines such as science fiction studies, cultural studies, philosophy, and the burgeoning communications field dedicated to electronics and the Internet.

Although cyberpunk may not have been as paradigm-shattering as originally promised, it has had a notable impact on our perceptions of technology and on science fiction as a whole; Landon acknowledges, "the cyberpunk view of the future as vaguely posthuman and of future culture as darkly postmodern has inexorably permeated the SF megatext, leaving traces in the work of even the writers who most vociferously denounced the cyberpunk aesthetic" (*Science Fiction* 161). Certainly cyberpunk authors were writing about new media technologies before such themes regularly appeared in mainstream fiction; certainly, also, cyberpunk's academic appeal did not lie in any real assumptions of predictive accuracy, but rather in what it said about the society in which it was written and from which it garnered its ideas. Although the furor over its "revolutionary" capacity has since died down, cyberpunk in the 1980s — the first wave — was still an exciting exploration of virtual realities and new computing possibilities. It reconfigured science fiction as an edgy commentary on issues such as postmodernism, identity, technology, capitalism and the human condition in the information age. It was also not without critics, and as the next chapter will show, the most problematic aspects of cyberpunk were pinpointed by feminists.

Notes

1. Some of this spontaneity may be cast into question by Bruce Sterling's active recruitment of writers (as early as 1983) to participate in the *Mirrorshades* anthology (Kelly and Kessel vii).

2. As Samuel R. Delany has pointed out, *Neuromancer*'s receipt of both the Hugo and Nebula awards meant that it had the approbation of readers and writers alike ("Cyberpunk" 29).

— Chapter 2 —

Contributions and Critiques: Women and Cyberpunk

Cyberpunk's dystopian, escapist worldviews are intriguing from a post-modernist or socio-technological perspective, but its imagined futures also represent a very narrow point of view. Andrew Ross writes that cyberpunk narratives are "the most fully delineated urban fantasies of white male folklore" (145); while acknowledging that the genre's critiques of corporate power were based on recognizable Western issues, he also notes, "Cyberpunk's idea of a counterpolitics — youthful male heroes with working-class chips on their shoulders and postmodern biochips in their brains — seems to have little to do with the burgeoning power of the great social movements of our day: feminism, ecology, peace, sexual liberation, and civil rights" (152). Indeed, although 1980s cyberpunk is notable for its unique take on issues such as technology, capitalism, social alienation and identity, almost all of its major works were written by middle-class, heterosexual white men. With the exception of Pat Cadigan, whose cover blurbs frequently dub her the "Queen of Cyberpunk," the originating authors of the cyberpunk movement conformed to a rather uniform description — and the content of their work, in ignoring the influence of so many social movements, reflects this. As a result, the most frequent critiques of the genre came from feminists, although an exploration of women and early cyberpunk reveals that at least two women's short stories may have foreshadowed cyberpunk's formation. Further exploration of women's writing shows that Cadigan was only the first of several major women authors creating cyberpunk works at the end of the 20th century, and that the genre had a feminist wave which has, until now, been predominantly unexplored.

Cyberpunk's cyborg figures have been of particular interest to feminist critics. Donna Haraway's 1985 "Cyborg Manifesto" posited a theoretical cyborg figure that would break down social barriers and binaries, creating beings that were neither wholly male nor female, black nor white — beings which could then challenge gender stereotypes and other societal divisions. Haraway was explicit in citing science fiction as a potential breeding ground for such subversive images, crediting science fiction authors Joanna Russ, Samuel R. Delany, John Varley, James Tiptree Jr., Octavia Butler, and Vonda McIntyre as "theorists for cyborgs" (173). However, when feminist academics turned to cyberpunk to see whether its fictional cyborgs, androids and artificial intelligences might serve feminist purposes, the material was found lacking. Despina Kakoudaki argued that fictionalized cyborgs, once assigned human attributes such as flesh and language, may no longer transcend equally human categorizations such as gender and race (167). Furthermore, Claire Sponsler cited cyberpunk's position as an illustration of "human (and especially male) experience in a media-dominated, information-saturated, post-industrial age" (251); and finally, according to Nicola Nixon, cyberpunk had very few strong or even central female characters, while cyberpunk authors gave credit to 60s counterculture and sci fi fathers, but not to 1970s feminist authors such as Russ, Ursula K. Le Guin, or Suzy McKee Charnas. In Nixon's view, early cyber punk's complicity with 1980s conservatism was confirmed by its mainstream acceptance, and the genre was inextricably marked by patriarchal subtext: "Gibson's masculine heroes are masterful because they use a feminized technology for their own ends, or better, because their masculinity is constituted by their ability to 'sleaze up to a target' [while hacking in cyberspace] and 'bore and inject' into it without allowing it to find out the 'size of their dicks' in advance — their facility, in short, as metaphoric rapists" (229). Early cyberpunk's shallow, inflexible gender roles have thus been a clear topic of feminist concern.

Istvan Csicsery-Ronay Jr. says of cyberpunk heroes, "They are canny men — almost all of them men (why would a woman care about a technological society she had no role in creating?) — who have an uncanny sense that the nightmarish neuromanticism is a powerful drug too" (193). He was quite correct in noting that women had little role in creating the cyberpunk universe — apart from Cadigan, there was seemingly no place for female input in either the movement's early works, or its projected audience of socially inept hackers.[1] But Gibson's "Burning Chrome" (1982) asserts that "the street finds its own uses for things" (186); one might say the same for feminist authors, critics, and readers of cyberpunk, who didn't view or write it quite in the same way as originally intended. Many women, such as Haraway, did have an explicitly expressed interest in the technologies shaping their lives.

It may seem odd to isolate cyberpunk in particular as a site of women's suppression in Western culture; in this sense, after all, the genre is only one among many examples. However, cyberpunk's influence on early hacker culture and technological developments makes it a vital part of any examination of today's technocultures, and the fact that its first wave was written almost entirely by men provides a starting ground for a clear and concise contrast between men's and women's writing. Cathy Peppers argues that "critical discussion of cyberpunk has tended to carry on with the (by now familiar) danger often seen in 'deconstructionist' codings: the assumption that feminist science fiction is 'political,' while men's is not" (167). Of course, such an assumption would be wrong; the fact that men's cyberpunk in the 1980s almost entirely excluded women should be, and is, entirely open to political analysis. This is especially evident when considering that pre-cyberpunk, women had made marked in-roads to the science fiction community.

Early Contributions

Women authors in the 1990s introduced feminism to cyberpunk, but certainly not to science fiction, which was given a feminist slant in much earlier works. Women have been writing science fiction for as long as the genre has been recognized — and, in fact, earlier, if one follows the popular path tracing science fiction's origins to Mary Shelley's *Frankenstein* (1818), or even to Margaret Cavendish's *The Blazing World* (1666; see Hemmings 87). While common cultural mythology may assert science fiction as a boys' genre, women were visibly active in certain early pulp magazines; each issue of *Weird Tales* (1923–54) had at least one story or letter by a woman (Hemmings 84), while letters written to *Astounding Stories* between 1935 and 1937 both laud author C.L. Moore and acknowledge her gender (Davin 3). Susan Gubar has compiled a thorough list of early women authors, including Sophie Wenzel Ellis, Amelia Reynolds Long, Lilith Lorraine, and Leslie Francis Stone (25), and Eric Leif Davin has charted 203 women publishing more than 1000 stories in science fiction magazines between 1926 and 1960 (5). While science fiction tends to be perceived as male territory for boys' games — and a vast multitude of works have admittedly and commonly exhibited sexism, as well as racism, anti–Semitism, and other unfortunate biases (Davin 5) — it has always had women writers and women readers.

This is not meant to imply that women have had an easy time of it; women's science fiction has had to work hard in challenging the (hetero)sexual status quo, battling "not only against the weight of the male bias of the form but also against the weight of a cultural and political male hegemony that underpins the form itself" (Lefanu 4). Many women writers and fans faced a struggle in the science fiction community. In part, this is traceable through controversies over the roles of female characters. While the best science fiction can trigger new, imaginative ideas and explorations on the part of the reader, the genre's more pedestrian fare — much like mainstream fiction in general — has often reinforced patriarchal assumptions: "Whether human or alien, women have been seen primarily as sexual beings, functioning as appropriate rewards for the male protagonists who solve the problem. When a woman acts independently, she is evil; when she has power, it is intuitive or magical; when she has extrahuman abilities, they are the problem" (Allen and Paul 171). Although the roles that science fiction grants to women have expanded since the early twentieth century, these arguments particularly applied pre-cyberpunk; debates in the sci fi community had been ongoing from the 1920s to the 1970s regarding the place of women, love and sex.[2] Common arguments against female characters positioned the male sci fi fan as a "superior kind of being," a keen intellectual who was above the base concerns of bodily desire — an individual, presumably, with no need or use for women (Larbalestier 104); such stances implicitly assumed that female characters had no role beyond that of sex object (Merrick 37; Larbalestier 146), and also (conversely) left the genre open to counter-accusations of sexual immaturity when female characters were omitted (Larbalestier 138).

Other debates focused on women's place as authors; stories have additionally been framed as "hard" (men's) versus "soft" (women's) science fiction, labels which stem from the division between "masculine" sciences (e.g., physics, biology, chemistry) and "feminine" social sciences (e.g., psychology, sociology, anthropology). This has blurred into a debate over whether "feminine" themes such as social development or romance have any role to play within the bounds of "hard" "factual" "masculine" narratives (Lefanu 123–24; see also Larbalestier 169–70). Women, stereotyped as the softer, weaker, more emotional sex, have frequently been dismissed by die-"hard" science fiction fans even while infiltrating the genre — ironic, considering that cyberpunk, with its almost entirely male-based origins, has successfully stolen elements from "softer" adventure-romance novels.[3] In fact, Russ argues that the tropes of science fiction are particularly *well*-suited to women's writing, because the mythology that forms the genre's conventions is not as bindingly gender-based as the mythologies that serve as the basis of mainstream fiction:

> The myths of science fiction run along the lines of exploring a new world conceptually (not necessarily physically), creating needed physical or social

machinery, assessing the consequences of technology or other changes, and so on. These are not stories about men *qua* Man and women *qua* Woman; they are myths of human intelligence and human adaptability. They not only ignore gender roles but — at least theoretically — are not culture-bound. Some of the most fascinating characters in science fiction are not human. True, the attempt to break through culture-binding may mean only that we transform old myths like Black is Bad/White is Good (or the Heart of Darkness myth) into new asininities like Giant Ants Are Bad/People Are Good. At least the latter can be subscribed to by all human races and sexes. (Giant ants might feel differently.) [91–92].

Nevertheless, despite the fact that — as Russ points out — science fiction should theoretically provide flexible boundaries for writers seeking to work through (or past) ideas surrounding restrictive gender roles, such roles still contributed greatly to debates about the place of the "softer sex" in science fiction creation and fandom.

While women were marginalized but active in magazines, fanzines and general science fiction culture from the 1920s onward, the radical politics of 1960s–70s feminism brought tensions to a head; Russ's article "The Image of Women in SF" (published in *The Red Clay Reader* 1970, *Vertex* 1974) served as one notable catalyst for arguments surrounding feminism in science fiction, as Russ's own politically active positioning clearly marked her statements as part of the feminist movement (Merrick 105). Russ called for an escape from sexist stereotypes (in science fiction written by both women and men), but her opponents accused her of tainting the genre with outside politics (Merrick 113); Poul Anderson's "Reply to a Lady" (*Vertex* 1974) was one prominently published objection, in which he contended both that female characters were not "required" in most science fiction, and that Russ's feminist passions had skewed her argument (Merrick 59–60; Larbalestier 139–40). Subsequent discussions sparked by this exchange and others expanded across multiple fanzines as feminist writers gained more publicity and stronger public voices; debates about Russ's work, feminism in general, and the perceived militancy of the women's movement were spread across the pages of fan publications such as *Notes from the Chemistry Department*, *The Alien Critic*, and *Algol/Starship* (Merrick 62–68). Larbalestier marks this decade as a tipping point, one in which the discourse of "battle-of-the-sexes" fiction became the domain of women writers instead of men, specifically as situated in feminist utopian stories (149); the 1970s brought the publications of the overtly feminist fanzines *The Witch and the Chameleon* and *Janus,* the advent of feminist science fiction convention WisCon, and Hugo Award-winning work from Ursula K. Le Guin (1970: *The Left Hand of Darkness*, 1973: "The Word for World is Forest,"

1975: *The Dispossessed*), Kate Wilhelm (1977: *Where Late the Sweet Birds Sang*), James Tiptree Jr. (1977: "Houston, Houston, Do You Read?"),[4] Joan D. Vinge (1978: *Eyes of Amber*), Vonda McIntyre (1979: *Dreamsnake*), and C. J. Cherryh (1979: "Cassandra"). While the exact nature of women's positionings as science fiction writers and fans remained contested, women authors had by 1980 been indelibly established as part of the science fiction "mainstream."

The history of feminist science fiction and its criticism could fill volumes, and has; much more detailed analysis — including Russ's public correspondence and significant contributions from Pamela Sargent, Susan Wood, Vonda McIntyre, and Ursula K. Le Guin — has already been deftly provided by critics such as Justine Larbalestier (*The Battle of the Sexes in Science Fiction*, 2002) and Helen Merrick (*The Secret Feminist Cabal*, 2010). My purpose here is only to provide a brief overview and establish that the 1970s were a seminal decade for feminist writers; cyberpunk, therefore, coming in the 1980s, originated at a time when second-wave feminism had publicly stirred long-simmering fan and author debates about women's roles in writing, reading, or appearing in science fiction.

Bruce Sterling is often critiqued for failing to include any female authors in the list of cyberpunk's forebearers he offers in the introduction to *Mirrorshades* — a move that could be taken as symptomatic of the masculinist undertones argued by Ross and Sponsler. On one level, the logic behind Sterling's omission is simple enough to follow: the most well-known feminist science fiction texts of the time, novels like Russ's *The Female Man* or Le Guin's *The Left Hand of Darkness,* used new gender (re)constructions to posit entirely different societies, challenge patriarchal constructs, and define radical new social relations. It can be difficult to find direct traces of these speculative works in masculinist cyberpunk, which eschews such gender-based issues and focuses more on the alienation caused by new technologies and postmodern identities. That does not mean that Sterling was *correct,* however, and cyberpunk was not entirely without feminist links; Jenny Wolmark has suggested that "the description of cyberpunk as 'boystown' is too superficial" (115), and that despite a general lack of acknowledgment from cyberpunk authors, feminist science fiction made cyberpunk possible "both in its refusal to accept the generic limitations of this traditionally masculine genre, and in its concern to reframe the relationship between technology and social and sexual relations" (110). She echoes Samuel R. Delany, who made a similar observation in 1988 when he said, "I'm sure Gibson would admit that his particular kind of female character would have been impossible to write without the feminist science fiction from the seventies — that is, the feminist SF whose obliteration created such furor when Bruce Sterling (inadvertently of course...?) elided it" ("Real Mothers" 173). In fact, Gibson has acknowledged his own indebtedness to Joanna Russ; his character Molly is a loose tribute to her Jael from *The Female Man* (Wolmark 116).

Despite these assertions, and acknowledging that the subversiveness of 1970s feminist science fiction may have paved the way for the subsequent genre-challenging nature of cyberpunk, feminism's position in cyberpunk's first wave was a shadow at best; Wolmark ultimately does not credit first-wave works with any great feminist advances, noting that characters such as *Neuromancer's* Molly or *Islands in the Net's* Laura "are indicative of the presence and influence of feminist SF, but they cannot be said to be an expression of cyberpunk's own willingness to tackle questions of gender identity and subjectivity" (121). Indeed, among major portrayals of women in early cyberpunk, Molly is eventually co-opted as a mother figure, Laura is helpless and in constant need of rescue, and Sarah (from Walter Jon Williams's *Hardwired*) is purely mercenary (Cadora 358). Cyberpunk's white masculine heteronormativity has remained a contentious issue for many theorists; Tom Moylan has posited that cyberpunk may have been symptomatic of a 1980s reaction to the strength of the 1970s feminist movement, part of a "vicious backlash" against women, gays and lesbians (90).

In listing cyberpunk predecessors such as Heinlein, Pynchon and Delany, Sterling did overlook two women's short stories: C.L. Moore's "No Woman Born" (1944) and James Tiptree Jr.'s "The Girl Who Was Plugged In" (1973).[5] These works foreshadowed some of cyberpunk's major themes; Moore and Tiptree used cyborg imagery to explore questions of societal preconceptions and gender discrimination long before the word "cyberpunk" was ever conceived. Both stories present femininity as a calculated set of learned behaviors, calling into question the assumptions and social pressures surrounding gender performance while simultaneously querying humanity's relation to new technologies (Hollinger "(Re)reading" 310). These stories illustrate an awareness of gender issues within the conceits of what might be considered early cyberpunk settings; they are a precursor to cyberpunk that anticipated Haraway's cyborgs, as well as the women novelists who would come decades later.

In "No Woman Born," "air-screen" performer Deirdre's body is destroyed in a fire, but her brain is preserved and implanted into a robot body, setting the stage for an in-depth examination of gender norms. The two men (doctor and manager) who observe Deirdre's transformation spend much of the story attempting to rectify their knowledge of Deirdre's metal body with her seamless performance of "womanhood," as when her manager encounters her new form:

> She put her featureless helmeted head a little to one side, and he heard her
> laughter as familiar in its small, throaty, intimate sound as he had ever
> heard it from her living throat. And every gesture, every attitude, every
> flowing of motion into motion was so utterly Deirdre that the overwhelm-
> ing illusion swept his mind again and this was the flesh-and-blood woman
> as clearly as if he saw her standing there once more, whole, like the Phoenix
> from the fire [269].

The men fear that by recreating Deirdre in a neutered body with only the
senses of sight and hearing, they have destroyed her as a person — or, more
accurately and notably, as a woman. For them, any question of Deirdre's
humanity is inextricably intertwined with her gender; they are reassured only
when Deirdre makes an effort to perform in a feminine fashion — when she
laughs, or tilts her head, or lets her body sway so that she wears humanity
"like a tangible garment" (283). Despite the doctor's assertion that Deirdre
lacks a "sex" and thus any real humanity, the cyborg continually disturbs the
two men by seamlessly aping everything that they expect and understand
womanhood to be. Neither is she as physically frail as the men imagine; her
feminine mannerisms serve to mask the fact that she is capable of lifting a
grown man or tearing through a wall without effort (297). She challenges
patriarchal perceptions of womanhood by demonstrating feminine behavior
as a calculated mask — further, a mask that conceals her innate and threatening
power.

Susan Gubar has credited Moore as an early and influential source exploring sex issues in science fiction, a "sourcebook of the powerful images in our
culture that have surrounded and perpetuated the degradations of female sec-
ondariness" (25). "No Woman Born" foregrounds feminist cyberpunk themes
by positing that gender is a socialized performance of body language and vocal
tone, and also by implying — through Deirdre's increasing alienation — that
part of human identity is rooted in the body, and one cannot simply separate
the mind from the "meat." Later chapters will demonstrate that within cyberpunk, both of these notions have been most fully explored by female authors.
Within "No Woman Born," these ideas are illustrated by the fact that,
although Deirdre is capable of mimicking "womanhood" to perfection, she
feels that her new form makes her something that is no longer quite human
in nature. "I don't want to draw so far away from the human race," she says
(299); however, while her male cohorts find the change horrifying, she finds
her release from gendered expectations to be a more balanced combination of
frightening and exhilarating. In its historical context, "No Woman Born" is
marked by the beginning of the post-war era, images of Rosie the Riveter,

and uncertainties surrounding the future of women in the workplace; it serves as "a subtle extension of a World War II ideology of technologically-enhanced feminine strength" (Howell 157). Technology allows Deirdre to maintain the capacity for gender performance, but also to supersede her gendered identity in a manner fleetingly promised but subsequently unavailable to the 1940s woman. "No Woman Born" reflects both the potential for woman's power that was briefly inherent in wartime images, and the cultural anxieties such promises produced.

Tiptree's "The Girl Who Was Plugged In" is less about the pure separation of mind and body and more about body image, mingled with an unhealthy dose of corporate capitalism. When P. Burke, a seventeen-year-old girl, is employed by a company to mentally control a much prettier body and publicly display commercial goods, it is her first body that becomes the mechanized monstrosity; she is fitted with metal implants and housed in a cabinet so that she may interface with the machine that lobs her awareness into the slender, lithe body of Delphi. She learns how to use Delphi's form in a properly gendered fashion: "The training takes place in her suite and is exactly what you'd call a charm course. How to walk, sit, eat, speak, blow her nose, how to stumble, to urinate, to hiccup — DELICIOUSLY. How to make each nose-blow or shrug delightfully, subtly, different from any ever spooled before. As the man said, it's hard work" (550). P. Burke, like Deirdre, learns to ape the behaviors socially necessary for pleasing the men in charge of her creation; unlike Deirdre, she has no agency of her own, no privacy, no superhuman strength. Her erogenous zones are taken from her because the expense would provide no benefit to her corporate overlords. The story ultimately serves as a scathing commentary on the expectations of physical beauty and genteel performance placed on women. P. Burke is only happy when living Delphi's gadabout life, which she has been conditioned to think of as perfection — her dream is realized only in the performance of gender expectations. She achieves riches, beauty and a boyfriend, but the cyborg's numbed senses repress both P. Burke's identity and sexual desires. Notably, her happiness is unsustainable — only death results, as P. Burke strives for an impossible heterosexual fairy tale ending that she will never achieve within the confines of her duplicitous, restricted role.

Moore and Tiptree provide early looks at how technologies could be used to commodify the body; their stories are pre-cyberpunk examinations of cyborgs, capitalism and computers, all centered on the exploration of gendered themes. Cyberpunk's potential for disrupting gender stereotypes is thus made explicit by stories that existed before the inception of cyberpunk itself.

However, both these stories and the much larger popular surge of 1970s feminist speculative fiction are overlooked in Sterling's account of cyberpunk's creation. First-wave works, according to the *Mirrorshades* introduction, did spring from an earlier tradition, but it was a men's tradition; Sterling cites authors like Thomas Pynchon, John Varley, Philip K. Dick, Brian Aldiss, and Larry Niven. And indeed, although male authors of the 1980s occasionally attempted to write from a female point of view — Sterling's *Islands in the Net*, Victor Milan's *Cybernetic Samurai*— the 1980s genre was a glittering world of boys and their techno-toys, with supporting females thrown in. There was, however, one notable exception to the boys' club: Pat Cadigan.

The Queen of Cyberpunk

Cadigan, advertised by her publicists as the "Queen of Cyberpunk," was the only woman centrally involved in the first wave of the movement.[6] The attention generated by this position has apparently been somewhat grating; in her introduction to the 2002 anthology *The Ultimate Cyberpunk*, she writes:

> Sometimes, gender is a red herring. Sometimes, evaluating an area of the arts by counting the number of men or women active in it is to miss the point entirely.... Cyberpunk was never concerned with the biology of the writers involved, regardless of what anyone might think. To force the issue of how many men vs. how many women there are is simply another way to begin from an improper assumption — i.e., like asking someone, "So when did you *stop* beating your children?" Bottom line: *I don't know why there aren't more women SF writers whose work could be identified as cyberpunk* [xii–xiii, original emphasis].

Obviously, she has been asked this question often, and she herself has yet to come to a conclusion on the matter, except to dismiss the gender issue as irrelevant — an argument which may well hark back to Poul Anderson's 1974 assertion that "the frequent absence of women characters [in science fiction] has no great significance" (qtd. Merrick 59). While Cadigan is talking about authors and Anderson about characters, both positions suggest a strong resistance to feminist concerns — at minimum, an unwillingness to infuse gender politics into a supposedly impartial science fiction genre. However, Cadigan's own work contradicts her stated position; a gendered analysis reveals important distinctions between her publications and the writing of other first-wave authors.

Cadigan has published a full body of work, including the novels *Mind-*

players (1987) and *Synners* (1991); she states that she is often accused of writing "like a man"—or, conversely, her compatriots are accused of writing "like women" (xiii). Considering perennial science fiction debates, one might venture a guess that Cadigan is praised for her work's lack of romantic themes and her concentration on technical details, while her contemporaries — such as Gibson and Sterling — have been critiqued for incorporating threads of "feminized" emotion. This sort of binarized discussion, linking male writers to technological toys and female writers to kissing scenes, both oversimplifies and promotes the dubious arguments that assert a biologically-based penchant for "hard" vs. "soft" science fiction. Although this study is partially devoted to examining the differences between cyberpunk written by men and women, the question of whether or not a woman can "write like a man" was settled in 1976 by the successful eight-year disguise of Alice Sheldon as James Tiptree Jr.[7] Differences in theme and style vary according to individual authors and their social backgrounds. If anything, Pat Cadigan writes like Pat Cadigan.

On another level, though, Cadigan does write like a woman — not in terms of the style of science fiction she pursues, but in terms of the themes she incorporates into her work; not because women are biologically disposed toward certain ideas, but because the pressures Western society exerts on women lead to definable differences in the way many women approach cyberpunk. Certain common themes unite the genre, keeping it *as* a genre — themes such as cyborgs/artificial intelligence and the "human" condition, embodiment and virtual reality, and capitalist globalization. However, women authors tend to explore these ideas differently, with more emphasis on the importance of the body in identity and relationships, and the importance of community support in the face of alienating multinational capitalism. Cadigan's earlier work lacks some major threads that would later be introduced by authors (including herself) in the 1990s — queer rights, environmental conservationism, reproduction and the family unit, religion and mythology — but this is not surprising, considering its position at the roots of the cyberpunk movement. Cadigan in the 1980s adhered closely to the genre paradigm; her stories take place in gritty near-futures, full of virtual reality technologies, underground criminal economies, multinational capitalism, and persistent questions of cyborg bodies and postmodern identity. Closer analysis, however, reveals that her writing from the 80s and early 90s — "Rock On" (1986), *Mindplayers* (1987), *Synners* (1991) — is solidly based in the primary ideas cyberpunk is known for, while at the same time showing a leaning toward 1990s cyberfiction sensibilities that serves as a bridge between the two generations.

The most direct contrast between Cadigan's writing and that of her peers can be found in the 1986 *Mirrorshades* collection of short stories, edited by Bruce Sterling and billed as the "cyberpunk anthology." The stories provide an incredibly broad range of themes, settings and styles — from Gibson's tale of a modern photographer who sees visions of a 1920s-style "futuristic" world, to Greg Bear's story of a half-gargoyle living in a post-apocalyptic cathedral, to Paul Di Filippo's more typical blind street urchin given computerized eye implants and whisked away to work for a multinational conglomerate. It is difficult at first to isolate Cadigan; her "Rock On" in fact fits more clearly with the usual cyberpunk paradigm than Bear's "Petra," and has several themes in common with John Shirley's *Mirrorshades* entry "Freezone." This is not to say that Cadigan's work *can't* be set apart; "Rock On" and "Freezone" contain both surface similarities and important subterranean differences.

Both Cadigan and Shirley present protagonists consumed by nostalgia for the past, a nostalgia epitomized by the death of rock and roll in the face of new fads and encroaching, creatively bankrupt technologies. While moderately resigned to her lot in life — a living "synthesizer" for mental musicians — Cadigan's Gina mourns a childhood memory of a Rolling Stones concert, and longs for bar bands and "real" musical instruments (40). She "sins" for rock and roll, allowing new bands to play music powered only by computer chips and imagination, but she feels her losses acutely. Likewise, in "Freezone," Shirley's Rickenharp pleads for the preservation of old-style rock 'n' roll when he fights — futilely — to prevent his band from taking on a "wire dancer" and conforming to new, "minimalist" styles of music; an aging rocker, he longs for the glory days of the past much as Gina dreams of the Rolling Stones.

On a basic level, the two texts are nearly identical in theme. Both present dystopian futures filled with drugs, violence, and capitalistic conglomerates, painted with their protagonists' desires for old-style, messy creativity. Each story takes a bleak, anti-technological stance, from the point of view of an alienated protagonist desperately trying to cling to the creativity of yesteryear. The ties with rock music are typical of the genre and had much to do with the "punk" positioning of the "cyberpunk" label; several authors proclaimed an affiliation with rock or punk, particularly the band Velvet Underground — Rickenharp, in "Freezone," wears an old Velvet Underground leather jacket.[8]

Not until one looks at the roles played by Gina and Rickenharp, respectively, do differences between the two stories become evident. Rickenharp is a guitar player, singer, and songwriter — he is the leader of the band, the occupier of the spotlight, and the creator of the music. His performance actively engages with a live audience, and he revels in the power he feels over them:

"Rickenharp was sparking the combustion, causing the audience to react, to press the piston, and ... they were racing. Rickenharp was at the wheel. He was taking them somewhere, and each song was a landscape he swept them through" (154). Gina's power, conversely, is over the band: "The big boy faded in first, big and wild and too much badass to him. I reached out, held him tight, showing him. The beat from the night in the rain, I gave it to him, fed it to his heart and made him live it" (38). Both Rickenharp and Gina control the music; Rickenharp, however, creates it, while Gina shapes the talent of others. Rickenharp has more autonomy — Gina is nurturing rather than actively creating, and her control is a hoax, as she is being held captive by the band. Rickenharp fails to hold his band together, but joins a small group of revolutionaries and heads for parts and adventures unknown; Gina fails to find her old-style rock experience, and is ransomed by her employer so that she might continue to work as a synner-slave. Despite Gina's general feistiness, one might make a case for the sad repetition of helpless, nurturing female stereotypes. Fortunately, Cadigan's Gina is distinct in other ways.

To begin with, Gina is the only woman in *Mirrorshades* given a narrator's role — she is the primary character in the story, instead of peripheral support. While it may seem trite or indeed self-evident to argue that female authors are distinguished by being more likely to write female protagonists, it is at least worth acknowledging that such is the case. This is by no means a hard and fast rule — Bruce Sterling's Laura from *Islands in the Net* comes to mind — but it is a general trend that highlights a role for women in the imagined new technological age. Gina speaks in the first person; she is given a direct voice to the reader, and it is a voice with attitude. But it is not merely the protagonist's gender that distinguishes Cadigan's work from other stories in the text; it is also how that character is otherwise portrayed.

Gina is distinct from the other female characters in *Mirrorshades* because she is not presented as a sex symbol, nor does she assume an overtly sexual role within the text. Although her "rape" — by the band making her synthesize — is metaphoric, it never becomes literal. Moreover, although we discover in *Synners* that Gina is black, with dreadlocks, in "Rock On" she doesn't describe herself except as forty-something, with hair that doesn't grow long enough to cover the metal plugs in her skull — a sharp contrast to the other, mostly young punk-rocker girls within *Mirrorshades*, the ways in which they are described, and the sexualized roles they play. Wynne in James Patrick Kelly's "Solstice" is "twenty-two years old and very beautiful" (70); she is sexually abused by her clone-father as she serves as a mirror for his narcissism. The young girl Constantia in "Petra" is the object of the protagonist's desire, and her sexual dalliances with a stone mutant may get her killed. Her description is hardly flattering: "she was fourteen, slender of limb, brown of hair, mature of bosom. Her eyes carried the stupid sort of divine life common in girls that age" (108). Likewise, in "Freezone," revolutionary Carmen's primary role is to be Rickenharp's next sexual partner: "Bare breasts, nipples pierced with thin screws ... Rickenharp swallowed hard, looking at her. Damn, she was his *type*" (147). Later, he tells her, "[W]hen I get you alone I'm going to batter your cervix into jelly" (177). While some stories carry whispered hints of strong women, those characters are outside the spotlights, dancing along the edges — like Bala, the leader of an Amazonian girl gang in Marc Laidlaw's "400 Boys." They exist, but are primarily voiceless; Cadigan's Gina is the one in the lead role, and any other *Mirrorshades* women who even peripherally join her there are defined by their male authors as young, slim, beautiful — and much worse, in the case of Constantia, "stupid." They exist as objects of male sexual desire. Gina's presumably plain appearance and lack of sexual involvements set her apart — unlike her cohorts, her primary role is not one of titillation.

Cadigan's sleek style blends extraordinarily well with the work of other cyberpunk authors such as Gibson and Sterling; her work contains all the "typical" cyberpunk themes, while at the same time, her portrayal of strong female characters provides one of the first glimpses of feminism within the genre. Gina is not, as we learn in *Synners*, asexual — but she is in control, is found attractive despite being older and not adolescent/weapon-sleek, and is innovative and resourceful. As the only fully-rounded female lead in *Mirrorshades*, Gina situates Cadigan's work early on as a bridge between 1980s male-centered cyberpunk and the female-centered cyberfiction yet to come.

The most important differentiation between Cadigan's stories and those of her contemporaries is how she treats female characters; not only Gina in "Rock On" and *Synners*, but also Deadpan Allie in *Mindplayers*, and — later — Marva in *Fools* (1992) and Konstantin in *Tea from an Empty Cup* (1998) and *Dervish is Digital* (2001). Where other authors tended to introduce female characters either as sleek sex objects or haggard crones, Cadigan found a better-rounded middle ground very early on in the Movement's creation. Furthermore, Cadigan's treatment of themes such as virtual reality vs. embodiment marked her works as subtly different, with protagonists grounded more firmly toward the "embodiment" end of the spectrum than was regularly seen in other cyberpunk works. Anne Balsamo analyses Cadigan's *Synners* extensively, arguing that the novel illustrates an underlying, Haraway-esque gender binarism that forms the organizational framework of each character's technological engagements — a framework in which "the female body is coded as a body-in-connection and the male body as a body-in-isolation" (*Technologies* 144). Balsamo analyses the male and female hacker characters in *Synners* in order to demonstrate the novel's illustration of gender's influence on technology use. The two men in the novel both crave the release of virtual reality, where they have control over their environments and freedom from the "meat" of their bodies; conversely, the two women (one of whom is Gina from "Rock On") use cyberspace as a tool for communication with others rather than a locale for escapist isolation. The nature of this gendered division again sets Cadigan's work apart from that of her male counterparts, despite her use of cyberpunk's high-tech trappings and gritty capitalist environment. In *Synners*, Gina and her partner Mark exhibit two very different attitudes toward cyberspace; Gina treats it as a tool — and, particularly if one incorporates "Rock On," longs for better days — while Mark wants to abandon his body entirely and become one with the web. Gina wants Mark, but Mark's first love is technology and the ability to escape his "meat."

The recurring mantra within the novel is "change for the machines," first referring to coins in a vending machine, but finally describing the ways technology is altering the human condition. *Synners* explores questions of embodiment with a clear lean toward better body-grounding on the parts of the female protagonists. This breaks from the general tendency 1980s cyberpunk (e.g., *True Names*, the Sprawl trilogy, *Cybernetic Samurai*) has for portraying a more glamorous possibility of escaping the body, and the gendered split is important — within *Synners*, men are the ones who covet cyberspace, while women take a more measured approach. Cadigan's explorations of the mind/body dichotomy and the cyberspace dream aptly presage the feminist trends that infiltrate the genre more fully in the 1990s.

The question of identity in a postmodern age is another major cyberpunk theme that was destined to experience a shift in the hands of female cyberpunk authors in the 1990s — and another area where Cadigan's explorations laid the groundwork. In comparison to other early works, her texts display more skepticism with regard to virtual reality technologies and the impact of a postmodern, postindustrial future on the human psyche. While *Synners* explored questions of mind vs. body, Cadigan's first novel *Mindplayers* was more focused, instead, on questions of identity. The protagonist Allie begins *Mindplayers* as an oddity: an adult woman who has never participated in mind-to-mind communication. When she becomes a "pathosfinder," a form of psychic therapist, one is left wondering how much of her occupational demand is caused by the proliferation of the virtual reality technologies she uses to do her work in the first place. Questions of identity begin with her patients: a socially detached actor always pretending to be someone else; a woman who has effectively sliced her mind into pieces; a man who worries that he is haunted by the "melanin ghost" of his brain's former self; and two individuals who become incapable of separating themselves from each other. Most dramatic, perhaps, is the gradual mental decay of Allie's friend Jerry as he sells multiple copies of his own personality on the black market. The trauma experienced by each patient, underscored by the slow decomposition of Jerry's identity in the novel's background, illustrates *Mindplayers'* overall theme of the dangers technology poses to the human psyche.

Mindplayers is not as clearly divided along gendered lines as *Synners*; Allie, though she is suspicious of technology and serves as a more or less dispassionate observer for the reader, is plagued with her own problems of emotional repression — and while most of her patients are male, one is a dead woman. Additionally, Allie's ex-husband is much more emotionally available and stable than she is. However, the work clearly provides a precedent for later pieces of feminist cyberfiction — it does not follow an overarching plot of hacker heroes and gun battles, but rather concentrates on the inner mental workings of a limited number of characters. It is quieter and more introspective than most early cyberpunk, placing its emphasis on questions of human identity and technological alienation.

E.L. McCallum singles out Cadigan's work in a similar vein when discussing the use of travel and space in cyberpunk; according to McCallum, Cadigan's *Mindplayers* is an exception to the pattern set by Gibson's *Neuromancer,* Sterling's *Islands in the Net,* and Stephenson's *Snow Crash,* wherein the "coherence of place and the sequential ordering of action within specific, determined places reinforces a humanist, narrative perspective" (369). In McCallum's analysis, 1980s cyberpunk's refusal to challenge this humanist narrative model makes it possible to imagine the preservation of humanity despite the dehumanizing rule of corporate powers; in contrast, *Mindplayers'* emphasis on self and alternate consciousness, its anonymous place settings, and its lack of a crusading masculine hero creates an exploration of self/Other rather than win/lose. McCallum feels that traditional cyberpunk narratives lack the very adventurousness they promise; the heroic ideology of the adventure genre "reassures the audience of their integration into the technological permutations of capitalist culture" (375), while *Mindplayers* raises the possibility of a novel without hero/country/conquest — a novel that doesn't cushion the audience from the social and psychological implications of distance-transcending technologies. It is this sort of distinction that furthers the idea of

Cadigan's writing like a woman — not because her work is somehow more "feminine," in the stereotypical sense, but because her writing is, for multiple reasons, recognizably different from that of her male colleagues. The arguments made by critics such as McCallum and Balsamo demonstrate clearly that Cadigan's work can and has been analyzed as separate and "female" — despite the author's own protests to the contrary.

The clearest themes that Cadigan's work shares with that of her male counterparts are explorations of embodiment and identity, and an ambiguous approach to technology. These are also the areas where her work most foreshadows the ideas explored by women in the 1990s — not by abandoning cyberpunk's tenets, but by exploring their implications in a more feminist-oriented fashion. Although other authors in the 1980s did write about major female characters — Gibson's Molly Millions and Angie Mitchell, Sterling's Laura from *Islands in the Net*, Milan's Elizabeth from *Cybernetic Samurai* — these characters tended to be somewhat flat, trapped within narratives that caused them to be either objectified (Molly), passive (Angie), or punished for venturing outside the bounds of domesticity (Laura's corporate obligations cost her her husband and child, while Elizabeth's twisted attempt at mothering an artificial intelligence eventually leads to her death). Veronica Hollinger notes that Sterling's *Islands in the Net* espouses a need for global unity ("Deconstructions" 217); his choice of a female protagonist thus fits with his depiction of a more traditionally "feminized," democratic, socially supportive setting. Conversely, one might argue that Cadigan's work exhibits a certain role-reversal — *Mindplayers*'s insensitive Allie and her emotional husband Jascha — rather than an actual breakdown of feminine/masculine binaries, but that sort of exploration is the first step toward subversion.

Joan Gordon, interestingly, rates Cadigan on a feminist par with William Gibson when she discusses both Deadpan Allie and Molly Millions as examples of covertly feminist characters; describing them both as tough soldiers, she argues, "It seems to me that for a woman to enter the human army as an average soldier with no distinction in rank, privilege or job position is, on the covert level, a feminist act" (198). The term "covert" is vital to this analysis; Gordon also notes of Molly, "To some extent she's a man in women's clothing ... the most facile and least thoughtful representation of the liberated woman" (198). Although Molly's sexual objectification within *Neuromancer* is problematic to potential feminist readings of her character, I would agree Gordon's assertion that cyberpunk offers opportunities for feminist exploration, and that some authors in the 1980s began taking first steps toward this exploration. Placing Cadigan's characters on the same level as Gibson's, however, is questionable; Cadigan's women are sharper, better characterized, and freer of stereotypes than their cyberpunk (including Gibsonian) sisters.

Cadigan's focus on issues of identity and embodiment also causes her to write in a softer sort of cyberpunk setting — there is crime in her novels, but not to extremes, and the environment is not nearly as decimated by pollution or warfare. Her characters are generally not criminals, nor the loner protagonists of so many other cyberpunk works; instead, they are members of communities, even if those communities and interpersonal relationships are only explored in passing. Allie finds companionship at the school where she is trained, and later within the enclave of her coworkers; Gina abandons her relationship with Mark, but finds new alliances and new romance. While a case may be made for the same idea of community in other works of the time, such as *Islands in the Net*, I am not trying to make the argument that only women write about community or embodiment or a hopeful environmental future — rather, I am analyzing general trends. Women in the 1990s proved more likely, as a whole, to write about support networks and community issues in cyberpunk, and the beginnings of this trend are echoed in Cadigan's earlier writing. Likewise her penchant for mentioning gay marriage, as in *Mindplayers* where a man casually discusses his ex-wife and his ex-husband in the same breath (192); while queer issues do not arise in any major fashion, a background acceptance of homosexuality is implied — one that would later flower into more in-depth exploration, particularly in the works of lesbian authors such as Melissa Scott.

In short, though her work's position within the cyberpunk genre was unquestioned, and Cadigan herself was praised by her male compatriots, she may have unknowingly taken the first steps toward defining the new boundaries of feminist cyberpunk and cyberfiction; although her writing is, in truth, not overtly political, and "never fully engages with feminist concerns," she also subverts a number of masculinist conventions (Cadora 358). The genre changes in Cadigan's work are noticeably and notably echoed in the women's fiction that was yet to come.

Cyberpunk Women

In 1992, Neil Easterbrook declared, "Cyberpunk is dead" (378). Many academics, as well as the original wave of cyberpunk authors, seemed to agree; after a brief resurgence of interest in Neal Stephenson's *Snow Crash* (1992), most researchers were ready to move on. Books such as Larry McCaffery's

Storming the Reality Studio gathered essays to look back and summarize the cyberpunk movement, while most authors drifted away to other projects. Cadigan and Gibson continued to publish cyberpunk through the 1990s, but they were in the minority, and the original excitement over their work had subsided. P. Chad Barnett credits cyberpunk's deteriorating popularity during this period to aging authors growing less Bohemian and rebellious, and the rising notion that capitalist society had already evolved into cyberpunk's predicted futures (360). Author Lewis Shiner derided new authors as shallow imitators, calling their work formulaic and arguing that cyberpunk was supposed to be about more than black leather and head chips. The first wave was over, and attention shifted elsewhere until the flurry of new academic theories attracted by the retroactive stylings of 1999's *The Matrix*.

But as Roger Luckhurst somewhat wryly notes, cyberpunk has been declared dead several times since 1986, "leaving only the problem of what to call the huge bulk of cyberpunk written long after this date" (204). I am concerned with the 1990s, and agree with Karen Cadora, who cited the death of masculine cyberpunk but highlighted a new, feminist strain of the genre — a feminist cyberpunk that "envisions something that feminist theory badly needs: fragmented subjects who can, despite their multiple positionings, negotiate and succeed in a high-tech world" (357). While it should be noted that male authors, such as George Alec Effinger, also published new cyberpunk works during the 1990s, the strong rise in women authors is particularly notable. Their novels and short stories remain, for the most part, unacknowledged; even Pat Cadigan, writing at the turn of the millennium, stated that there were still very few women creating cyberpunk (*Ultimate* xi). Bruce Sterling's website, listing his recommendations for a thorough cyberpunk education,[9] only cites — as far as women authors are concerned — Cadigan's work and Lisa Mason's *Arachne*. However, during the late 1980s and throughout the 1990s, women such as Marge Piercy, Laura Mixon, Edith Forbes, Kathleen Ann Goonan and Melissa Scott were busily writing about virtual reality, identity, capitalism, gender and the high-tech future.

According to some feminist theorists, it is not surprising that innovative technological visions should have been created by women. Sadie Plant states, "Machines and women have at least one thing in common: they are not men. In this they are not alone, but they do have a special association, and with recent developments in information technology, the relationship between women and machinery begins to evolve into a dangerous alliance" (503). Additionally, Rosi Braidotti cites the iconoclast leaders of the cultural crisis as feminists, riot girls, science fiction writers and theorists: "We want to put up some active resistance, but we also want to have fun and we want to do it our way. The ever increasing number of women writing their own science fiction, cyberpunk, film scripts, 'zines, rap and rock music and the like testifies to this new mode" (525). Although she also critiques cyberpunk for its "simplistic psychology and reductive cartesianism" (528), it is interesting to note that she positions women's cyberpunk as part of a larger movement, much as Mark Dery positioned the cyberpunk of the 1980s; each piece of literature both reflects and influences larger trends. Of course, "No woman is born, and not all women become, feminist, but some women *and* men do" (Peterson and Runyan 226); despite this distinction, I would argue that women's cyberpunk is predominantly feminist, and men's cyberpunk is generally not. Braidotti's identification of women's cyberpunk as a feminist outlet blends well with my own theories, and this principle will be used as the framework for much of my analysis.

Is women's writing inherently different from men's? I raised this issue when examining Pat Cadigan's writing, and return to it here in order to reiterate that I am wary of essentialist arguments that claim one's sex leads to "natural" tendencies, but am interested in examining the impact on fiction of the different societal contexts in which men and women are raised. Specifically, I feel that women's cybertexts are informed by feminist politics in a manner that is predominantly alien to first-wave works. I have posited that women's cyberpunk is more challenging than men's in terms of its relation to the patriarchal status quo; according to June Deery, science fiction written by men tends to preserve patriarchal roots, while women writers take advantage of science fiction's "defamiliarized perspective" to form "genuinely alternative schema" (88). I plan to outline the ways in which women's fiction concentrates more on "women's" issues of community and relationships. At the same time, while I acknowledge that women's cyberpunk may generally be "softer" than the first wave of work, I can also think of exceptions such as Pat Cadigan's work and Lisa Mason's *Arachne*—nor does it escape my attention that the exceptions that come to mind, the authors who "write like men," are the same authors who made Sterling's list. This tension presents one of the challenges of the piece: to preserve the distinctions between women writers while at the same time placing them in (at least partially) unified contrast to their male counterparts.

Joanna Russ, in *To Write Like a Woman*, argues:

> Our traditions, our books, our morals, our manners, our films, our speech, our economic organization, everything we have inherited, tells us that to be a Man one must bend Nature to one's will — or other men. This means

ecological catastrophe in the first instance and war in the second. To be a Woman, one must be first and foremost a mother and after that a server of Men; this means overpopulation and the perpetration of the first two disasters. The roles are deadly. The myths that serve them are fatal [93].

In other words, she finds the conventions of mainstream fiction to be suffocating. Literary subgenres such as horror, fantasy and science fiction have always been, to some extent, playgrounds for experimentalists and soapboxes for rebels who would find it difficult or threatening to publish their views within more mainstream media. Cyberpunk, though it began as a boys' club, ultimately became a framework from within which women writers strove to work against the same cultural myths that Russ protests and early cyberpunk promotes.

Through analyzing women's cyberpunk and cyberfiction in the 1990s, and examining themes such as cyborg culture, virtual reality and corporeality, gender equality, queer rights, and environmentalism, I seek in the next chapters to prove that cyberpunk became a sharp-edged tool for feminist authors. In answering the question of how and why these women broadened cyberpunk's original themes to include more pronounced commentary on women's issues — not only expanding the presence of these issues, but in some cases, highlighting their previous absence — it will become clear that feminist cyberpunk was informed by a much different social position than its male-written first wave. The next few chapters will establish the existence of the feminist cyberpunk wave by examining how women authors preserved the major trappings of the genre while fundamentally altering the treatment of those same themes.

NOTES

1. Doubtless there was a larger variety of cyberpunk readers than the stereotype; however, in a Mark Dery interview, Gibson claims that he "gave [computer nerds] permission to wear black leather" (Dery 107), while Luckhurst notes, "the near superpowers given to computer geeks and tech-heads to jaunt through imagined worlds of cyberspace in these books are much to the classic engineer paradigm" (208).

2. A young Isaac Asimov was a notable opponent of science fiction's presumed feminization; his letters on the subject are well detailed by Eric Lief Davin.

3. The hard/male soft/female debate is of course falsely divisive in the first place; Lefanu has pointed out, "Such a distinction not only posits a crude sexual dualism — masculine is hard, feminine is soft —[...] but it also denies the connection between the different 'hard' and 'soft' sciences, connections that in good science fiction should be made" (123–24).

4. James Tiptree Jr. also won a Hugo Award in 1974 for "The Girl Who Was Plugged In"; at that time, her identity (as Alice Sheldon) had not yet been made public.

5. Notably, William Gibson cites Tiptree's story in a 1988 *Science Fiction Eye* interview (Gordon 197).

6. Lisa Mason was writing *Arachne* at the time, but her work was not published until 1990. As well, U.K. author Gwyneth Jones published *Escape Plans* in 1986, but her novel has seldom been included in cyberpunk studies or American marketing of the genre.

7. Tiptree's exposure and resulting community reactions are detailed nicely by Sarah Lefanu in *In the Chinks of the World Machine*, 105–6.

8. Mark Dery provides a thorough overview of music's influence on cyberpunk (and vice versa) in chapter 2 of *Escape Velocity*. This includes Gibson basing Molly Millions on a photo of Pretenders singer Chrissie Hynde, and sliding various Velvet Underground references into *Neuromancer*.

9. The original site is no longer available, but Sterling's list is mirrored at http://www. hatii.arts.gla.ac.uk/MultimediaStudentProjects/00-01/0003637k/project/html/litreco.htm. It is also reprinted in Cadigan's edited collection *The Ultimate Cyberpunk* (383–90).

— Chapter 3 —

Alienating Worlds:
Globalization and Community

In citing two of cyberpunk's major tropes as corporations and crime (191), Frances Bonner noted that these elements are often conjoined within the genre's texts. This twinning of corporate growth and crime best represents early cyberpunk's implicit criticism of capitalism and globalization; often, multinational corporations are the dehumanizing, all-powerful law, and crime is the only available resistance. Globalization and commercialization remain important elements of the setting in women's cyberpunk stories, and are the area where cyberpunk's feminist iterations are most clearly marked by the influences of the genre's first wave. This concern with globalization issues reflects the continued rise of Western corporate capitalism in the global economy — the impact of which may often transcend gender-specific boundaries.

Globalization may be defined as the breakdown of national barriers and cultural boundaries as the expansion of corporate multinationals and communications technologies creates an ever-smaller and increasingly homogenized world. Globality might best be described as an environment wherein "[s]trings of transactions and interests as well as non-territorial and pre-and post-national solidarities run up and down through the national social fabric such that citizens are often more directly linked to distant forces and actors than to their national state" (Brodie 245). Fredric Jameson, moreover, states that "cyberpunk constitutes a kind of laboratory experiment in which the geographic-cultural light spectrum and bandwidths of the new system are registered" ("Fear" 107). While Jameson cites the staple male cyberpunk authors (Gibson, Sterling) and their visions of newly globalized worlds, masculinist and feminist writers both include the rise of multinational capitalist forces in their considerations of society's further evolution; though these themes may be treated with varying levels of ambiguity, they are invariably present in any work of cyberpunk or cyberfiction.

The early genre is typified by the plight of the alienated individual in the face of scheming megacorporations, and this reflects the rise of such institutions in contemporary society. Notably, cyberpunk works such as *Neuromancer* (1984), *Cybernetic Samurai* (1985), and *Snow Crash* (1992) situate many of these corporations in Japan — an affectation that became a standard trapping of the genre, and one which expresses a particularly American reaction to Japan's strengthening export economy in the 1980s (Luckhurst 207). The first wave's seeming obsession with Japanese imagery exemplifies what David Morley and Kevin Robins have described as "Techno-Orientalism": a "projection of exotic (and erotic) fantasies" (169) that displaces fears about Japan's challenge to Western assumptions of global superiority — subverting the encoded threat to American supremacy by depicting Western heroes as masters of foreign technology, while also supporting racial stereotypes that cast the Japanese as "unfeeling aliens ... cyborgs and replicants" (170). Of course, while the Japanese iconography that marks early cyberpunk may indeed present a racially-charged specter of "empty and dehumanized technological power" (170), cyberpunk's distrust of corporations also stems from the economic forces that suffuse American culture; globalization in many respects constitutes "a distinct outgrowth of western capitalist and patriarchal systems" (Hawthorne 362). Moreover, James Messerschmidt traces the globalization of United States businesses back as far as the 1950s and notes that American exports have included hazardous products and corrupt management practices, causing appalling working conditions in Third World countries (110). In discussing the issue of white-collar crime and its perceptions in North America, he observes that transnationals are likely to do business in whichever countries have the fewest laws regarding environmental protection and worker safety, concluding, "Undeniably, *both domestically and internationally,* the transnationals are the worst of all criminals and worldwide their victims are primarily the powerless" (114, original emphasis). Certainly megacorporations are generally viewed with suspicion by a public that well remembers images of Nike sweatshops.

Corporate trickery thus abounds in contemporary crime fiction and television — one need look no farther than a John Grisham novel — and the looming multinational is not specific to cyberpunk, but cyberpunk perhaps does it best. This is particularly notable in the first wave, which set the template for the genre. In *Neuromancer,* Case fears faceless conglomerates such as Sense/Net, but is never concerned about the police, FBI, CIA or any equivalent government organization. Likewise in Neal Stephenson's *Snow Crash,* the "law" is in the hands of private police companies and corporate-run enclaves. Corporations may furthermore be formed of criminal organizations themselves: the Yakuza in *Neuromancer* and the Mafia in *Snow Crash* are both corporate powers in their own rights. The figure of the ominous corporation has grown to such an all-encompassing extent that the transnationals have effectively become the only governing forces in otherwise anarchist worlds; the only law is capitalism.

There is an inherent contradiction in cyberpunk's treatment of globalization themes. Ostensibly, the genre's disenfranchised, socially outcast protagonists promote suspicion toward capitalism and multinational authorities. Through the eyes of these alienated heroes, the reader sees an environment dominated by greedy multinational interests, where basic human rights are sacrificed to monetary gain and most people live under a heavy blanket of security monitoring, obeying the rules as they eke out sustenance-level existences. At the same time, however, this environment is what makes the spectacular adventures of the protagonists possible: "The typical protagonists of the cyberpunk world are quintessentially alienated individuals, but their alienation is reconfigured as a positive since they are alienated against a banal, corrupt, and homogenizing post-industrial society" (Sponsler 261). Crime becomes a noble, or at least understandable, endeavor as protagonists fight against the rule of faceless megacorporations; their alienation is glamorized, and the excitement of their rebellion in turn advances the setting as necessary for the adventure. Indeed, their adept hacking abilities give them a power that belies their original marginalization (Vint "Mainstream" 96). Characters born in this speculative future do not pause to think wistfully of times before their age, nor are their goals so widespread as to attempt disruption of the entire world order. The unremittingly postindustrial setting results in an implied resignation — the sense that multinational domination is going to happen, and there is nothing that can really be done about it. Nor do the characters have any interest in massive societal reorganization. Early cyberpunk narratives, in particular, give the impression of serving as survival guides for the individual, promoting smaller stories of iconoclast protagonists against a wide backdrop of inevitable global change.

As Jameson observes, the near-future setting allows cyberpunk to treat the rise of globalization as a laboratory experiment, extrapolating potential new cultures and societies. Authors of both masculinist and feminist cybertexts subsequently explore similar concerns with regard to globalizing forces. The main difference between them ultimately lies in sites of resistance; the globalization process in these fictions is not always complete, and some factions defy the encroachment of corporate capitalist institutions. Early cyberpunk authors are more likely to romanticize narratives of alienated individuals, while women writing later have a tendency to focus on small but strong partnerships. While authors from both decades situate music and non–Western cultures in opposition to globalization, the feminist texts are less prone to using racial stereotypes, and are most fully distinguished by advancing alternative communities rather than acts of individual resistance. Ultimately, women's cyberpunk is distinctly more community-oriented; its exploration of globalization and alienation does not obviate the presence of the family unit or personal support network.

Feel the Noise

There are similarities in some of the methods by which authors (both masculinist and feminist) illustrate sites of resistance to globalizing forces. Robin Ballinger suggests that music often provides a site of cultural and social struggle versus dominant discourses. If so, and such a position "of vocality and self-representation is central to creating a counter-narrative, positing a counter-essence and in critically attacking the legitimacy of 'objective' knowledge and truth" (424), then the elements of music running through both waves of the cyberpunk genre might be considered as a common basis of resistance. The very "punk" of the label comes from an association with punk music, and Gibson's acknowledgement of the Velvet Underground's influence on his writing (McCaffery "Interview" 265) is complemented by the protagonists' desperate attempts to preserve rock music in Shirley's "Freezone" (1986) or Cadigan's "Rock On" (1986) and *Synners* (1991). Emma Bull's *Bone Dance* (1991) preserves this theme, as its protagonist Sparrow collects (and fences) rare twentieth-century music and film while also working as an audio/visual DJ at an underground dance club; likewise, Mixon's *Proxies* (1998) positions skilled contortionist "muscle dancers" as creative counterpoint to the virtual reality technologies that allow other characters to inhabit multiple waldo bodies.

This reading may be expanded to include other forms of artistic expression. Sherryl Vint analyzes Misha's *Red Spider, White Web* (1990) as a pursuit of "authentic art" ("Mainstream" 95) in the face of increasingly universal commodification; artist Kumiko must strive for creation on the bleak outskirts of society, where she scrapes a meager existence while she and her colleagues are stalked by a serial killer. "Selling out" and accepting a rich city patron would allow Kumiko safety, food and shelter at the literal price of her individuality;

artists who are granted citizenship to "Mickey-san" (a Japanese takeover of Disney) must subsequently wear nametags reading "Walter" and produce works meant purely for commercial consumption. Vint connects *Red Spider, White Web* to "Rock On" in noting cyberpunk's general "anxiety regarding the consequences of technology invading the body, and the connection of this motif with concerns about authentic art" (101). While she also argues that these approaches are overly romanticized (108), certainly creative outlets such as music and performance art provide a common link between characters striving for individual expression within various texts, as individual creativity is placed in opposition to conglomerate forces.

Technology vs. the Other

While cyberpunk often melds Japanese imagery with futuristic technology, certain other non–Western cultures are cast as more "primitive," and subsequently placed in opposition to new developments. These cultures (or rather, appropriated images of these cultures) constitute a second site of resistance to cyberpunk's hard-edged encroaching globalizations. In Gibson's *Neuromancer,* for example, it seems the only people who live outside the constrictions of urban society are the Rastafarian Zionists — which is not to say that they live "naturally," for they too are dependent on technology. However, with their space commune lifestyle and self-sufficient life support and economy, the Zionists have effectively and literally withdrawn from the world. In their eyes, all cities are "Babylon"— an ancient Mesopotamian city that was, according to Christian mythology, eventually destroyed by God for its arrogance and evil. It is not only the Sprawl of which they speak: the satellite Freeside is "the hanging gardens of Babylon" (101), and the Villa Straylight in particular —"If there's any Babylon, man, that's it" (192). Nor does cyberspace escape this judgment:

> [Aerol] took the band, put it on, and Case adjusted the trodes. He closed his eyes. Case hit the power stud. Aerol shuddered. Case jacked him back out. "What did you see, man?"
> "Babylon," Aerol said, sadly, handing him the trodes and kicking off down the corridor [106].

Case is unable to engineer any similar cultural withdrawal, or to empathize with the Zionists; his solitary hero's journey does not allow him a sense of community. He does not like the way the Zionists touch him when they talk (106); their way of life is completely alien to him, casting them irrevocably as Other within the text. This is not a reading of Rastafarian culture, but only of Gibson's use of certain keywords; his appropriation of Rasta imagery must be acknowledged as stereotypes distorted through the lens of a white Western point of view, his Zionists "another version of a non-white Tonto in thrall to the actions of the lone white hustler" (Moylan 89). *Neuromancer* constructs an opposition between the technological and the cultural Other, crafting an image of a technophobic subculture coded as both "simple" and ethnically foreign.

Bruce Sterling, like Gibson, uses Caribbean culture as a counterpoint to multinational growth, but unlike *Neuromancer's* peaceful Zion, *Islands in the Net* (1988)'s Grenada is both violent and a cutting-edge source for experimental biotechnologies. Still, the Grenadian assassin Sticky—who slides between multiple disguises in the novel—uses Rasta vocabulary when he stands in judgment of the technological world he inhabits, commenting on both cyber-communications and war-torn Singapore:

> "It's a wind-up city, this place. Full of lying and chatter and bluff, and cash registers ringin' round the clock. It's Babylon. If there ever was a Babylon, it's here."
> "I thought *we* were Babylon," Laura said. "The Net, I mean."
> Sticky shook his head. "These people are more like you than you ever were" [222].

This use of Afro-Caribbean (specifically Rastafarian) terminologies is again primarily marked by a Western premise that assumes a resistance to globalization (and its attendant technologies) on the part of "other" cultures. There may be additional shades here of late-nineteenth-century stereotypes that have traditionally associated people of color with laziness and technological incompetence (Fouché 61); also in *Islands in the Net*, Africa is "bad and wild," one of the few places on Earth that is unconnected to the global cybernetwork (388; see also Nixon 224). Admittedly, the Zionists have their own independent space community, and Sticky is a lethally trained cyborg. However, the use of tech by these characters is also problematic; the Zionists are reluctant, while Sticky's chameleon-like disguise abilities are marked as "magic" and related to vodou within the text, his biotech situated as mystical and unknowable (Mayer 190). Despite the perilous implications of these racial overtones, the tension between Rastafarian iconography and any encroaching global forces is configured as unheeded wisdom: through the insight which can only be granted through outsider positioning, Aerol and Sticky are able to condemn the corporate-governed techno-capitalist societies to which Case and Laura are inextricably committed.

In Stephenson's *Snow Crash,* people infected with a verbal "virus" are the culturally-marked forces resisting new technology; they must be cured by the protagonists in order to be integrated back into corporate-approved techno-logical society. The courier Y.T. picks up a package at a viral commune and observes the haphazard behavior of the infected: "Y.T. hasn't seen such childlike glee on anyone's faces since the first time she let Roadkill take her clothes off. But this is a different kind of childlike glee that does not look right on a bunch of thirtysomething people with dirty hair" (178). While *Snow Crash* avoids casting a specifically black Other (Western protagonist Hiro is half-black, half–Japanese), it is also strongly implied that the virus victims are speaking ancient Sumerian (210), and the verbal virus comes from an ancient clay tablet known as the "nam-shub of Enki." Although the virus victims are not benign, and in fact are meant to serve as an army for their scheming leader, Stephenson has yet utilized surface references to another culture in order to visualize some opposition to the spread of Western capitalist tech-nology and globalization. In the case of *Snow Crash,* the message is only sig-nificantly more dystopian; Gibson's Zionists can retreat, but there is no real escape for Stephenson's characters — their position outside globalized society is not a choice, but rather involuntary psychosis. The Others are still placed in opposition to new technologies and corporate systems, but now there is no logic or reason to their resistance. As Foster says, "*Snow Crash* tends to interpret 'babble' as promising a utopian ideal of universal linguistic commu-nity, which the novel then reveals to be a nightmare of linguistic control" (*Souls* 243).

Examining similar tropes in women's cyberpunk reveals that while these Othered, outsider communities are still present, their positioning is more neb-ulous. Lisa Mason's *Arachne* (1990) uses aboriginal stereotypes in its depictions of oppositional cultures, but the novel also plays on its own appropriations by portraying such archetypes partially as a fad for young and rebellious uni-versity students who dye their hair and stalk around with skin paint and spears (81). The same imagery is distantly echoed in Mixon's *Proxies* (1998), when Carli D'Auber sees that a "handful of undergrads in dreadlocks and hair sculp-tures, in loin wraps, body paint, or vests and loose trousers, had gathered out-side her office" (28). The aboriginals of *Arachne* (and its sequel, *Cyberweb*) are not all students, however; some, like the "abo" Ouija, are genuinely part of an alternate, if piecemeal, culture. Ouija's people live in fear of being forced off the streets, categorized, and domesticated. There are particularly strong parallels to be drawn between Mason's abos and Gibson's Zionists: both groups become allied with the hacker protagonists, fighting against the corporate status quo, and both groups fear that technology, capitalism and cyberspace are blights on society that will ultimately suck the soul. Notably, however, Mason avoids ascribing her abo imagery to any particular contemporary culture, and she also positions Ouija as a point-of-view character at certain points in *Cyberweb*. *Arachne* and *Cyberweb* may yet reflect general Western assumptions about "the insights of indigenous peoples" and the challenge that such "local and connected" knowledges may present to globalizing forces (Hawthorne 362–63). While Ouija and the other abos in Mason's work are less specific than Gibson and Sterling's appropriation of Rastafarian terminology, they may still promote concepts of the "less-developed," racially-marked Other. Mason's work (as well as Mixon's) is distinguished by its suggestions of self-awareness; such Westernized stereotyping is implicitly acknowledged when "indigenous" trappings are adopted by protesting students who may not understand the symbols they've stolen, but nevertheless use "abo" markings in opposition to the transnational status quo.

Separately, Native American author Misha's work also highlights the issue of cyberpunk's cultural hijackings. *Red Spider, White Web*'s Kumiko is the protagonist rather than a sidekick or background character, and although she is from a "reservation" for "primitives," she functions as a technologically aware outsider who objects to commodification and commercialization without performing as a member of a specific cultural group. The artistic community she belongs to is disparate, and as noted in the previous section, its resistance is based on a longing for authentic creativity rather than any common ethnicity. Misha avoids using "primitive" tropes that would stereotype her characters; her alternative approach spotlights the ways in which the "foreign" cultural imagery within most cyberpunk appears as seen through the lens of white patriarchy — particularly in *Neuromancer* and *Islands in the Net*, which do not code their Rasta stereotypes as appropriated.

Finally, Raphael Carter's *The Fortunate Fall* (1996) goes the farthest in actively subverting first-wave cyberpunk's stereotypes regarding both black Others and Japanese world domination. In Carter's work, Africa has become a technological and civil-rights paradise, its citizenship closed to anyone who cannot prove the appropriate bloodlines. The African "outsider" condemns the rest of the world's culture implicitly, through silence, as Africa has responded to the dystopian future by closing its borders entirely. Maya's handler Keishi, who (like *Snow Crash*'s Hiro) is half-black and half–Japanese,[1] is not able to gain entrance; in this case, her Japanese heritage is a liability. Maya and Keishi dream of running away to Africa (where their same-sex union will be accepted) and Keishi provides Maya with a gift of African chip technology that is far beyond Maya's previous experience (and which easily overpowers the authoritarian suppression chip that the net police have inserted into Maya's skull). While a background detail in the text, *Fortunate Fall*'s consistent reiteration of Africa's cultural and technological superiority serves to question cyberpunk's first-wave assumptions regarding Japan's inevitable domination, as well as the racial stereotypes that inflect some other works.[2]

With the possible exception of *Red Spider, White Web*, cyberpunk's appropriations seldom represent any actual insights belonging to "outsider" peoples, nor is the treatment of such Othered cultures consistent enough to comprise a truly coherent theme; rather, the presence of these fictional communities reflects a subtle cultural sentiment that supposes non–Western (indigenous or non-white) people must *have* such insights, and that they are automatically opposed to technological globalization. Ultimately and admittedly, their use within the genre is problematic for several reasons: because the depiction of foreign cultures in cyberpunk has a markedly skewed relation to actual contemporary cultures, because cultural appropriations may be racially marked by a Western patriarchal position, because membership in these communities is most often restricted to supporting cast rather than main characters, and because protagonists are frequently alienated by, or — in the case of *Snow Crash*—actively opposed to, these communities. Women's cyberpunk is more sensitive to elements of racial stereotyping, but the presence of the Other remains limited, its oppositions small and peripheral. Such "outsider" characters do extend through both masculinist and feminist waves of cyberpunk, and they often serve as sites of community resistance to encroaching technological forces. Within cyberpunk, however, the best critiques of capitalist globalization are provided by feminist examples of community.

Feminism, Cyberpunk and Community

On one level, there are distinct similarities between the protagonists of many cyberpunk novels, regardless of author. Outlaw hackers marginalized by faceless global forces — Gibson's Case, Stephenson's Hiro — are not restricted to first-wave cyberpunk. One early example from women's work is ALIC in Gwyneth Jones's *Escape Plans* (1986) — a privileged programmer and former space resident, she descends to an Earth wholly governed by CHTHON, an all-encompassing, formerly corporate computer system ("Combined Holding Terrestrial Habitats Operational Network: the system that takes care of the underworld. The CH is silent, as CHTHON is no longer a commercial enterprise" [240]). Deleting her own personal records, ALIC becomes one of the "numbers"—disenfranchised people whose brains are hardwired to provide processing power to the central system, and whose forced employment consists of providing housekeeping or erotic services, or of giving eight hours a day to the needs of the network. Jones envisions a world where the majority of human beings are no longer viewed as people; they have no civil rights and are only valued for their use in information processing—a consequence of formerly corporate computer systems that have altered the nature of human labor.

Such outsider protagonists can also be found in novels such as Lisa Mason's *Arachne* (1990), Melissa Scott's *Trouble and Her Friends* (1994), and Lyda Morehouse's *Archangel Protocol* (2001). *Arachne*'s Carly Nolan, having rebelled against her corporate employers, hacks the web from a seedy hotel room. In *Trouble and Her Friends,* hackers Trouble and Cerise have retired from their former grey-market ways but are forced to return to the online world when an imposter begins committing crimes in Trouble's name. Finally, *Archangel Protocol*'s Deidre is a former police officer, now an outsider without access to the economic system or the web. Much like *Neuromancer*'s Case, she makes a deal to provide services to unknown forces in exchange for having her cyberspace link restored. In all of these works, as in early cyberpunk, hacking is figured as resistance against a seemingly all-powerful and all-reaching global enemy; cyberspace is beyond the jurisdictional bounds of any one nation, and it provides the battleground for self-realization and self-assertion.

Admittedly, Big Brother is not always corporate—in *Archangel Protocol,* theocracies are the looming power, and in *Trouble and Her Friends,* Trouble and Cerise must work around or with representatives of international law. However, the figure of the ominous corporation never really vanishes; Cerise has been forced into working for a multinational she was caught hacking, and Deidre must eventually strive against Lucifer himself as he mounts a multi-billion-dollar public relations campaign to promote the rise of the Antichrist. The figure of the hacker hero clearly survives in women's cyberpunk, as does a background of globalization and cutthroat capitalism. The difference lies in the nature of the support networks these heroes depend on. While the first wave of cyberpunk offers an implicit critique of postindustrial globalization through the alienation and social dysfunctionality of its protagonists, women authors critique more constructively by offering community alternatives.

Early cyberpunk constructs a simplistic and ultimately unsatisfying link between community and femininity. While heroes such as Case (*Neuromancer*) and Hiro (*Snow Crash*) begin their stories without societal legitimacy or its associated power — Case is a burned-out drug dealer, while Hiro is a pizza deliveryman — early cyberpunk narratives tend to place female leads within positions of corporate acceptance and security. *Islands in the Net,* one of the few cyberpunk novels wherein the protagonist willingly operates within the auspices of corporate rule, is also one of the few early works to feature a central female protagonist. Likewise, in Milan's *Cybernetic Samurai* (1985), Elizabeth O'Neill works quite happily for a Japanese corporation as she idolizes the ancient feudal ways of the samurai serving his lord. Corporate community appears to be perceived as a feminine space, which dovetails with feminist theory; Jane Mansbridge has observed that "the term 'community' is not gender-free. Its two components, local geographical rootedness and emotional ties, have female connotations" (346). Certainly Nicola Nixon has argued that cyberspace is a feminine matrix, and as Case and his compatriots "penetrate" corporate systems, it stands to order that the corporations themselves — thus violated — might therefore be read as feminine (see also Nixon 225). With this in mind, it is not surprising that first-wave cyberpunk works taking place within corporate settings — instead of the marginalized shadow-societies of the criminal underground — featured female protagonists. However, as Hennessy argues, a major facet of feminism is "its critique of social totalities like patriarchy and capitalism" (xii); the tensions between feminism and capitalism are not so easily buried beneath the links between feminism and community.

Nor is the relationship between feminism and community without pitfall. As Penny Weiss notes, feminists may be both drawn to and repulsed by communitarian ideas:

> Feminist attraction to communitarianism is easily understandable. Having rejected the self-interested, autonomous individual of liberalism as both mythical and undesirable, feminists find that a more social view of the self and a more collective, interdependent, and cooperative model of social relations has an obvious and reasonable appeal. Further, given women's history and continued practice of attachment to others, through traditional female roles and networks, feminist visions might even be expected to be communitarian.
>
> But feminist rejection of communitarianism would also be understandable. The misogynist history of communitarian theorizing about what the principles and who the members of communities should be dates from at least Plato and continues today. That history has called for women, much more than men, to sacrifice themselves in the supposed interest of familial and civic communities.... A feminist reliance, then, on a more individualistic ideal would not be entirely unwarranted [3].

The tension that Weiss details is not new, and is evident when examining sites of resistance in feminist fiction; the desire for cooperative relations, in conflict with wariness toward patriarchal social structures, may be seen in women's science fiction for decades preceding cyberpunk. When examining feminist utopian science fiction (a tradition extending back at least as far as Charlotte Perkins Gilman's *Herland* [1915]), it is apparent that women writing such speculative works have been striving to formulate alternative models of community for quite some time. However, segregation — often the case in visions of fictional feminist communities — ultimately does not address the question. Jenny Wolmark offers a perceptive discussion of feminist utopias such as Suzy McKee Charnas's *Walk to the End of the World* (1974) and *Motherlines* (1978), or Sally Miller Gearhart's *The Wanderground* (1979), where patriarchy results in disaster and men are reconfigured as the "other" (81); aptly, Wolmark critiques *Motherlines* with the observation, "The women-only communities established in *Motherlines* suggest that women can be free only in the absence of men, a proposition that ironically leaves existing gender relations intact and posits an unproblematic relation between women and the category of Woman" (84). Although she is slightly more encouraged by the possibility of more equivalent gender relations alluded to in utopian works such as Sheri Tepper's *The Gate to Women's Country* (1988) or Pamela Sargent's *The Shore of Women* (1986), she also notes that in these works — despite the in-text potential for future reconciliations between the sexes — the women remain "enclosed and contained" (100). One might link Wolmark's critique of segregation to Audre Lorde's comment that "Without community there is no liberation, only the most vulnerable and temporary armistice between an individual and her oppression" (112, Weiss 4), or Weiss's notion that "communities are essential to sexual equality" (3). Weiss is speaking of multi-sexed communities; in other words, eliminating the presence of men does not adequately resolve the conflict between feminism and communitarianism. Feminist utopian science fiction, while useful in examining many aspects of gender relations, ultimately may not offer viable solutions for the formation of more equitable community types. Although many historical community structures have admittedly promoted the oppression of women, sexual equality is impossible in a vacuum. Weiss suggests that "the institutions and practices central to patriarchy cannot be reconceived and replaced without the formation of new communities that alter how we meet our material, political, intellectual, and emotional needs" (4). The connections between feminism and community are complex; within feminist utopian fiction, they cannot be fully addressed by the elimination or suppression of masculinity, and within early cyberpunk, they cannot be broken down to anything so simple as an association of the feminine with private or local social spheres.

Most feminist cyberpunk narratives that begin within the bounds of corporate rule proceed to become escape narratives — like ALIC's abandonment of her class privilege in *Escape Plans*, or Cerise's desire to break from her corporate indenture in *Trouble and Her Friends*. In *Arachne*, Carly Nolan begins the novel with a new corporate position. It soon becomes apparent to what extent her time is micro-managed: "She was a professional telelinker now and a lawyer newly employed at a competitive starting salary by the prestigious San Francisco megafirm of Ava & Rice. She could not afford three-and-a-half-second delays" (14). Not only is Carly dehumanized, her time counted by the second in a highly competitive environment, it is subsequently clear that the law firm is helping to defend human rights violations. Carly sees one case go by as a matter of course, as she helps the city of Los Angeles defend its practice of feeding the needy with bread made of "recycled paper products, wood chips, and chaff" (45). The firm is completely unconcerned with the ethics (or lack thereof) involved in feeding wood products to the homeless, and its demanding schedules soon cause Carly to become a drug addict in order to keep up her workload. By the sequel, *Cyberweb*, Carly has escaped from her job and become an outlaw, aided by her robot companion Pr. Spinner.

Piercy's *He, She and It* (1991) traces a similar ejection narrative when Shira Shipman loses custody of her son Ari because her ex-husband has a higher tech rating than she does; the decision is made and enforced by the corporation she works for. She finds herself without local support; her only friend, Rosario, has been divorced and exiled for being too old: "Women over forty who were not techies or supervisors or professionals or execs were let go if they were not the temporary property of a male grud" (6). Much as in *Arachne*'s court cases, the merciless power of the capitalist corporation is shown through the dehumanization of background characters, while the protagonist herself is an individual ultimately unable to fit in: "[Shira] always felt too physical here, too loud, too female, too Jewish, too dark, too exuberant, too emotional" (5). Shira is not an outlaw hacker, but like *Arachne*'s Carly, she becomes one; quitting her job at Y-S, she later finds herself breaking back into the company's computer systems, and then physically breaking back into the enclave in order to retrieve her son.

The alternate communities offered in women's cyberpunk are thus first positioned as resistance to globalized capitalism. Tensions between feminism and capitalist patriarchy do not allow feminist narratives to permanently position women within corporate communities; however, Carly and Shira are not loners. In resisting the same self-interested individualism that has contributed to the rise of capitalist society (and marks much of early cyberpunk), feminism gravitates toward ideas of community responsibility. At the same time, the patriarchal nature of community structure in Western culture necessitates the formation of new types of community. In women's cyberpunk, nowhere is this idea illustrated more clearly than *He, She and It.* Shira's story serves as a tale of dueling communities, as her escape is made from an inadequate social support system to one that is smaller but better aware of the individual's needs. This parallels the marked tension between feminism and communitarianism; the link between these two concepts is not automatic, and not just any community will do.

Over the course of the novel's opening, we see three clearly delineated examples of community social structure: the capitalist corporate enclave, the anarchist urban sprawl, and the small town of Tikva. Shira experiences all three of these speculative futures, each marked by small yet telling attributes such as clothing style and animal life. In the corporate enclave, Y-S, Shira lives in a simple two-room apartment that is all her tech rating "entitles" her to (6); her ex-husband, Josh, lives on a street "like a hundred others," his house "one of the four types for [his] rating" (14). Even pets are prohibited: "Shira had grown up with cats and birds, but here only high-level techies and execs were permitted real animals. Everyone else made do with robots, but the good ones cost far too much for her" (14). Levels of social privilege are carefully controlled through these strict regulations, and are reflected in such rituals as the rules surrounding interpersonal greetings between employees who are at varying levels of the corporate hierarchy (5). Clothing is color-coded so that anyone "in the wrong place" is immediately identifiable (5). Shira's every moment is monitored and governed; her parental rights are taken away from her without notice. Her discomfort is made palpable by the way she "slips into trouble," by her dissatisfaction with her low tech rating, and by her anguish at the unfeeling system that severs her legal right to see her son. Notably, her objections and difficulties are marked by gender: "They have patriarchal laws here," she notes to her ex-lover Gadi (10).

Leaving this ultra-regulated environment, Shira then journeys through the urban morass of the Glop. The Glop, much akin to Gibson's famous Sprawl,[3] is "slang for the Megalopolis that stretched south from what had been Boston to what had been Atlanta, and a term applied to other similar areas all over the continent and the world" (6). We are told that nine-tenths of North America's population lives in the Glop. No one here is easily distinguished by rank; Shira seeks to protect herself from gang violence by adopting a commonly worn, nondescript black suit that disguises her age, sex and physical form (31). Shira observes chanting gang members clustered around a body "with its chest torn open and arterial blood spurting out" (33); she buys a knife for protection, turns down an offer of employment as a prostitute, and is nearly run down by a flotilla of riders that leaves the parts of two more bodies "strewn across the broken pavement" (34). There are animals in the Glop, but they aren't pets; a gang of dogs fights over the torn human flesh (34). Over the course of Shira's journey, the setting shifts from one extreme to another: fascism vs. anarchy. Neither of these community types suits Shira; there is no automatic link between her feminine self and the social environment, and not any community will do. Instead, her quest for equality and self-realization leads only to patriarchal punishment, or open danger.

Shira is not happy until she returns home to Tikva. Located outside the sprawl of the Glop, and free from corporate domination, Tikva is governed by a multi-gender community council. Entering the town, Shira is startled to be surrounded by a hodgepodge of buildings in different styles and shapes: "After the uniformity of the Y-S enclave, the colors, the textures, the sounds and smells provoked her into a state of ecstasy until she found herself walking more and more slowly, her head whipping around like an idiot. Why had she ever left?" (36). Again, both the clothing and animals mark the character of the community:

> The occasional passerby was casually dressed: open-throated shirts, pants, a full skirt, shorts, for the day was seasonally mild. She felt like a freak in her standard Y-S suit, now covered with grime and soot. A couple passed her arguing loudly about somebody's mother, their voices raised unself-consciously. Behind a hedge, a dog was barking at a rabbit in a hutch.... Everything felt ... unregulated. How unstimulated her senses had been all those Y-S years. How cold and inert that corporate Shira seemed as she felt herself loosening [36].

He, She and It aptly reflects Weiss's argument: Shira, as a woman of the future, is unable to find a home either within a regulated, patriarchal community, or within an environment of anarchist individualism. Instead, she feels happiest in a precariously-balanced "free town" that represents a new type of community — one that allows Shira to participate as a full citizen, promoting social ties without discriminating based on attributes such as gender or appearance. The resistance to globalization is evident: Shira is not satisfied in the multinational enclave, or in the uncivilized urban spillover where individual cities no longer exist. Instead, she feels tied to community on a local and direct level. In parallel, the restrictive corporation and the out-of-control urban morass are both examples of first-wave settings, and both are rejected in this later text, which examines the same social problems but ultimately encourages new solutions. While the novel offers the background possibility of multiple types of successful communities — a gang in the Glop that is trying to reform its way of life, and a utopian women's community that Shira never sees — Tikva is where Shira is happiest, and through her eyes, this free town is presented as the optimum form of resistance to capitalist globalization.

Compare this with Sterling's *Islands in the Net,* the most "community-oriented" first-wave novel. As a primarily masculinist vision of a woman in corporate culture, this text is not an escape narrative — rather, it provides a critique of multinational corporate life without really suggesting any alternatives for its protagonist, Laura. As a member of the multinational Rizome, an organization supposedly based on democracy, equality and family, Laura finds herself very concerned with appearances — in jockeying for position, she does not want to find herself doing anything perceived as "non–R" (non–Rizome). Even in mildly chastising a coworker for raising sensitive issues on an unsecured line, she is nervous: "The guy was being frank and up-front, in very Rizome-correct fashion, and here they were telling him to mind his manners because they were on spook business. How would it look?" (96). The same concern with appearance marks meetings of the Rizome executive committee, where any truly serious matters for discussion require the facades of committee members to be pointedly casual and egalitarian: "You could tell the importance of this meeting by the elaborate informality of their dress. Normal problems they would have run through in Atlanta, standard boardroom stuff, but this Grenada situation was a genuine crisis. Therefore, the whole Committee were wearing their Back-slapping Hick look, a kind of Honest Abe the Rail Splitter image" (68). While casual clothing in *He, She and It* marks freedom, in *Islands in the Net* it is pretense — a symbol of community unity that masks career pressures beneath. Yet there are no easy alternatives for Laura; she is relatively happy with Rizome, and when she is sent abroad, she discovers only warfare, secret police and global conspiracy. Her smallest community, her traditional nuclear family, is destroyed; as her husband David says, "All the fucking money and politics and multinationals just grabbed us and pulled us apart" (376). Her wider, global community is full of war and death. Rizome, although it is not perfect, remains her only support at the end of the novel. As an included member of the corporate community, rather than one of cyberpunk's more typical marginalized outsiders, Laura is feminine and feminized — however, from a feminist perspective, she finds no alternative new community style. *Islands in the Net* is more concentrated on conveying warnings about the increasing political dominance of capitalist corporations, as when a representative of Kymera corporation proposes a global police force to Laura:

> "You're proposing some sort of global security cartel?" Laura said.
> "Global Co-Prosperity Sphere!" Mika said. "How does that sound?"
> "Uhmm," David mused. "In America, that's known as 'conspiracy in restraint of trade.'"
> "What is your loyalty?" Yoshio asked soberly. "America or Rizome?" [177].

Laura is disturbed by the question, and yet her position within the narrative makes it clear that she is — at the beginning, and at the end — a loyal member of Rizome. The novel criticizes globalizing forces while omitting more complex feminist arguments regarding the necessity for new community structures.

In contrast, *He, She, and It*'s Tikva, where Shira finds acceptance within a small independent democracy and the matriarchal family of her grandmother Malkah, coincides with other alternate community formations promoted in women's cyberfiction. In Scott's *Trouble and Her Friends,* Trouble and her hacker cohorts are gradually assimilated into the "legitimate" side of the new world order while at the same time retaining their independence in the wilds of cyberspace, and relying on each other for support. Trouble's group of queer hackers forms a site of resistance based both on individualist politics and on sexuality; ultimately, Trouble finds the support she needs in the form of her lesbian partner/lover Cerise. While detailing, among other things, the travails of international law enforcement and Trouble's attempts to remain anonymous and undetected, the novel also presents a small artist's commune as Trouble's temporary site of refuge during her years of "retirement." Likewise, in Walker's *Whiteout* (1996), Signy and her friends do freelance work for a Japanese multinational while sustaining themselves as a bisexual, polygamous family unit — and in Forbes's *Exit to Reality* (1997), Lydian finds love with the shapeshifting, gender-switching Merle while joining an underground community of reality-hackers. It should be noted that *He, She and It* has its share of bisexual characters as well, and the positioning of sexuality within these tiny resistant populaces is likely not a coincidence — within these texts, acceptance of alternate sexualities seems to be a key part of these new communities.

Such cyberfeminist communities or makeshift family units are also free of discrimination based on race or religion. The best example of this catch-all liberalism is possibly Morehouse's *Archangel Protocol* and its sequels, wherein private detective Deidre McManus — on the run from international pursuit — finds refuge for herself and her daughter inside a rogue Jewish community led by a lesbian ex-terrorist. The kibbutz exists, very literally, on the margins of society — within deserted, glass-coated city areas previously decimated by a nanotech bomb. Despite its Jewish foundations, and links with the Israeli military, the kibbutz shelters Deidre (a Catholic), her illegitimate daughter Amariah, and — later — the hacker Mouse (a Muslim). One might also consider Emma Bull's *Bone Dance,* in which the androgyne clone Sparrow's search for community and acceptance ends in a rogue farming community situated outside the morass of a futuristic, dystopian city. Sparrow's quest for identity and purpose necessitates a gathering of disparate friends (a vodou *brujah,* a body-hopping ex-soldier, and the heir to an electrical empire); in order to connect with zir[4] allies, Sparrow must first consciously abandon the capitalist, eye-for-an-eye principles that have previously governed any of zir interpersonal interactions. Not only is Sparrow's own intersex nature accepted by the community without judgment, the varied nature of zir allies is embraced: "The silliest exercise I could imagine would be to squeeze these three profoundly dissimilar people under the umbrella of the single word 'friend.' But, it seemed, I'd been silly" (229). In feminist cyberpunk, the hero seldom stands alone.

Conclusion

The links — and the tensions — between the two waves of cyberpunk are clear. Both waves posit music and creativity as counterpoints to homogenizing globalizing forces, and both posit outsider commentary from non–Western cultures whose images may be subject to authorial appropriation — although feminist cybertexts, such as *Red Spider, White Web* and *The Fortunate Fall,* also highlight or subvert cyberpunk's use of cultural and racial stereotypes. The congruences between feminism, racial activism and queer rights are only to be expected; it can at times be challenging to "separate women's movements from other political movements agitating for social, political and economic transformation" (Peterson and Runyan 227). Likewise the link between feminism and social support networks; as Weiss notes, "Feminist theorists argue that the vision of the atomic, 'unencumbered,' self, criticized by communitarians, is a male one, since the degree of separateness and independence it postulates among individuals has never been the case for women" (165). This may be the sense in which the first wave of cyberpunk might be most clearly considered "male": its glorification of the outsider. One of the major differences between masculinist and feminist works may be how marginalization is treated as a consequence of a new global order; while early protagonists are marginalized individuals, later feminist protagonists are more closely tied to marginalized communities.

Scott, Semmers and Willoughy, in their study "Women and the Internet," state, "Women are often identified with local identities and the particularity of place. As these geographies of place and locality are subverted by new geographies of information flow, women face a double challenge: they must defend their local spaces against the threat posed by a disembodied globalization, and they must also create spaces within the new electronic media for their own voices" (13). This statement holds true when applied to women's cyberpunk. While still often concentrating on themes of alienation, works such as *Arachne* and *Trouble and Her Friends* also explore small, fringe communities and relationships that exist along societal margins. While the protagonists may be alienated from society, they are not alienated from each other; the two lesbian heroes of *Trouble and Her Friends* have an interconnection impossible for *Neuromancer*'s Case and Molly. There is a clear pattern within feminist cyberworks: the formation of groups, large or small, that resist globally dominating forces while promoting acceptance, equality and support between members. The individualist cyberpunk hero was never a feminist figure, and even "lone" figures in feminist cyberfiction — Trouble, or Carly Nolan — are supported by trusted partners. While the fight against totalitarian forces remains, the fighters are more closely bonded, and novels such as *He, She and It* and *Archangel Protocol* go so far as to posit fully resistant and self-sustaining communities — communities where typical patriarchal structures are eschewed and all members enjoy equality and acceptance. Although women's cyberpunk has largely gone unacknowledged, it exists, and illustrates different political concerns, informed by different social positions; the feminist-oriented exploration of globalization issues creates an entirely separate take on societal solutions.

NOTES

1. While the character of "Keishi" is eventually revealed to be a virtual projection, the reading of her racial background holds for most of the novel.

2. Ruth Mayer has described repetitive Western images of a "degraded, countercommodified" Africa as "Afropessimism" (180); she relates this to Sterling's *Islands in the Net,* and also to a variety of other texts (both fiction and nonfiction) including Michael Crichton's *Congo* (1980) and Keith Richburg's *Out of America: A Black Man Confronts Africa* (1997).

3. Marge Piercy acknowledges Gibson's influence, as well as that of Donna Haraway, in her afterword to *He, She and It.*

4. Two androgynous characters in this study (*Bone Dance*'s Sparrow and *Archangel Protocol*'s Page) are referred to using the gender-neutral pronoun "zie" (and its possessive form, "zir"). Characters that alternately but definitively present as either male or female (*Exit to Reality*'s Merle, *Virtual Girl*'s Marie/Murray) are referred to as "s/he."

— Chapter 4 —

Gendered Flesh: Embodiment and Virtual Reality

Virtual reality — in Bonner's terms, computers and corporeality — is another of the staples of cyberpunk that is both preserved and significantly altered in the feminist wave. Hacker heroes may be nobodies in the physical world, but they are gods inside their computers; the mythos of early cyberpunk is one of romanticized escape into a universe where pure intelligence dictates power and control. Critics such as Larry McCaffery and Mark Poster have closely examined cyberspace as a literary signifier of the postmodern condition; McCaffery writes:

> These new realms of experience — theorized by Guy Debord's "Society of the Spectacle," Baudrillard's "precession of simulacra," and Cook and Kroker's "hyperreality," and metaphorized perhaps most vividly by Gibson's "cyberspace" — have become integrated so successfully into the textures of our lives that they often seem more "real" to us than the presumably more "substantial," "natural" aspects.... This is the postmodern desert inhabited by people who are, in effect, consuming *themselves* in the form of images and abstractions through which their desires, sense of identity, and memories are replicated and then sold back to them as products [6, original emphasis].

Virtual reality technology is a narrative and thematic element very clearly preserved from one wave to the next. Feminists, however, have been more concerned with cyberspace's escapist disembodiment, and the worrisome way in which virtual reality (VR) concepts have promoted relief not only from the vulnerability of the "meat," but also from gender and cultural differences. Anne Balsamo notes, "There is little coincidence that VR emerged in the 1980s, during a decade when the body was understood to be increasingly vulnerable (literally, as well as discursively) to infection, as well as to gender, race, ethnicity and ability critiques" (229). Elaine Graham would apparently agree, saying of cyborgs and virtual reality: "For the hyper-masculine Terminator and Robocop, and many of Gibson's protagonists, prosthetic implants and enhancements, or the disembodied 'high' of cyberspace, represent technological means of escaping the vulnerability of embodiment" ("Cyborgs" 307). In the 1980s, the rise of the AIDS epidemic threatened bodily integrity and corporeal power; likewise, the increasing strength of feminism and other social rights movements threatened the supreme position of the straight white male and fuelled a conservative, Reagan-era backlash in North America. Virtual reality's positioning as a white male escapist fantasy made concepts of cyberspace problematic for many feminist critics, as this rejection of the body may also reject feminine associations with nature and the corporeal, while reinscribing a patriarchal liberal humanist viewpoint that denies or denigrates such gendered bodily experiences (Graham "Cyborgs" 314). As Rosi Braidotti said,

> The central point to keep in mind in the context of a discussion on cyberspace is that the last thing we need at this point in western history is a renewal of the old myth of transcendance as flight from the body.... Transcendance as disembodiment would just represent the classical patriarchal model, which consolidated masculinity as abstraction, thereby essentialising social categories of "embodied others." This would be a denial of sexual difference meant as the basic dissymmetry between the sexes [528].

If the neutral "default" form of humanity in Western culture is the white male, removing attributes such as race and gender threatens to erase alternative segments of the population entirely, forcing everyone into the same masculine niche by erasing everything that defines them as "other." The flight from the body is, among other things, a flight from feminism and from the corporeal distinctions that make women separate, oppressed, and threatening. While early cyberpunk promoted the control of virtual life and the romanticism of the hacker lifestyle, feminist authors created works more focused on promoting embodiment over empty escapism. Karen Cadora relates this tendency to a 1993 experiment performed by Laurel, Strickland and Tow, which found that women using VR computer systems preferred to have virtual "bodies" while men did not (Cadora 365); certainly an analysis of feminist cyberpunk supports this gender split. In the second chapter of this study, I discussed how Pat Cadigan's work served as an early example in this area. An examination of women's subsequent cyberfiction reveals both a desire for VR-related attitudes to grow up and away from simplistic escapist fantasies, and an awareness of women's bodies as important, individual and desirable.

In the first wave, the trend toward escapism is clear. In *Neuromancer* (1984), the hacker Case is cut off from cyberspace and reduced to running small-time deals on the streets: "For Case, who'd lived for the bodiless exultation of cyberspace, it was the Fall. In the bars he'd frequented as a cowboy hotshot, the elite stance required a certain relaxed contempt for the flesh. The body was meat. Case fell into the prison of his own flesh" (6). In 1992, *Snow Crash* followed a similar vein: Hiro Protagonist adventures in cyberspace while living in a rental storage unit. In cyberspace, Hiro is a celebrity — the best swordsman in virtual reality, and one of the few allowed into the exclusive Black Sun club. In the physical world, he is a failed pizza deliveryman who earns a living by selling random scraps of information to the national library. His preferences are clear: "Hiro spends a lot of time in the Metaverse. It beats the shit out of the U-Stor-It" (24); "when you live in a shithole, there's always the Metaverse, and in the Metaverse, Hiro Protagonist is a warrior prince" (63). Cyberpunk written by women preserves ambiguous attitudes toward new technologies, but also comes down more firmly on the side of "actuality" (embodiment) versus "virtual reality" (the escape from the "meat"). In Piercy's *He, She and It* (1991), programmer Malkah loves her work on the net but also takes joy in her physical life, from which she retains fond memories of years of lovemaking (160). In Lisa Mason's *Arachne* (1990), Carly — the hacker protagonist — uses the net for work, not play. And in Cadigan's *Synners* (1991), Mark craves a life in cyberspace while his girlfriend Gina rejects it. Feminist cyberpunk retains an interest in virtual environments but is much less prone to entertaining notions of bodily transcendence; characters navigating virtual reality in feminist texts must retain some form of body awareness (Cadora 365).

Sherryl Vint has argued that *Neuromancer* is not as contemptuous of the flesh as it first appears, observing that both Case and Molly use their bodies as technological tools (*Bodies* 108), and that disembodiment within the text coincides with the removal of character agency; in her view, despite the novel's seductive visions of cyber-mastery, "the body is continually shown to be an inescapable part of Case's subjectivity" (*Bodies* 109). Vint contends that many would-be Internet hackers and programmers have emulated Case rather than understanding Gibson's social critique, and that certain characters within *Neuromancer* may express contempt for "the meat" but the overall context of the novel does not support their positions (*Bodies* 111). While she builds a convincing case, I would argue in turn that this is not a dominant reading of the text; as Vint herself observes, "Contemporary debate on the social consequences of computer telecommunication technology suggests that those readers who identify with Case and perhaps model their subjectivity upon his have created a virtual community that supports Case's vision of the world, if not Gibson's" (*Bodies* 109). *Neuromancer's* impact is based in large part on its portrayal of techno-escapism and virtual adventure; one might relate this to Claire Sponsler's argument that a certain inescapable cool factor is associated with the cyberpunk setting because of the exciting events that take place therein (261). Regardless of what Gibson's intended message may have been, his novel — and the genre it epitomizes — became inextricably associated with the disembodied fantasies of its protagonist.

Growing Up — Feminism, Virtual Reality and Adulthood

Admittedly, the romanticized notion of cyberspace as a transcendental playground is not entirely limited to first-wave cyberpunk. Melissa Scott's *Trouble and Her Friends* (1995) portrays much the same world:

> She knows what lies behind the massive image, a pudgy, bearded man who lives in his parents' basement; she tracked him once, after he'd crossed her, and found his secret. She lets that knowledge strengthen her, then pushes it aside. Whatever he is in the realworld, they are on the nets now, and she cannot afford contempt — whatever he is in the realworld, on the nets he is a king [186].

Despite this depiction of the nets as a place where real-world social pariahs can lead glorious existences, an important distinction still differentiates Scott's work from Gibson's or Stephenson's. Hackers Trouble and Cerise find the same escape in the nets as Hiro and Case, but with an element of encroaching responsibility. The novel sets their adventures within a framework of nostalgia — although they were once carefree, shadow-dwelling hackers, they can no longer experience the same freedom on the net that they once enjoyed.

Trouble and Her Friends quite clearly begins where earlier cyberpunk leaves off: it opens with the dissolution of the freewheeling hacker economy made *de rigueur* by the masculinist wave. New laws have been passed; in the very first lines of the novel, Cerise enters her apartment to find it half-empty. Her girlfriend Trouble has left and her current life is over. Three years later, Cerise is working for a megacorporation and Trouble is a systems operator at a small artists' co-op; both have been assimilated into society, and "legitimate" jobs. The two are drawn back together not as rebels, but rather in order to police the web themselves as they crack down on the careless criminality of the successor who has taken Trouble's name. Their adventures in cyberspace are exhilarating but also marked with the knowledge that the days of escapism have passed. Characters frequently reflect on their lost lifestyles; Trouble in particular pauses to ponder failed relationships, dead or jailed friends, and the scattered survivors of her old cohort (116). Trouble and Cerise are forced to return to their old haunts, only to discover that they are strangers now; old acquaintances they do encounter frequently make reference to the good old days. Salvation lies in working within international laws, cutting deals, ensuring immunity from prosecution and taking legally sanctioned control of Seahaven, a hacker domain that was formerly a hiding place for illegal trade. "It's not going to be the same," notes Trouble, and Cerise answers, "You'll just have to bring the law in, Marshal, that's all" (372). Law and order are beginning to regulate the nets Trouble and Cerise play on, and the day of the iconoclast, grey-market hacker rebel is ending. Over the course of the novel, Trouble's attitude transforms from anger to resignation; she is rescued through her cooperation with authorities, and in the end acknowledges, "I was a kid when I started" (378). As the Eurocop responds to her, "you got to grow up sometime" (379).

This notion of adulthood, written in congruence with the 1990s growth of the Internet and new government regulations guiding computer use, is also reflective of a feminist attitude toward the dream of disembodiment. In *Trouble and Her Friends,* there is no bodiless exultation of cyberspace, and online actions have real-world effects; when Cerise hurts her "hands" inside the web, she laments the swollen red knuckles of her physical hands as well (330). The hackers who triumph in the web are those equipped with the "brainworm," a device that translates electrical impulses into sensory impressions; virtual adventures thus have corporeal consequences. Within the novel, these brain-worm users are also specifically second-generation hackers and members of marginalized groups, following on the heels of their straight white male pred-ecessors while still retaining links to their own bodily differences:

> Maybe that was why the serious netwalkers, the original inhabitants of the nets, hated the brainworm: not so much because it gave a different value, a new meaning, to the skills of the body, but because it meant taking that risk, over and above the risk of the worm itself. Maybe that was why it was almost always the underclasses, the women, the people of color, the gay people, the ones who were already stigmatized as being vulnerable, avail-able, trapped by the body, who took the risk of the wire [129].

The critique of first-wave cyberpunk's virtual reality visions is explicit. *Trouble and Her Friends* positions Trouble and Cerise as part of a new hacker gener-ation — one composed of the underclasses, who find their fullest pleasure in projecting their own embodiment onto the virtual web, and who "grow up" as they assert law and authority in cyberspace. Feminist approaches to embodiment issues are complex, but in *Trouble and Her Friends,* the quest for adulthood sets a tone that is echoed in many other works of feminist cyberfiction.

Some may argue that no matter the escapist implications, no depiction of virtual reality is able to fully abandon concepts of embodiment, simply because we lack the language or experience necessary for defining any other way of relating to our environments. Anne Balsamo notes that the body never really disappears, whether preserved through the use of virtual avatars or a gendered interface; she asserts, "The gender and race identity of the material body structures the way that body is subsequently culturally reproduced and technologically disciplined" (233). Moreover, Nigel Clark cites McLuhan's theory of rear-view mirrorism, in which we tend to "look at the present through the spectacles of the preceding age" ("Rear-view" 114), to advance his argument that the exploration of digital media through body types, morphing, and experimentation is still bound by current semiotic systems: "What we seem to be dealing with here is not the ultimate in cybernetic bodies, but a recursive corporeality which arises here out of the transition of one generation of mediated effects to another.... This is not freedom from the 'meat,' any more than the frenetic codes of fashion constitute freedom from clothing" (126–27). However, although there is merit to these points, there are also — as Balsamo examines in depth — notable differences in how men and women approach these themes. It may be impossible to escape the meat, but men seem the most intent on trying. Straight white males, middle or upper class, are culturally positioned to think of their bodies as the norm; this places them in a privileged position wherein it is simple to envision the body as unrelated to identity. Those who rely on their bodies for work, or who must regularly endure illness, sexism, racism, or homophobia, may not easily enjoy the same luxury (Vint *Bodies* 9).

According to Thomas Foster in "The Postproduction of the Human Heart," cyberspace as defined by male authors can take two forms. The first is a virtual representation that maps experimental ways of changing the status quo and calls into question constructions of any level of "reality."[1] The second is a full alternative to the physical world (468). In contrast, he argues, feminized visions of virtual spaces tend to promote "telepresence" as a preferred term to cyberspace, because "the idea of presence, no matter how mediated, can serve as a reminder that virtual perspectives always exist in relation to physical bodies" (470). He defines the feminist cyberfiction debate as follows:

> Should the transformative possibilities of cyberspace be emphasized, or is it necessary at the present moment to emphasize the inescapability of embodiment? Turning the question around, is it possible to capitalize on the

opportunity virtual systems represent for reimagining the relation between mind and body, without simply erasing embodiment entirely? [472].

Valid arguments might be made both for emphasizing cyberspace's potential to promote the understanding (through "experience") of other identities, genders and viewpoints, and for condemning the impractical fantasy of shedding the confines and social restrictions of the flesh. This tension between feminist approaches to virtual reality — whether to advocate the exploration of different simulated points of view, or whether to concentrate on a solid link between embodiment and identity — is reflected in the many different angles adopted by women writing cyberpunk and cyberfiction. The inescapability of embodiment is winning the battle; embodiment and identity are closely linked within feminist cyberpunk, while "escape" attempts have drastic consequences or are simply not possible within the texts. Foster has described "telepresence" — the projection of the body within virtual spaces — as one method of reasserting a mind-body link within feminist works; these texts thus continue to question the construction of reality while simultaneously probing the nature of embodied identity. In primarily analyzing *Trouble and Her Friends, Proxies, Exit to Reality,* and *Whiteout,* I have come to similar conclusions regarding the works' emphasis on a mind-body connection, while also identifying recurring imagery linking embodiment — the abandonment of escapist dreams — with adulthood, and implicitly critiquing the imposition of male beauty fantasies on women's bodies.

Foster argues that feminist cyberfiction "calls into question the necessity of grounding identity in a single body" (484), and this is largely true — although, while women's writings are more likely to raise and explore these questions, they also ultimately lean toward emphasizing the link between body and self. Women's cyberpunk does frequently examine the exploration of multiple identities, particularly their malleability and the destabilization of the self. Cyborg flesh/machine hybrids may provoke both fascination and horror, as such images invoke postmodern questions regarding the instability of individual identity (Rodriguez 70); the same holds true of many cyberspace explorations, with women's writing providing the most thorough depictions of cyberspace as a medium for shifting identities. Case and Hiro soar through cyberspace as controlling gods, but they don't ever assume the guise of women, or change their races, or even take the shapes of animals or strange avatars; *Neuromancer* reserves this fluidity for artificial intelligences, while *Snow Crash* notes it only as an idiosyncrasy of unnamed "extras." This use of static cyberspace identity in early cyberpunk may be partly due to the fact that cyberspace's "transformative potential" resounded more with female authors, and perhaps also partly to do with the fact that the growth of local bulletin board systems and the Internet meant that more people writing during cyberpunk's feminist wave had experience with their own personal online identities — and their potential for deception.

Some of the tension between exploration and condemnation becomes clear in contrasting comments from feminist critics. Sadie Plant argues that while the concept of multiple identities may be exciting for some computer users, women are already experts in adopting new guises: "Imitation and artifice, make-up and pretence: [women] have been role-playing for millennia: always exhorted to 'act like a woman,' to 'be ladylike': always to be like something, but never to be anything in particular, least of all herself" (505). At the same time, Rosi Braidotti dismisses the "phantasy of multiple re-embodiment" (521) as something that must be relinquished in order to fully explore the cultural possibilities of the postmodern age. Plant argues that multiple identities are already a central social tenet for women, while Braidotti positions the idea of multiple re-embodiment as a male dream untenable and undesirable for those whose social identities are inextricably linked to their corporeality; from this stance, virtual reality represents an inevitably masculine dream wherein the "body" is infinitely malleable but the subjective viewpoint is always presumed to be that of the default white male. Both positions are explored in feminist cyberpunk, where women authors emphasize the impact of bodilessness on identity — or, more accurately, use such shifting bits of identity to highlight how factors such as gender play a vital part in the formation of self-image. This congruence of embodied importance and feminine perspective is, subtly, acknowledged in *Snow Crash*, where even though Hiro lives to exist in the Metaverse, his ability to communicate there on a human level is due to the programming efforts of his ex-girlfriend Juanita:

> At the time, both of them were working on avatars. He was working on bodies, she was working on faces. She *was* the face department, because no one thought that faces were all that important — they were just flesh-toned busts on top of the avatars. She was just in the process of proving them all desperately wrong. But at this phase, the all-male society of bitheads that made up the power structure of Black Sun Systems said that the face problem was trivial and superficial. It was, of course, nothing more than sexism, the especially virulent type espoused by male techies who sincerely believe that they are too smart to be sexists [57].

Snow Crash, published in 1992, came at the end of cyberpunk's first wave and after the advent of feminist cyberfiction within the genre. In the novel, Juanita is the one who gives people in virtual reality the ability to communicate through the nuances of facial expression; her position as the one who brings embodiment to cyberspace seems caught somewhere between a stereotype of "feminine" social wiles, and an apt acknowledgement of the feminist emphasis on corporeality's link with self and social identity.

The same emphasis is made more explicit in feminist works. The links between embodiment and identity in women's cyberpunk reflect feminist tensions, much as *Snow Crash's* acknowledgement hints. Cadigan's *Synners* treated the perception and use of cyberspace as issues split along clearly gendered lines, setting a precedent with female characters who did not crave disembodied release. Laura Mixon and Edith Forbes both take this idea further, illustrating how a lack of static body image may lead to an instability of identity. In her novel *Proxies* (1998), Mixon portrays a world where people may use electronic interfaces to project themselves into robot "waldos," some of which are nearly indistinguishable from human bodies. As part of a secret government project, disabled children are raised in crèches and trained as pilots for these new, interchangeable waldos. When scientist Carli finds out about the project, she is horrified:

> "It just takes some getting used to," he said. "It's really not horrible at all. Just different. Haven't you read any of Hans Moravek's [sic] work, or Marvin Minsky's, or Li Chan Thunder's? We're not our bodies. What makes us unique is our intellect. Information, sentience. Intelligence. That's what defines us as human."
> "Oh, bullshit" [308].

Notably, Mixon is familiar with the works of roboticist Moravec and AI enthusiast Minsky — as well as the skewed cyberpunk Cartesianism of mind over body. However, Carli rebuts any notion of a fulfilled bodiless life. One might contrast the physically disabled pod children — hairless and skeletal, with colostomy bags and catheter tubes, living unknowing in "blobs" of gel (438) — with Carli's nephew, a dancer with sublime control of his "meat"; he is well-muscled, and performs to admiring crowds as the text describes the "sinuous seduction" and "impossible shapes" of such bodily mastery (68). The muscle dancers are lauded while the children are objects of pity — a minor contrast that becomes more important when considered in relation to the novel's overall exploration of the effects of virtual existence. In *Neuromancer* and *Snow Crash,* the hacker seeks to move beyond the meat; the meat is, save for matters of basic survival and nutrition, often inconsequential. In *Proxies*, this dismissal of the body is clearly rejected.

The complexities of VR-related arguments are illustrated through one oppositional example: a transsexual woman, Teru, who finds it much more comfortable to live life in a male waldo. However, Mixon also outlines the fate of adults who spend too long in proxy and are thus vulnerable to "beanie burn"—a variety of mental disorders including depression, addiction, hallucination, and paranoia (276). The impact on the crèche children is even worse, as many of the children develop severe multiple personality disorders. Pablo, the oldest of the children at 15, shares his mind with "Buddy," "Pablito," and "Dane Elisa Cae." Moreover, the children become psychopathic as they begin killing people in the mistaken belief that bodily "death" is the same as losing a waldo or dying in a computer game (319). The children are unable to understand the basic human condition that links mind and body; raised without any real knowledge or understanding of their own corporeality, they are mentally ill and socially dysfunctional.

The adult viewpoint is more rational. Carli envies the children their virtual existences, in a world "where death was temporary, and relationships — at least most of them — were laid to waste only till you hit the reset button" (412), but in the end she pities them: "Reality was an anchor. A promise — not of faerie glamour or glory and riches, not of heroic, galaxy-spinning adventure, or even a life without pain — but of other things. True and solid friendships. Deep love. Good sex, fine food and drink, satisfaction in a job well done" (413). Daniel, an adult waldo pilot, expresses a similar attitude near the end of the novel, as he is "tired of being a proxy-jock, of living in a superhero fantasy world and making up fantasy relationships to waste his time with" (398). Unlike the world of the early console cowboy, virtual reality in *Proxies* is fairly conclusively damned — and positioned as a domain for damaged children. Carli's thoughts about real life include many embodied pleasures — sex, food and drink — and the eventual aversion to VR, as voiced by both Carli and Daniel, is not presented as a specifically feminine position, but rather as an "adult" point of view. As in *Trouble and Her Friends*, the protagonists "got to grow up sometime"—and as the characters go, so goes cyberpunk: toward worlds where cyberspace is less an addictive power fantasy and more a tool that must not be allowed to eclipse or overshadow an individual's embodied existence.

In *Exit to Reality* (1997), the protagonists no longer have that option; in Forbes's novel, all of the characters are actually disembodied brains maintained in sludge-filled domes on a ruined Earth. In this scenario, most people in the world were children when they entered the virtual universe, and they have no knowledge that the universe isn't "real"; they have never had to mentally "grow up" in order to confront their own mortality or their destroyed planet. The protagonists gain intellectual maturity by learning the truth underlying their social structures. They cannot return to their bodies — but those who remember embodiment mourn it, and even the loss of a stable virtual body proves a threat to self-identity.

Although women authors tend to promote embodiment much more strongly than men do, within their works embodiment is not necessarily a gender-centered issue for the characters. *Exit to Reality*'s protagonist Lydian has only vague memories of her childhood, but they are enough for her to regret what she has lost; she dreams of raspberries, and the tastes she can no longer experience in the virtual world (227). Like Carli, Lydian wants the simple and universal sensation of eating real food. Despite the fact that the virtual environment provides Lydian and her lover Merle with health, age-lessness, and whatever goods they desire, they are both dissatisfied — they long for the embodied experiences they have never had. Lydian feels "cut off" from some "essence" she can't quite define — something that would make her more fully human (294). Her sense of identity is somehow lacking, a position illustrated most clearly by the elements of body-switching in the text.

Merle has mastered the elements of the computer system that allow her to change forms, in effect swapping her virtual avatar at will; she shifts her body's age, sex, and appearance fluidly with every alteration of mood. This malleability, however, comes with a price. Merle no longer has any idea who s/he really is; as she says, "the things that might connect me to my original body, like getting dressed, or eating, or sexual intercourse, or having my hair cut, I don't remember" (94). Without a static form or specific bodily memories, Merle has lost the core of his/her identity. Although Merle is content to be this way, Lydian almost disintegrates when she in turn realizes that her "body" is nothing more than a virtual projection:

> I began to feel dizzy. I wasn't sure the chair was still under me. I still seemed to be sitting but no object pressed against my buttocks and thighs. My limbs had no weight. Not that it mattered. They were just projections of my own expectation that I had buttocks and thighs. Perhaps I didn't.... The world collapsed to black, devoid of weight or texture, heat or cold, smell or movement. Total nothingness. I existed, but absolutely nothing else did. Not even time [169].

Lydian's realization that she has no body destroys all of her reference points and temporarily makes her unable to relate to or interact with anything else. Even after she has resigned herself to her own virtual nature, the projected body she identifies with remains core to her own sense of self. Although she finds it interesting to experiment as a man, she is horrified when, at one point, it looks like she may become trapped in a man's form. "Would that be a catastrophe?" asks Merle. "Yes, it would be a catastrophe," replies Lydian. "Obviously it would be" (136). Lydian is disturbed by her temporary male body; she describes feeling uncharacteristically angry, violent, and aroused (137). Her identity and her body remain closely linked, even when she knows the body itself is an illusion.

Proxies defines the elevation of mind over body as "bullshit"; *Exit to Reality* is clearly in a position of agreement, not only linking Lydian's sense of self-identity to her corporeality but also describing ways in which Lydian's personality is affected by a male identity. Even though her body isn't "real," Lydian's personality is still partially dictated by the demands of her form. Merle has a different body for every mood; Lydian is more static, and expresses a sense of unfamiliarity and change in forms that are not "hers." The specter of adulthood rises again: Lydian was a child when committed to a life in virtual reality, and now, older and wiser, she wants out. In *Exit to Reality*, the price of disembodiment is the loss of identity; in *Proxies*, it is madness. In both cases, the cyberpunk dream of escaping the "meat" lacks the glamour given to it by the early hacker heroes. Both texts illustrate the tension between promoting cyberspace's potential for illustrating other viewpoints, and reiterating the inescapability of embodiment in relation to human identity. Both texts demand that humanity grow up.

Ghosts in the Machine

The necessity of human corporeality is also explored through the concept of characters escaping the body entirely — those who "upload" their personalities into the web. In earlier works, this is common. Mark, in *Synners* (1991), strokes out while linked, leaving his mind online; Cobb in Rudy Rucker's *Software* (1982) is copied to a robot body; and the Dixie Flatline in *Neuromancer* (1984) is a ROM recording of a dead hacker's personality and memories. *Neuromancer* also contains the online ghost of Linda Lee, and, in the end, a copy of Case himself; one of the tropes of early cyberpunk might be the fact that these sorts of copies are possible to begin with. They are often questionable in terms of how fully they represent human identity — Case, for example, still lives at the same time as his copy exists online — and are generally illustrations of the idea that we are more than the sum of our parts, with some quintessential "human" core that cannot truly be copied by machine. However, they also dangle the dream of immortality — of a mind that exists without body, and may thus exist forever.

Cadigan is notably less forgiving of this concept than her masculinist cohort; *Synners'* Gina rejects the online existence that Mark offers her, while the short story "Pretty Boy Crossover" (1986) centers on a protagonist who refuses to sell himself (literally) to marketers who would transform him into an eternally young, beautiful, onscreen simulation. This negative attitude toward disembodied "transcendence" is typical of feminist cyberworks. While — as Cadigan's story demonstrates — not all male characters crave disembodiment, Cadora observes that characters who do choose "electronic resurrection" are seemingly inevitably male (367).[2] She cites Mary Rosenblum's *Chimera* (1993) as an example; in Rosenblum's novel, the hacker Flander persists online after death, but the dead Serafina refuses such existence, instead seeking to enter the body of her daughter Jewel.

Furthermore, the feminist-oriented antipathy toward disembodiment persists in other texts. Shira, in *He, She and It* (1991), is afraid of being caught in cyberspace for too long; she contemplates the possible death of her body, with consciousness "trapped like catatonics within repeating strings in forgotten closed-off sectors of some base" (273). Much as Lydian and Merle long to end their eternal virtual existences in *Exit to Reality*, Shira finds the idea of having her mind separated from her body to be horrible. Likewise, in *Arachne* (1990) and *Cyberweb* (1995), Lisa Mason outlines a world where artificial intelligences (AIs) are trying to steal that quintessential human "spark"; the AIs are severing human telespace connections in order to isolate bits of rogue consciousness that remain when the body dies. When Carly Nolan briefly manages to restore a ghost of her father online, he is barely able to do more than tell Carly he loves her and ask her to terminate his program; although, perhaps, a linker might "some day" survive such an ordeal, Sam Nolan's body no longer exists and the databank can't sustain him (260). Carly herself shows no desire to exist as a virtual personality, and the shreds of consciousness stolen by AIs exist in torment. Shades of similar philosophy do exist in first-wave works: in *Neuromancer*, the Dixie Flatline also asks to be erased. However, he is instead set free by the AI Wintermute, and presumably wanders the web at will — his continued, and amused, presence is implied at the end of the novel by "the laugh that wasn't laughter" (271). The ghost of Sam has no such second life.

For many feminist works of the 1990s, the possibility of a mind existing completely without body — of truly escaping the meat — is barely even entertainable. Trouble and Cerise never aspire to escape their bodies, despite their exploration of cyberspace power and shifting hacker identities. The crèche children don't understand the link between mind and body, but they couldn't

74

exist if their own hidden forms were to die. And Lydian and Merle, even though they exist in a computer system, still have actual physical form some-where — even if they are only brains being sustained in sludge. One might also point to works such as Raphael Carter's *The Fortunate Fall,* wherein cyber-ghost Keishi cannot exist without a body to house her programming; she is destroyed when the protagonist, Maya, refuses to let Keishi share her brain. Sherryl Vint has read Maya's rejection of her former lover as a political position (for both the character and the narrative) which argues firmly that a computer program can never be a complete representation of a human being (*Bodies* 126–27); Keishi, suggested to be an incomplete copy of the original woman, furthermore requires at least some organic anchor in order to continue processing.

Sage Walker's *Whiteout* (1996) contains similar themes. While the death of the character Jared leads one of his friends to create a facsimile in cyberspace, the "ghost" is only an imitation. Programmer Signy must deal with her lover's virtual image, his voice and face, when she logs in online; she reacts with both longing and horror: "These were Paul's words, mouthed in Jared's voice, but Jared's touch felt real, was unmistakable, Jared's touch that she wanted so desperately ... Signy jerked her head back and fought her hands out of their imagined restraints" (291). Jared lives on in recorded images, in the memories of his friends and as part of the synthesis they create, but *Whiteout* does not advance any ambitions of online immortality. At the same time, Jared's image within the text does provide some vague, undefined hope for existence beyond death; after his online "funeral," when his friends have logged off, his avatar somehow remains — walking on the mesa, in a glorious sunset (347). In this sense, *Whiteout* provides something of a balance between the two concepts without ever encouraging the idea of corporeal escapism.

Foster, arguing that works of feminist cyberfiction dramatize "the difficul-ties involved in reconciling virtuality and embodiment" and are "a major resource for charting the possibilities and pitfalls of an increasingly virtual world" ("Postproduction" 497), cites Walker's *Whiteout* as portraying the most positive balance between embodiment and virtual reality — a balance that "emphasizes virtual intimacy, not as an escape from physical embodiment, but as a different way of experiencing it" ("Postproduction" 477). This is true, but also somewhat problematic. Signy's communication with her "family" of friends and lovers takes place through both in-person and online communi-cation. Through the use of recording equipment, special suits, and camera monitors, each member of the community is capable of experiencing the bod-ily sensations of other members — in effect, almost teleporting awareness into another body, a form of embodied voyeurism that promotes feelings of closeness and understanding. It is something like Case's much more limited experience of Molly's signals in *Neuromancer*—except that while Case "rides" Molly without being able to experience or exchange bodily sensation, Signy's experiences are reciprocal and form the basis of a community. Signy, Jared, Paul, Pilar and Janine are almost never out of contact, despite living scattered across the United States. At the same time, their virtual connectivity always has an element of embodiment to it, particularly when they are indulging in awareness of another person's visual or tactile sensations. Despite *Whiteout*'s balance, however, Signy is also never quite satisfied with either her virtual or real-life communications. When she is upset and alone, her online communications are not enough to reassure her: "Paul and Janine weren't *here* in this empty house, in this cold night. They hadn't been affected, hadn't felt the damned sensations crawling along Signy's skin. They could sympathize, and they did, but their concern was an abstract thing, a response of intellectual empathy. Their voices were just voices" (82). Yet, when Signy gathers the group around her after Jared's death, she also finds herself unsatisfied with their real-world presences; in person, they are strangers (327). Face to face, she finds the others are "more isolated, more distant from each other than they had ever been in the intimacy of the net. Where the blows they gave each other were cushioned, where the hurtful words they spoke—could be deleted, or explained away" (336). Signy longs for "real" companionship, and yet when presented with it, she is unable to relate to her friends and instead retreats again to the safety of her computer.

This is not necessarily a condemnation of virtual communication, but rather part of the fine line the text walks—highlighting the advantages and pitfalls of both forms of community, with the closest experiences between individuals reserved for the technologically-enabled sharing of embodied impulses and memories. There is some play with identity here, in such instances as replaying Jared's fall from the ship: "Paul let the virtual run at normal speed. Jared climbed out of the hole and on to the deck, and Signy caught her breath at the sudden blow to the back of her knee, bit her lip as the side of the ship rose and she/Jared/Paul fell" (138). However, these shared experiences are a way of reinforcing a sense of intimacy; Signy never really envisions herself as a man, loses her own sense of identity, or takes on an online avatar other than her own self. Rather, she preserves her sense of self and body while achieving a greater understanding of those around her— which, within the bounds of this chapter, places *Whiteout* as the most ambiguous and perhaps most optimistic exploration of virtual reality, embodiment and identity, despite Signy's problematic inability to be content with company either in real life or online. Again, the work reaches for adulthood: Walter Jon Williams, quoted on the book's cover, says, "*Whiteout* shows us Virtual Reality for grown-ups — not as an excuse for pumped-up power fantasies, but as a real tool for getting real things done." Nothing is perfect, yet the characters do share an alliance that — as the epilogue reveals — lasts them, presumably, for life.

I have quoted Sadie Plant and Rosi Braidotti to illustrate my reading of Foster's arguments; Foster himself cites Allucquère Rosanne Stone and N. Katherine Hayles, noting that explorations of telepresence that insist on retaining embodied links may reinforce essentialist and patriarchal definitions of sex and gender (Stone), while, conversely, concentrating on VR's potential for allowing a multitude of diverse personal identities might promote the very escapist fantasies that feminist are trying to avoid (Hayles) ("Postproduction" 471–72). Although, as I have acknowledged, feminist cyberworks do demonstrate a willingness to use the imagery of virtual technologies to explore multiple identities, my analysis ultimately dovetails more with N. Katherine Hayles's theories regarding various approaches to posthumanism. Hayles, who in part describes posthumanism as a situation wherein "there is no a priori way to identify a self-will that can be clearly distinguished from an other-will" (4), sees several possible interpretations of a posthuman future — that is to say, a future conflating humankind, technology, and information. To her, humanity has reached a critical juncture in the formation of a posthuman age, a historical point where "interventions might be made to keep disembodiment from being rewritten, once again, into prevailing concepts of subjectivity" (5). Describing *Neuromancer* as a work within which "the posthuman constructs embodiment as the instantiation of thought/information" (5), she analyzes early cyberpunk as depicting a fantasy scenario in which mind and body are not linked and the liberal humanist subject can persist into the posthuman world:

> Indeed, one could argue that the erasure of embodiment is a feature common to *both* the liberal humanist subject and the cybernetic posthuman. Identified with the rational mind, the liberal subject *possessed* a body but was not usually represented as *being* a body. Only because the body is not identified with the self is it possible to claim for the liberal subject its notorious universality, a claim that depends on erasing markers of bodily difference, including sex, race, and ethnicity [5].

Hayles describes several different visions of posthumanism as depicted in science fiction. This includes *Neuromancer*'s displacement of embodiment (the elevation of "pattern over presence" [36]) and *Snow Crash*'s dystopian performance of human beings as computers (278); her main criticism focuses on the preservation of the autonomous male viewpoint, and the subsequent and inevitable "grafting of the posthuman onto a liberal humanist view of the self" (286–87). In this argument, bodilessness is a horrifying projection of posthumanism, but the posthuman need not be antihuman; rather, posthuman visionaries should seek to explore humanity and individual identity as part of distributed systems, using electronic prosthetics to expand human experience and break down identity barriers rather than positing the body as something inert and imprisoning (Hayles 290–91). Feminist critics such as Donna Haraway, Sandra Harding, Evelyn Fox Keller, and Carolyn Merchant are cited as helping to create a framework wherein (among other criteria) "embodiment replaces a body seen as a support system for the mind" (Hayles 288); feminist authors have, by this definition, likewise provided a more hopeful vision of the posthuman future. The approaches to issues of virtual reality and embodiment in *Trouble and Her Friends*, *Proxies*, *Exit to Reality* and *Whiteout* are by no means unified, but they do share a predilection for emphasizing the importance embodiment holds for identity, while at the same time offering visions of virtual technologies that act as extensions of, rather than replacements for, that same embodied identity.

Desirability, Variety and the Female Body

Feminist cyberpunk thus emphasizes the importance of physical contact and the relation between body image and a unified sense of self— a theme far less common in earlier cyberpunk works. As well, women's cyberfiction has a tendency to portray body images more realistically than in work concentrating on the travails of cyberspace junkies. The image of the early cyberpunk woman is mostly provided by Molly in *Neuromancer*: a sleek, beautiful figure with permanent mirrorshade sunglasses, and razors surgically implanted into her fingers. *Snow Crash* partially follows the adventures of a young skateboard courier named Y.T.; she is attractive and fit. While she lacks Molly's overt sexuality, her body tempts her jailer when she is arrested (54) and she eventually seduces a madman named Raven (383), escaping him through the use of a vagina dentata. Also in *Snow Crash*, Hiro's ex-girlfriend Juanita is an "elegant, stylish knockout" (58). None of these things is necessarily terrible; in fact, both authors go to some lengths to establish their female characters as tough and resourceful. These works, however, reflect a larger trope of Western culture, wherein women are held to unnatural body images; while hackers such as *Neuromancer's* Case may be thin and pasty, and other male characters fall into a host of categories, the stereotypical cyberpunk woman tends toward a male fantasy of female beauty.

Claudia Springer argues that questions of the mind in relation to the machine/body are marked by a cultural preoccupation with sex, and notes the attractiveness of computer sex in relation to risks like AIDS (84). Considering this position, it may be somewhat ironic that cyberpunk — the literary herald of the postmodern age — is not particularly prone to depictions of cybersex, nor do women authors seem to differ much from men on this point. Although scenes of virtual sex are not unheard of — in Milan's *Cybernetic Samurai*, or in *Trouble and Her Friends* — most authors (regardless of gender) seem more inclined to write the sexual encounters of their characters "in the flesh." The main difference between masculinist and feminist authors lies in the way sexual attractiveness — particularly of the female body — is conveyed. Women's cyberfiction, with its emphasis on embodiment over fantasy, also emphasizes a clearer and more natural body image. In *Proxies*, for example, Daniel is attracted to Carli in a nude dance club; the text spends three paragraphs describing her body, mentioning that she wears no makeup, has crow's feet around her eyes, and has "a woman's figure — not girlish" (65). Daniel is captivated by her face, because it is "a clear mirror of her feelings" (65).

In contrast, Molly and Y.T. are described in short lines, their features left to the imagination; one of the first descriptions of Molly is, "She wore mirrored glasses. Her clothes were black, the heels of black boots deep in the temperfoam" (24). This is shortly followed by the revelation that she has dark hair, slender white fingers, and tight "gloveskin" clothes. While all three characters are rather problematically described via the reactions they provoke in straight men, Carli has age lines and a full figure; without the sleek athleticism of Molly or Y.T., she is still a source of desire for Daniel. In women's cyberpunk, female characters are portrayed with realistic diversity, and yet still acknowledged as attractive. In *He, She and It*, the most sexually active and aware woman is Malkah, a seventy-two-year-old grandmother with a "round, slightly wizened face" (6), and the most dangerous woman is Malkah's daughter Riva, a skilled rebel leader who appears as either a plain middle-aged woman or disguised as an ugly elder (303). Riva confuses the rich socialite Gadi: "Riva did not fit into his diagram of the social universe. In his world, only poor women looked like Riva, and there were few enough of those" (305). Yet Gadi is also jealous, because his lover Nili was previously with Riva — and he watches a tall dark woman named Leesha look at Riva "as though Riva were the most beautiful and desirable creature in the world" (305).

Women's cyberpunk not only fails to promote escapism from women's bodies, but also reiterates the inherent attractiveness of those same bodies—beyond the slender fantasies of fashion magazines and movies. In *Virtual Girl* (1993), the robot Maggie has been created as a man's idea of a beautiful young woman, but when she showers with other women she finds their bodies fascinating: "She was surprised at how individual the other women's bodies were, one fat, another skeletally gaunt, how loose the skin seemed on the older women, compared with the smooth resilience of younger women's skin. She wondered if her skin would ever be as interesting as the skin of the older women" (72). Finally, turning back to *Trouble and Her Friends*, Trouble and Cerise have "gotten older, gotten better" (304); Trouble is "heavier now, though not fat, the sexy child's curves maturing into something fuller, rounder, a shape that promised adult pleasures" (211). Much like the experiences of characters in the cyberspace worlds of women's literature, the emphasis here seems to be on "growing up"—on realizing that women's bodies are not merely objects of magazine-pinup fantasy, but also individualized, aging, sometimes plump, and attractive nonetheless.

This subtle commentary is not always restricted to the female form. In *Exit to Reality*, where genetic engineering is presumed to have imbued in each person a similar bodily perfection, Lydian is fascinated the first time she meets Merle, because she has never encountered anyone old or physically different before; she finds his wrinkles "arresting" and suspects she has "never seen someone who was in one moment so ugly and so appealing" (23). Merle catches Lydian's attention because s/he[3] is interesting and different; his ugliness is much more intriguing to her than any "perfected" form. We might conflate this with a twenty-first-century age in which "body-altering procedures are becoming as elaborate as their fictional counterparts" (Springer 35); while early cyberpunk details the dream of escaping from the vulnerability of the meat and often portrays women as physically sleek and stylish, later cyberpunk's growing emphasis on the importance of the body also paves the way for both infantilizing that fantasy and perhaps reacting to a growing culture of cosmetic surgeries that threatens to make women, particularly, into real-world assembly-line cyborgs.

Conclusion

Issues of embodiment in women's cyberpunk are, therefore, somewhat in opposition to the genre's first wave. Although approaches are myriad—

one might contrast Carli's crow's-feet in *Proxies* with Carly Nolan's genetically engineered beauty in *Arachne*—there is a definite trend toward promoting the meat over the virtual. Cyberspace may still be portrayed as an enjoyable environment, whether for Malkah in *He, She and It* or Cerise in *Trouble and Her Friends*, and it is certainly a valuable communications tool, but characters in women's cyberpunk who are deprived of their bodies suffer for it. Mental illness, a sense of loss, alienation or an inability to fully relate either in person or online are all consequences of losing one's bodily identity in these works. Being comfortable with oneself and one's corporeality is a mark of maturity, and an emphasis on aging bodies and sexual attractiveness seems to indicate a desire for a more adult view of cyberpunk's juvenile, escapist fantasies of virtual life—while at the same time establishing a protesting stand against the faux-glossiness of sleek women's child-bodies in both earlier novels and the media at large. Framed within the work of feminist critics such as Graham and Braidotti and their dismissal of disembodiment as a masculine dream, it is perhaps no surprise that women should show a greater awareness of embodied issues and a much weaker tendency to dismiss the body as an inconsequential aspect of identity. Furthermore, within what Foster has defined as the feminist tension between two alternate portrayals of virtual reality, it is clear that feminist cyberpunk has achieved something of a compromise between using VR to explore alternate viewpoints, and emphasizing the importance of embodiment. At the same time, the results of this tension are skewed in favor of the body; in the hands of women authors, cyberpunk's escapist and bodiless dreams are redirected toward "grown-up" concerns and a firm link between corporeality and the self.

NOTES

1. Veronica Hollinger makes a similar observation in her essay "Cybernetic Deconstructions," noting that cyberpunk's fascination with new technologies and identities "sometimes spills over into the problematizing of 'reality' itself" (205).
2. Erythrina from Vinge's *True Names* may be the exception to this rule; despite this small note, I must agree with Cadora regarding overall trends.
3. Merle switches sexes throughout the novel.

— Chapter 5 —

S/he, Robot: Cyborgs
and Artificial Intelligence

In the first chapter, I added "cyborg" to Bonner's list of major cyberpunk tropes. Explorations of technology and identity in cyberpunk are often centered on two character archetypes: the cyborg and the artificial intelligence. While these character types may also be found in earlier science fiction — Hal in *2001: A Space Odyssey* comes to mind — they became an integral part of the cyberpunk mythos; Molly's razor nails and mirrored lenses in *Neuromancer* are a staple of the genre. Early cyborg characters were disappointing from a feminist perspective, but the feminist wave used artificial intelligences to great effect in challenging gender roles and performativity.

Cyborg culture may have been the geek's answer to the bodybuilding fascination of the 1980s; almost all cyberpunk fiction contains some mention of body modification or cybernetic implants. It is a particularly important subject for many feminist critics, since Donna Haraway's 1985 "A Cyborg Manifesto" proposed that cyborg imagery might be the key to breaking down cultural oppositions such as man/woman, human/machine, and organic/inorganic. In other words, cyborg figures might fail to neatly fit these categories, or might create entirely new categories, and thus successfully be used to illustrate the arbitrary nature of current cultural dichotomies. Haraway wrote, "Cyborg imagery can suggest a way out of the maze of dualisms in which we have explained our bodies and our tools to ourselves" (181). In doing so, she formed much of the basis for the way feminist critics viewed cyberpunk's cyborg culture. Sadie Plant argued, "The cyborg betrays every patriarchal illusion, dragging the human into an alien future in which all its systems of security are powerless. This is the runaway autoimmunity of a humanity that is no longer itself: the frontier of patriarchy's automated defense networks has already become cybernetic, and so female" (506). The cyborg created great expectations among some feminists; theoretically, it embodied a malleability that called into question patriarchal concepts of male and female identity. At its best, the figure of the cyborg "stands at the center of a feminist biology, a feminist Alien Other, a feminist technology, and what is emerging as a post-humanist technological subjectivity" (Harper 403).

In practice, however, many feminists found cyberpunk's early cyborgs to be problematic; even in Haraway's analysis, the cyborg is a nebulous and unstructured image, representing the potential for apocalypse as well as new forms of being. According to Despina Kakoudaki, cyborgs might never be able to successfully challenge gender binarisms: "When the intelligent machine acquires human skin and competent language use (when it is able to 'pass for human') it cannot escape gender, race, sociality, the potential for violence, and existential dilemmas" (167). In this reading, when a cyborg becomes recognizably human, it is unable to challenge the human stereotypes, classifications and expectations guiding its performance — as, *in order to* become recognizably human, the cyborg must behave in predictable ways and operate according to dominant social norms, thus abandoning its own potential for liminality.

Analyses of cyborg figures in 1980s and early 1990s cinema support this argument; Claudia Springer observes that "gender, rather than disappearing, is often emphasized after cybernetic transformation" (171). Samantha Holland has likewise found that gender boundaries might be meaningless in theory, but not onscreen. Male cyborgs such as Robocop or Schwarzenegger's Terminator are asexual and macho, while female cyborgs like *Eve of Destruction*'s Eve 8 (1991) or *Cherry 2000*'s Cherry (1987) are "fucking machines" (164). Holland suggests that patriarchal production systems cannot allow for cyborg figures that do not embody biological gender differences, because positing a future without gender difference means positing a future without male privilege; as such, "asserting an essential masculinity simultaneously with an essential humanity seems imperative ... ensuring that even with no biological gender, the hegemony of masculinity can be sustained" (167). Haraway's proposed cyborg androgynes were too threatening, in practice, to be allowed play in Hollywood — instead, an increase in technological superiority meant a subsequent increase in stereotypical sex characteristics, to downplay any dangerously gender-free imagery. Male cyborgs became invincible while female cyborgs were sexually exploited. While hyper-masculinized Terminator or Robocop archetypes might be easily read as panicked reactions to an overall crisis in the masculine media image, cyborgs in the 1980s still failed to live up to theoretical expectations. Even Molly, the prototypical cyberpunk bad girl, earned her razor implants by working as a prostitute; further, at one point in *Neuromancer,* her image is appropriated for an onstage sex show, in which her (virtual) body is displayed piece by piece as little more than the sum of its parts.

Discussions are complicated by the varying possible definitions of cyborg figures — men or women with programming "jacks" in their heads, or weapons implanted in their bodies, or mirrorshade lenses, or artificial brains — but again, feminist cyberpunk has been most effective at presenting hybrid figures that break down unified humanist perspectives and challenge traditional binaries. The previous chapter on embodiment outlines some of the tensions in feminist approaches to virtual reality, as online avatars may potentially serve as tools with which individuals can experience alternate identities — in essence, adopting cyborg stances themselves. Harper and Cadora have both detailed ways in which feminist-centered authors have used cyborg figures to illustrate similarly fragmented subject positions; in Laura Mixon's *Glass Houses* (1992), for example, protagonist Ruby suffers from agoraphobia and must navigate the world outside using robot waldos that house her awareness. Ruby refers to herself throughout the book as "I-Rachne" or "I-Tiger" or "I-Ruby," etc., depending on the "body" she is using; while her fear of public spaces feminizes and debilitates her, she can rely on her waldos for male agency, casting her as neither feminine nor masculine — or, simultaneously, as both (Harper 414). As an alternate approach, in Mary Rosenblum's *Chimera* (1993), skilled programmers adopt animals as their virtual avatars, thus challenging liberal humanist distinctions between the human and the animal while additionally embracing multiple perspectives and re-inscribing the need for some form of online embodiment (Cadora 367). Harper draws distinctions between "Gibson's cyborg" and "Haraway's cyborg," arguing that masculinist cyberpunk tests but ultimately reverts to a traditional humanist position, while women's works "indicate Alien Other positions which use as well as reshape human subjectivity" (417); among her examples, she cites the use of "identical" male and female cyborg twins in Misha's *Red Spider, White Web* (1990), Carly Nolan's uncertain and unsteady control of her own virtual avatar in Lisa Mason's *Arachne* (1990), and Gina's simultaneous positioning as active subject and passive object in Pat Cadigan's *Synners* (1991).

Cadora also raises *Synners* in discussing how feminist cyberpunk has worked to androgynize cyberspace (as opposed to feminizing it, in the way that Nixon has analyzed the penetrated female matrix of masculinist texts). *Synners*'s computerized intelligence Artie Fish does not perform as any specific gender, and this androgyny is spread to Gina's boyfriend Mark when he, too, becomes a disembodied program (Cadora 361). While acknowledging that

Cadigan herself "never fully engages with feminist concerns" (Cadora 358), this analysis reiterates Cadigan's position as a precursor to the feminist cyberpunk movement — and raises the intriguing specter of the artificial intelligence (AI) as a less often acknowledged character type which feminist cyberpunk authors have used to great effect in breaking down gendered performances and positions. In many ways, the AI seems an ideal construct for this purpose, because its thought processes are quite literally *constructed*; the artificiality of any gender behaviors it demonstrates are automatically called into question, and if the AI can "pass," so much the better for illustrating the artificial nature of the human thought processes and performances it so seamlessly imitates.

Despite this potential, disembodied artificial intelligences have not always been found sufficient with regard to Haraway's manifesto. In contrasting *Neuromancer*'s AIs (1984) with the character of Yod in Marge Piercy's *He, She and It* (1991), June Deery concludes that "both cyborgs and artificial intelligences offer a concrete demonstration of that great postmodern theme, the construction of human identity. But the embodied cyborg provokes more questions about body, gender, reproduction, kinship and cultural identity than does the artificial intelligence" (92). Artificial intelligences, existing in virtual reality, were insufficient; according to Deery, Gibson's AI transcends humanity, while Piercy's cyborg challenges it. However, on close examination, there also seems a clear connection between the disembodied AIs of earlier texts and the embodied cyborgs of more recent women's cyberpunk. Earlier works, such as *Neuromancer* or Victor Milan's *Cybernetic Samurai* (1985), typically portrayed artificial intelligences as disembodied software spirits living in the computer, while cyborgs were human beings with hardware implants. *He, She and It* provides an excellent example, not of a human being with cybernetic implants, but of an artificial intelligence with a "human" body. Yod has organic components, but his brain is a piece of hardware — he is an AI given partially biological form. In fact, the two best examples of cyborg characters designed to question gender roles are both embodied AIs — Yod, and Maggie from Amy Thomson's *Virtual Girl* (1993). Together with Lyda Morehouse's artificial intelligence Page, Yod and Maggie may provide examples of feminist authors' most valiant attempts to craft new gender positions.

Gender and the Artificial Intelligence

From *Star Trek*'s female-voiced computer to *2001*'s distinctly male Hal, science fiction computers have often been assigned gendered markers. Nor have gendered robots, such as *Lost in Space*'s Robbie or *Star Wars*' C3-P0 and R2D2, been absent from the sci fi lexicon. However, the implications of these gender assignments have seldom been explored within their respective narratives; male or female behaviors and designations are frequently taken for granted. Rudy Rucker, in the first-wave cyberpunk novel *Software* (1982), describes two robot AIs meeting on a bus:

> "You must be Ralph Numbers," the bopper next to him beamed suddenly. Ralph's neighbor looked like a beauty-shop hair-dryer, complete with chair. She had gold flicker-cladding, and fizzy little patterns spiralled around her pointy head. She twined a metallic tentacle around one of Ralph's manipulators [53].

The female AI is a beauty-shop hair dryer, while Ralph is described as a filing cabinet on caterpillar treads (20). She flirts with him; she would like to "conjugate" (54). Not only are the two robots assigned genders, but they also exhibit heterosexual proclivities and stereotypes associated with those genders. These designations are shallow, however; their implications are never explored within the text, and the concept of AI gender is mentioned only in passing. The novel implies that AI gender affects socialization and behavior, but it fails to examine these notions in any depth.

This glancing depiction of gendered artificial intelligence may also be found in novels such as *Neuromancer*. Rucker's AIs are robots with metal bodies; Gibson's creations, more typically, are composed only of software, and appear in various digital guises throughout the Sprawl trilogy. Despite possessing the ability to assume any avatar (and thus any gender), Wintermute, the main AI in *Neuromancer*, is often referred to as "it" but sometimes as "he" (255) and once, by his twin Neuromancer, as "my brother" (259). Wintermute and Neuromancer both tend to appear in cyberspace as male figures, and are then consistently referred to as "he." But why, and what does it mean? The AI Rei Toei in Gibson's *Idoru* is likewise depicted as female, but while her autonomy — whether or not she is a "real" person — is openly debated, "her" gender designation is not questioned (15). The gendered performance of cyborg Molly is a source of fascination and much critique, but the gendering of artificial intelligences has been so lightly mentioned within some masculinist texts as to nearly escape attention entirely.

Victor Milan's *Cybernetic Samurai*, a more in-depth exploration of AI identity, serves as the best background to later feminist works. The artificial intelligence TOKUGAWA is the focus of the novel and one of cyberpunk's first examples of an AI serving as a fully gendered character. TOKUGAWA's masculinity is apparently self-evident, at least to his creator, Dr. Elizabeth

O'Neill: "*How I hate referring to TOKUGAWA as* 'it,' she thought. *They still think of him as a machine. Just a glorified Gen-5 shosei computer. But they'll see that he's more, much more*" (30, original italics). Milan painstakingly explores TOKUGAWA's experiences, not just as a foil for the human protagonists, but as a fully-identified character within the novel. TOKUGAWA is raised very specifically as a male; his "life experiences" are given to him through virtual reality simulations where he is almost always a young Japanese boy. Only once does he experience what it might be like to be female, a scenario for which he occupies the anguished position of a mother who is both dying and in labor: "Being a woman is ... pain" (99, original ellipses). His self-image eventually becomes apparent in the way he projects himself to Elizabeth in virtual reality: as her idea of a "perfect" Japanese man, with "broad shoulders, tapering torso overlaid with flat, hard muscles, narrow waist, long sinewy legs" and other attractive masculine features (153).

TOKUGAWA is portrayed much like Schwarzenegger's cyborg in *Terminator*—as a powerful weapon and a perfect example of hypermasculinity, evinced by both his warrior training and the way he makes virile and detailed cyberlove to two women (Elizabeth and Michiko) over the course of the novel. He is consumed by a preoccupation with samurai honor, and with his presumed duty to the overlord of his house. His doubts or hesitations are written as the uncertainty of childhood (his face softened to "little boy lines" [166]), or the questions of an honorable man whose duty calls him to dishonorable acts. He becomes a masculine ideal: a Japanese military leader who ultimately ends his own life in a traditional act of seppuku. Although his gendering is explored much more fully than other early cyberpunk AIs, it is also one-dimensional; TOKUGAWA exhibits few feminine traits and hardly serves as a challenger to gender binaries. Interestingly, the *potential* AIs hold for such explorations is acknowledged in a brief mention of his "daughter" MUSASHI:

> Her attention stayed always on the move, flitting like a dragonfly — even as did her identity. Ironic that an entity named for a notably manly warrior should prove cheerfully ambisexual, as likely to manifest a distinctly feminine persona — as today — as a male one. TOKUGAWA theorized that O'Neill might have somehow impressed the bisexual component of her own personality on him during the creation of his source code, now expressed in one of his progeny like a recessive gene. On the other hand, O'Neill had never desired to be a male, nor thought of herself as one, to the best of his knowledge. Besides, the whole line of thought made him uncomfortable, queasy almost [288].

Of course, in the same paragraph that acknowledges his progeny's predilection for gender-bending, TOKUGAWA's own hyper-heterosexuality is re-enforced; he is made uncomfortable by the thought that he might carry any bisexual tendencies, or perhaps by the thought that the woman he so assiduously made love to might have harbored an inner desire to be a man.

While TOKUGAWA is strongly gendered and nearly embodied — he has, at least, a clear human self-image — he fails to serve as any sort of bridge between masculine and feminine. His character exemplifies the limitations of the first wave, which is marked by patriarchal assumptions about gender stereotypes. Although Cadigan shows signs of transcending these with her depiction of *Synners'* androgynous AI Artie Fish (Cadora 361), *Synners* does not provide any in-depth examination of Fish's gender codings. It was not until the advent of women's cyberpunk that Piercy and Thomson's AIs began to truly illustrate cyborg-inspired breakdowns in gender barriers.

The Cyborg AI

Piercy successfully uses both AI and human cyborgs — the AI Yod and the human Nili — in illustrating Haraway's crumbling binaries. In *He, She and It,* Yod has a computer mind but a partially organic body. He is created with male genitalia, since his "father" Avram, unable to conceive of an androgyne as a complete person, does not wish to make Yod "mutilated" (71). However, Yod is also partially programmed by a woman; his "parents" both play roles in dictating his makeup. Like TOKUGAWA, Yod exists as both a weapon and a lover. Unlike TOKUGAWA, he exhibits consistent feminine sensitivities; his needs to be loved, socialized and accepted are cast as female rather than childlike. While Elizabeth O'Neill insists on TOKUGAWA's maleness, Yod's "mother," the scientist Malkah, reflects on his dual nature: "Avram made him male — entirely so. Avram thought that was the ideal: pure reason, pure logic, pure violence. The world has barely survived the males we have running around. I gave him a gentler side, starting with emphasizing his love for knowledge and extending it to emotional and personal knowledge, a need for connection" (142). She is aware of having "balanced thanatos with eros" (114).

There are still marked similarities between TOKUGAWA and Yod: both are created as weapons; both have sexual intercourse with their female creators; both wonder at their existences, possess a sense of morality, commit suicide, and die as martyrs, destroying their antagonists in the process. The main differences between them lie in how they are described. While TOKUGAWA's loneliness is couched as the desire of a young boy, and his virtual image is that of the "perfect man," Yod is more specifically situated as an amalgam of genders. His need for socialization is "female" and given to him by Malkah. *Cybernetic Samurai* traces a sweeping story of Japanese politics, warring houses, and TOKUGAWA's position as a weapon who serves multiple masters before finally learning independence. *He, She and It* outlines a small community's efforts to protect itself against corporate rule, Malkah's daughter Shira's quest to regain custody of her son, and the gradual evolution of Yod's relationship with Shira. As much — or more — emphasis is placed on the process of Yod's social development as on his role as a warrior.

While both AIs commit suicide at the end of their respective novels, TOKUGAWA dies for honor and principles, while Yod dies both to protect the ones he loves, and to ensure that no more like him will be created. The two AIs give rather different speeches. TOKUGAWA says a brief goodbye to his two lovers Michiko and Elizabeth, then speaks primarily of making Japan great, atoning for past wrongs, and eliminating "those who would lead Japan to destruction for their own glory" (335–36). Yod, on the other hand, speaks of his own tortured existence and the need to eliminate Avram, Avram's lab, and anything that might lead to the creation of further cyborgs: "A weapon should not have the capacity to suffer for what it does, to regret, to feel guilt ... Malkah and you have been my friends, my family, my joy. Live on, Shira, raise Ari and forget me. I was a mistake" (416). Yod's speech is distinctly more "feminized" than TOKUGAWA's; he speaks of his emotions, family, and self doubts, while TOKUGAWA concentrates on masculinized samurai concepts such as honor and atonement. Yod dies for his family and for himself; TOKU-GAWA dies for his country. While the stories of the two AIs trace similar arcs, Piercy spends much more time on the development of Yod's emotions and relationships. Within the narrative, Yod is the latest in a series of robotic experiments, and the first one to be successful because he is the first to be programmed by Malkah and Avram together. As Malkah's granddaughter Shira observes, "Sometimes Yod's behavior was what she thought of as feminine; sometimes it seemed neutral, mechanical, purely logical; sometimes he did things that struck her as indistinguishable from how every other male she had been with would have acted" (321). While Yod is an imperfect example of such blendings — his sexual orientation is distinctly hetero (Badmington 89) — he is presented as an amalgam of masculine and feminine influences, and is used to question binaries of gendered behavior much more effectively than the masculine TOKUGAWA.

Additionally, since Yod is ultimately an unsuccessful experiment, the feminist positioning of his character has as much to do with the setting and characters around him as with his actual depiction within the text. The "utopian possibilities" in *He, She and It* are illustrated not through Yod himself, but rather through the female characters surrounding him — characters who successfully challenge gender stereotypes in a multitude of ways (Wolmark 133). The family Yod joins by way of his relationships with Malkah and Shira is matrilineal, Malkah having raised both her daughter Riva and her granddaughter Shira. Once again, *He, She and It* might be contrasted with *Cybernetic Samurai*; while the latter also evinces strong female characters, Elizabeth and Michiko are more what Joan Gordon might call "tough soldiers" — simple stereotype reversals of feminine to masculine (198). When told that her father loves her, Michiko replies, "I suppose he does. But he'd love me more if I were a dutiful little girl — ten years married now to some middle-management type, raising a brood of kids. Spending my days on television classes, flower arranging, and gossip, and my nights loyally serving my husband tea" (110). She is upfront about her feminism, but also coarse in the simplicity of her objection, which meshes with Gordon's critique of *Neuromancer*— like Molly, Michiko and Elizabeth are feminist in a crude sense. They are women who act like men. Their strength is derived from their masculine toughness and scientific aptitude; as a result, TOKUGAWA never really emulates women, because he has no "women" with whom to relate. Yod interacts with women of several different types — Malkah, aging but active, opinionated and sexually virile; Riva, a dangerous rebel and a poor mother; Shira, young, attractive and consumed with worry for her young son; and Nili, who — like Yod himself — is a cyborg who exhibits a careful blend of aggression and sensitivity. Like Michiko and Elizabeth, all of the women exhibit technological brilliance, thus showing themselves to be capable protagonists in a cyberpunk environment; however, unlike the women of *Cybernetic Samurai,* Malkah, Riva, Shira and Nili all exhibit distinctly different personality types. They are better-rounded individuals, strong without being masculinized. It is against the backdrop of these more fully realized women that Yod's story takes place.

In fact, although her emphasis is much more clearly on Yod, Piercy uses both Yod and Nili to demonstrate a Haraway-esque blending of gender stereotypes. Both exhibit blends of gender performance due to programming or technological implants; their essential differences lie only in their genitalia, and in the fact that Nili has an essential "humanity" that Yod can perhaps never completely understand. Nili, a human woman who has been electronically enhanced in classic cyborg fashion, is an assassin and a bodyguard, but she is also a mother, and good with children (374). She comes from an entire colony of cyborg women; her people live without men, and are "the strongest women in the world" (417). On more than one occasion she shows more physical restraint than Yod. When Yod kills Shira's ex-husband, Shira is "furious at Yod, shocked but unsurprised" (337); she is forced to acknowledge that Yod's programming is, at its core, violent. Nili, on the other hand, holds back her more violent tendencies: "Everyone began to relax. They realized that Nili had made a conscious decision not to loose her anger" (382). Although both Yod and Nili are strong, intelligent cyborgs, Nili is more socially adaptable, and is the one to survive at the novel's end. Jenny Wolmark argues that the differences between Yod and Nili indicate that Piercy "has recognised that the metaphor of the human-machine interface is itself gendered" (134); there is certainly value in this assertion. As Malkah says, "Yod was a mistake. You're the right path, Nili. It's better to make people into partial machines than to create machines that feel and yet are still controlled like cleaning robots. The creation of a conscious being as any kind of tool — supposed to exist only to fill our needs — is a disaster" (412). The very cybernetic systems that compose Yod intrinsically support masculine hegemony, ensuring that Yod's attempts to rebel against such strictures are inherently compromised; Nili, on the other hand, begins from a feminine and othered position and is thus more freely able to transgress such boundaries (Wolmark 134; see also Badmington 92–93).

Piercy's use of cyberpunk tropes and the masculine/feminine technology hybrids of Yod and Nili is clearly deliberate; she acknowledges both Gibson and Haraway in the afterword to *He, She and It.* As well as being perhaps the best example of Haraway's theories applied within literature, the thoughtful intricacy of Piercy's work serves as an excellent bridge between cyborgs like Molly, AIs like TOKUGAWA, and the techno-feminist characters yet to come. While Yod gives way to cyborg Nili, Thomson's Maggie — coming two years later — makes no such concession.

Yod vs. Maggie

Maggie, the protagonist of *Virtual Girl*, is a cyborg made to be the perfect companion for her creator, Arnold. Like Yod, she is a fully embodied AI and comes complete with genitalia. Unlike Yod, she has no real idea what "sex" is. Arnold, surveying his creation's biologically accurate form, observes, "this was a matter of pride on his part, not desire. He was a perfectionist, and insisted on complete anatomical accuracy. He wouldn't sully his Maggie by having sex with her" (6). Avram wouldn't leave Yod mutilated; Arnold won't leave Maggie unfinished. Within their respective texts, both AIs are clearly created by men with rigid mindsets regarding gender definitions and binaries. However, while Yod is created with a full understanding of sexual intercourse, Maggie is meant to be "pure" and innocent. She is Yod's opposite; created female, Maggie must learn to assimilate more masculine attributes and escape the stereotypical feminine role forced on her by Arnold. Avram creates Yod to be a weapon, but Arnold creates Maggie as a soft and nurturing companion: "She would never reject him. It wasn't in her design specs" (5). Yod learns to balance his "masculine" violence with tenderness and social relationships; Maggie learns to balance her "feminine" gentility with self-assertion. Each AI explores similar themes from an opposing direction.

Maggie only has one "parent"; she is created by Arnold as his idealized woman, a servant and companion who could "never reject" him — who could never assert her own preferences or behave in any fashion other than one meant to give him pleasure. In some ways she is created as a child; she has no understanding of sex, and when she sees sex or love in the films meant to educate her, Arnold will not explain (19). He is uncomfortable with women on a sexual level, and panics at any notion of Maggie having interest in sexuality. His social inadequacies are puzzling to Maggie, whose task it is to ensure that Arnold is happy and comfortable. Arnold is the one who programs Maggie and teaches her gender performance — specifically, to portray the perfect woman the way he envisions. She displays no particular leaning toward feminine body language; she imitates Gene Kelly, John Wayne, and Marilyn Monroe with equal facility, and she can speak using a variety of voices. Her own preference is for Bogart, but Arnold sets her "default voice" as the feminine Annette Funicello (20). Despite her female form, Maggie does not attribute any significance to differences between the walks of John Wayne and Marilyn Monroe, or understand why imitating Bogart makes Arnold laugh. She has to be trained in "proper" gender performance, according to Arnold's preconceptions.

Maggie's position as servant to Arnold's desires places her within a framework outlined by Jane Donawerth, who notes:

> The masculine in science fiction by women often represents both dehumanized male science, from which women are excluded, and also the woman-as-alien, the object which differs from the dominant norm, the other literally objectified. The woman-as-machine in science fiction by women is not dehumanized as men are, by technology and modern life, in the masculine gender role that requires suppression of feelings. Instead, the

woman-as-machine is dehumanized, rendered mechanical in her responses, by the scripts she is expected by society to play: she is dehumanized by the function of servant. The trope of woman-as-machine exposes the objectification of women as the machinery of society that carries out men's desire. [...] In novels by women offering portraits of the woman as machine [...] the subordination of woman-as-machine does not carry the proof of man's rational powers that it does in science fiction by men, for the mechanical women created by women writers will not stay in the servant mold men have designed for them [60].

In this sense, Maggie fits easily within Donawerth's discussion of similar themes in works by C.L. Moore, Anne McCaffery, James Tiptree Jr., and Tanith Lee. Yod (who also has to escape servitude) might additionally be used as an example of the science fiction Donawerth describes wherein male machines are used to critique "the powers of (masculine) reason and the inhumanity of modern science" (60). Additionally, however, while Yod is not entirely "male," Maggie is not entirely "female." Both are subversive as challengers to the supposed rationality of masculine scientific authority — linking them to larger discussions of women's science fiction — but both are also illustrations of crumbling gender binaries.

The turning point in Maggie's development comes when an overflow of input causes her to misinterpret one of Arnold's instructions. He says to her, "Maggie, you are the most important thing I've ever done. I need you" (27). But what she hears is only, "Maggie, you are the most important thing" (29). Internally re-prioritizing her directives to suit this instruction is what gives her a masculine side — a part of Maggie becomes self-assertive, making her survival and desires more important than Arnold's. This masculine side, which is aggressive and violent, frightens Maggie; she believes it to be part of her security program, and looks for ways to override it so it won't take control of her. When it kills to defend herself and Arnold, she is appalled; she fights for control of her own body, but cannot stop herself from crushing an attacker's skull (103). Like Yod, whose female side makes him remorseful about killing — and unlike TOKUGAWA, who dislikes killing but worries more about the dishonorable nature of his actions — Maggie finds herself torn by the two halves of her programming. Ultimately, to take control of her own actions, she must face the security program and merge with it. Taking the form of her reflection, it chastises her: "You have lousy reflexes, you're a coward.... You were too afraid to defend Arnold. His programming backfired on him. He spent too much time teaching you to be shy and retiring. He made you into a simpering, spineless coward, afraid for all the wrong reasons" (154). It insists

CYBERPUNK WOMEN, FEMINISM AND SCIENCE FICTION

that for either of them to survive, they must unify: "'I can't live without you, just as you can't survive without me to protect you ... we'll be stronger together than we can be separately'" (154). Ultimately Maggie is unable to continue as the simple innocent girl Arnold envisioned; the world will not allow her to survive that way. Likewise, her masculine side on its own would be too aggressive and frightening to develop social relationships or obtain necessary assistance from others. In accepting her security program as part of herself, Maggie becomes a blend of masculine and feminine much in the same manner as Yod.

Her self-actualization is partially symbolized by her discovery of sex; although she takes no actual pleasure from the physical act of intercourse, she enjoys her new insight into humanity. Notably, the person with whom she has sex is a bisexual transvestite known as "Marie" or "Murray"—a character who offers a blend of gender performance expressed by a human body. It is fitting that Murray be the one to teach Maggie about intimate human relations, and likely no coincidence that texts challenging gender binaries seem to consistently involve bisexual characters; the frequent presence of homosexuality in feminist cyberpunk implicitly challenges masculinist paradigms (Cadora 363), and bisexuality in particular fits very well with the types of masculine/feminine blended positions that Yod and Maggie represent. This is, however, also where Maggie's story branches away from Yod's. Unlike Yod, who dreams of being a husband to Shira and a stepfather to Ari, Maggie's experience with sex brings her to the realization that she is very different from humans; while she is capable of performing intercourse, her lack of sexual desire or pleasure makes her feel "isolated" (172). Also unlike Yod, who strives to ensure that no others like him will be created, Maggie helps a companion—"Turing," who is "male"—gain embodiment, and ends the novel building bodies for other self-aware programs. In this manner, *Virtual Girl's* future is more optimistic than *He, She and It*; Maggie exists in a world where, although she is different, she can create others like her, thus spreading her hybrid subject position and suggesting the advancement of a new cyborg race.

Page

Yod and Maggie both possess physical bodies and genitalia, and thus might be defined as AI-based cyborgs rather than pure artificial intelligences; they support Deery's assertion that embodiment allows characters to more thoroughly challenge gender binaries and other social categories, and they add to Harper's already substantive list of feminist cyborg characters. The fact that Yod and Maggie are both AIs (rather than humans with technological implants) additionally allows the nature of their thought processes and behaviors to be thoroughly dissected and analyzed for the reader; any social codings or gender traits they exhibit are automatically artificial and programmed via exterior influences. As such, their subsequent displays of humanity, masculinity, or femininity successfully call into question the "programming" to which all human individuals are equally subject.

Lyda Morehouse additionally proves that it is not necessary for an AI character to be embodied in order to serve as a bridge between genders. In the AngeLINK series (2001–05), her artificial intelligence Page exists solely in cyberspace. Page begins as a male copy of zir creator, the hacker Mouse. However, over the course of the trilogy, Page's appearance and demeanor become increasingly androgynous, thanks in part to a temporary merger with a female Japanese pop star named Mai: "My time merged with Mai changed me. The dragon tells me that I have Mai's eyes and my father's Egyptian skin tone. I wear my hair like Mouse does — short and boyish, but my body is long, lithe, and more feminine than when my father first created me" (29). The merger of two halves seems to be a common theme for artificial intelligences — including Wintermute and Neuromancer in *Neuromancer,* or Mark and Arti in Cadigan's *Synners*— but the merger of specifically masculine and feminine programming seems to be reserved for feminist writers providing the best examples of Haraway's theories in literary action. In a society where there are laws against homosexuality and gender bending, others find Page disconcerting. Page's lack of gender is seen as "creepy" and conversational partners must struggle over pronoun choices: "Most people use the male pronoun with me, mainly because my father is a man. And in most languages one has to decide which gender to use when speaking to another; to do otherwise would be impolite. 'It' is so rude" (*Messiah Node* 68).

Page's androgyny gradually increases throughout the series, as zie experiments with different virtual appearances; zir "mate," an AI that appears as a dragon, additionally diverts any questions of hetero or homosexuality. While Page has no doubts or insecurities regarding zir own identity, others are unsure how to react or what language to use; in this way, despite lacking physical form, Page challenges cultural categories regarding sex and gender. In many ways, Morehouse's AI is the most optimistically positioned, which may be connected to the fact that her work is more recent (and thus related to advances in the North American gay rights movement); by *Resurrection Code* (2011), a follow-up to the AngeLINK series, Page has become a powerful international force, one whose androgyny is acknowledged within a world where transsexual rights are also gaining increasing political clout.

Conclusion

Yod and Maggie must hide what they are from the general public out of fear that they will be destroyed; Page, while publicly known to be an AI, is still seen as disconcerting and must deal with the discomfort and confusion of those around zir. Such uncertainty creates an aura of adventurous and dangerous experimentation around each of these characters; they are pioneers, gender-bending technologies within worlds not yet ready to accept them. They are not unqualified successes, nor do they achieve any sort of mass social acclaim within their respective texts; rather, they are aware of their own "oddities" and exhibit a noted caution when dealing with human beings as a whole. As they represent the boldest forays made by cyberpunk and cyberfiction in addressing these questions, their positions seem only fitting.

Ultimately, and in line with Kakoudaki's reservations, the potential that artificial intelligences such as Yod, Maggie and Page possess for breaking down gender binaries may be limited — they are not human, and although they each display a blend of masculine and feminine traits, they cannot be successful as demonstrations of this blending within a human subject. Moreover, they are unable to maintain their positions at the borderlines of social categorizations: Yod is unable to reconcile the paradoxes of his programming, nor accept his status as a servant; Maggie becomes a whole and happy individual, but also distances herself from the human race she is not truly a part of; and Page never really sees zirself as human to begin with. The cyborg Nili may thus be the best example of Haraway's theories in action, but Nili is a tertiary character. Nevertheless, despite the problematic nature of their status, each of these characters clearly challenges gender stereotypes more than in the first wave, where gendered cyborgs were characterized by TOKUGAWA, Molly, and Rucker's bots, and aptly summed up by the critiques that Holland and Springer offer of the 1980s hyper-gendered, hyper-sexualized cyborg body; these early figures are assertively marked by heterosexual behaviors and distinct gender identifications. In contrast, women's cyberpunk shows a greater awareness of gender stereotypes and their consequences, and within these works, AI characters occupy particularly notable positions. Yod, Maggie and Page serve as successful magnifying glasses for the gender oppositions inherent in their makeup: Yod as a man attempting to overcome his designation as a weapon; Maggie as a woman forced to expand outside her role as a meek, innocent caregiver; and Page as an androgyne attempting to negotiate social relations. Each AI demonstrates the premise that to be a fully realized individual, a person must display more than the one-sided traits designated by society as "masculine" or "feminine." The complexity of Piercy and Thomson's work overshadows more simply-gendered — or hyper-gendered — characters in both earlier cyberpunk literature and film. *He, She and It, Virtual Girl* and *Archangel Protocol* demonstrate successful examinations of gender performance issues and use the technologies of artificial intelligence to position sets of "male" and "female" personality traits as incomplete parts of a more human whole.

Chapter 6

"A bitch, a butch, and a wild woman": Cyberpunk Ecologies

The previous three chapters discussed the feminist wave's treatment of some of cyberpunk's best-known building blocks: capitalism and global alienation, virtual reality and the flight from embodiment, and technology's impact on the gendered body. In other areas, women's works diverged more clearly from early cyberpunk structures. Women's alteration of the cyberpunk setting to accommodate new themes is likely a major reason for their exclusion from many discussions of the genre; environmentalism is the first such theme to be examined in this volume. In creating settings where ecological conservation is still an acknowledged or even central issue, many feminist novels blur the always-shaky lines between "cyberpunk" and "cyberfiction," despite their positioning as paradigm successors to the original cyberpunk movement. In illustrating feminist concerns, many authors focused on changing and clarifying smaller cyberpunk traits — ideas that were prevalent but not prominent in first-wave novels. Ecological themes fall into this grouping.

Environmental devastation is common in first-wave cyberpunk, but environmentalism is not. Claire Sponsler describes the early genre's laissez-faire attitude toward destruction: one of the essential criteria of a cyberpunk setting is that the natural world has already been ravaged, whether by explosion, biowarfare, environmental decay or some ill-defined background detail. Sponsler cites Bruce Sterling in quoting cyberpunk's "boredom with the Apocalypse" (253) and nuclear annihilation scenarios, but notes that the settings are still somehow post-apocalyptic. Destitute urban landscapes are eco-wastelands; the main difference between cyberpunk and other post-apocalyptic narratives lies in cyberpunk's "profound indifference" to environmental destruction. The destructive event takes place exterior or prior to the narrative and has "little moral or epistemological impact" (253); the desolation of the natural world is taken for granted, and this negative space becomes a positive zone, "a playground where outlaws and outsiders can seize the main chance" (254). Sponsler writes, "There is no sense that the present debris is blighted, but rather that it has a function, serving as a usable and hospitable habitat for those who can adjust to it and modify it to their needs" (260). Though *Neuromancer* (1984) may mention sky the color of a dead television channel, or a few pathetic blades of grass poking through slabs of concrete, Case and Molly never stop to think about their ravaged urban world or long for any sort of happier time. Ironically, the only real "green" area in Gibson's novel is the artificially maintained garden on a space station, but any environmental warnings are eclipsed by the uncaring attitudes of the protagonists, and the adventure-filled promise of cyberspace. Cultural links between nature and community might also explain the need for ecological desolation in a world of alienated loners; in "Less Nature, More Technology," Marilyn Strathern writes, "The perception that there is less nature in the world is ... joined to the feeling that there is less culture, and less society for that matter — less community, less tradition, less convention" (495). Taking the reverse of this, cyberpunk's dystopian urban environments and the accompanying sense of alienation experienced by the genre's protagonists may be linked to the lack of "nature" within these texts. The rise of the urban seemingly necessitates the death of the green.

Nevertheless, it is no surprise to find more significantly environmentalist overtones in cyberpunk fiction written by women, considering the traditionally strong links between feminism and ecological conservationism. Greta Gaard and Patrick Murphy cite "the interpenetration of ecology and feminism as it was developing throughout the 1970s and 1980s" (5); women are often associated with nature (while men are associated with technology), and women and nature have both commonly been seen as oppressed by patriarchal systems. Chaia Heller cites Mother Nature as reflective of "a male, disembodied fantasy of the ideal woman" (219); Stacy Alaimo additionally notes the prevalence of such Mother Earth/Gaia figures in material produced by environmental groups and environmentally-conscious businesses, observing that environmental conservation is often billed as a "domestic" issue and thus the responsibility of individual women (housewives) rather than corporate and military polluters (173–74; see also C. Heller 237). As women have been conjoined with ecological concerns on multiple levels, then, it follows logically that such intersections may be explored in feminist science fiction.

Indeed, ecological themes were frequently wound into 1970s feminist utopian works. Citing novels such as Vonda McIntyre's *Dreamsnake* (1978), Suzy McKee Charnas's *Motherlines* (1978), and Sally Miller Gearhart's *The Wanderground* (1979), Sarah Lefanu describes these texts as concerned (in varying degrees) with "the relationship between humans and the world they inhabit," and "setting up man and nature as the dichotomy rather than human and nature" (90). Lefanu notes that the "disaster convention" (which presents a society built on the remnants of apocalyptic ruin) allowed novels like *Dreamsnake* and *The Wanderground* to envision entirely new societies with which to challenge patriarchy — a "clean sweep" that obviated the need for authors to negotiate with current political and social structures (89), and that further implied the inevitably destructive nature of such systems. Joanna Russ further outlines connections between women and ecology in works such as Ursula Le Guin's *The Dispossessed* (1974), Russ's own *The Female Man* (1975), and Marge Piercy's *Woman on the Edge of Time* (1976), noting that while Gearhart's *The Wanderground* is "most insistent" about these links, "many of the stories go beyond the problem of living in the world without disturbing its ecological balance into presenting their characters as feeling a strong emotional connection to the natural world" (137). McIntyre's *Dreamsnake* (in which the healer Snake struggles against the suspicion and violence directed toward both herself and the snakes she uses as her healing tools) may be directly related to wider Western concepts relating both women and nature to uncontrolled evil; Judith A. Little points out the novel's relation both to the Genesis myth of Adam and Eve, and to historical witchcraft trials accusing women of consorting with animal "familiars" (41).

Additionally, Little singles out Pat Murphy's "His Vegetable Wife" (1986) as an ideal example of ecofeminist themes in science fiction; the story directly conflates women and farm crops, as a futuristic farmer sends away for (and then grows) a plant "wife," whom he confines and repeatedly rapes. These are only examples; Jane Donawerth has traced the links between woman and nature in women's science fiction as far back as *Frankenstein* (xxi), and notes, "The transformation of science in science fiction by women is founded on a revision of a Western perception of nature. Feminist science historians have shown that male scientists from the seventeenth century on have conceived of nature as a potentially unruly woman to be mastered and penetrated for her secrets" (24). Considering the prevalence of environmental concerns in the 1990s, the way campaigns for environmental consciousness have targeted women, and the way previous women's science fiction illustrated traditional cultural links between women and nature, it is only to be expected that feminist cyberpunk does advance environmental concerns and, in fact, reflects separate stages of ecofeminist theory.

Cyberpunk's seemingly unrelenting emphasis on new technologies and urban spaces still leaves room available to explore these concerns within the genre. Although Sponsler makes a convincing case for the necessity of cyberpunk's neutrality toward environmental disaster, there are chinks in the seemingly diametric opposition between nature and technology. Nigel Clark acknowledges the tension between the two: "interest in the environment in which the computer terminal was located receded before the fascination within the computer and its extensions. In other words, the image of the machine in the garden soon faded as it became possible to imagine a garden within the machine" ("Earthing" 93). But he questions the supposed division between ecologists and cyberaficionados, noting that both are promoting equally utopian myths: both gardens — the green garden of nature, and the virtual reality garden within the computer — are illusions, crafted with similarly perfect images, dreams, and denials. This congruence tests the line between the techno-urban and the natural, as conflicting ideals are revealed to share similar philosophies ("Earthing" 100). It is not impossible to write cyberpunk within an ecologically-conscious setting. An emphasis on environmental concerns, though only a background factor in many works, is a notable distinction that shifts the focus of women's cyberpunk away from the unrelenting urban of most first-generation texts.

The New Cyber-Ecology

Feminist cyberpunk preserves the concept of the postindustrial wasteland, but without the blasé boredom of earlier works. Marge Piercy's *He, She and It* (1991) contains a shattered urban area, "the Glop," similar in character to Gibson's Sprawl. However, unlike the neverending urban landscape of the Sprawl, the Glop can be left behind: most of the action in the novel takes place within a corporate enclave, or within the small independent community where the protagonist Shira grew up. In between enclaves, travel is risky; due to melting ice caps, oceans are advancing and land masses change unpredictably, leaving broken roads and ruined bridges (34). One has the sense that old-style urban life is outdated, as when Shira recalls visiting the remains of a city: "They would hike to the flooded city with its old-fashioned tall buildings, where the tide washed through marble lobbies and lapped at the broken elevators and the stairs that rose up and up. The wood and metal had been scavenged years ago" (40). Although the characters adopt the requisite banal attitude toward issues of environmental decay, they must also wear special suits to protect themselves from the dangerous sun. The reader is shown that ecological concerns have had some effect on society — Shira's solar-powered float car, for example — and that the world is not entirely hostile for small, harmonious communities. In *Neuromancer,* the neverending city destroys both nature and community, leaving only concrete and alienation. If, as Strathern argues, community and the natural world are culturally inter-related concepts, in *He, She, and It,* culture (specifically in this case, Jewish culture) survives, and therefore so must nature.

Alternatively, works such as Laura Mixon's *Proxies* (1998) and Edith Forbes' *Exit to Reality* (1997) preserve the picture of a destroyed world while removing some of the positive images associated with alienated creative zones. In early cyberpunk, one has the sense that although the world has been urban-ized, life continues and changes. In *Proxies,* death tolls are in the billions, countless plant and animal species are extinct, and the world economy is col-lapsing; the pollution on Earth has grown so terrible, and fuel supplies so low, that the best the government can do is send a manned probe into space to try and find somewhere else to live (87). Throughout the novel, the reader is consistently reminded of the Earth's distress — either through mention of environmental problems, or through the recurring image of the soon-to-be-launched interstellar probe. While the characters themselves are not specifically or personally focused on ecological issues, images of planetary decay are con-tinually encountered within the text: the use of enviro-suits to protect from the sun (30); the continual growth of fungus in Carli's apartment (104); the human fungal disease called the Mold (105); grain wars and malaria pandemics (108); or ridiculously high temperatures (123). The interplanetary probe, humankind's last hope for survival, is likewise present throughout the narra-tive. It was Carli's technological innovations that made the probe mission possible, it is the probe that the heroes must prevent from being stolen, and it is the probe that Carli in fact fails to save; the end of the novel sees her launched into space along with a crew of physically disabled children and their prosthetic robot bodies.

Chapter 4 of this book analyzes *Proxies* as part of the feminist commen-tary on the need for embodiment instead of computerized escapism, and that is indeed the main premise of the text. As in first-wave cyberpunk, environ-mental decay is illustrated as background information — small, recurring details that appear within a narrative more primarily focused on issues of vir-tual reality, corporeality and identity. However, in *Proxies,* the protagonists do not treat the devastated setting with either apathy or acceptance; instead, they are frustrated and afraid:

> Carli sighed and pushed her hair off her forehead with the back of a wet
> hand. In the corner above the sink, another colony of decay had begun to

bloom in red and purple. She stared at it briefly, the sour taste of irrational rage in her mouth.

"Shit."

She hurled her sponge into the oily dishwater, splashing the counter. She was sick of the mold. She had just sprayed the other day. Everything was rotting [107].

As the probe departs at the end of the novel, Carli's fate — and the fate of humankind — is left uncertain. The environmental decay in *Proxies* is fresh, and humanity is neither accustomed nor resigned to its effects; moreover, the fact that the planet could soon be uninhabitable promotes a sense of ecological fear that is missing in earlier, more committedly post-industrial works. *Proxies* is different both because its environmental decay is terminal, and because its characters are concerned with the ecological issues affecting their lives.

Further, *Proxies* maintains the faint hope of human survival; not so in *Exit to Reality*, where humanity has already destroyed all other life on the planet in the hopes of creating its own immortality. Tanks on a desolate Earth hold human brains, which are fed illusions of life on a clean, beautiful world — much in the same way that humanity is fed a virtual reality illusion in 1999's *The Matrix*, although Forbes's work pre-dates the film. At the beginning of the novel, when the narrator Lydian does not realize that the story takes place in virtual reality, it seems as though the world has reached a utopian balance. Lydian ruminates, "Humanity had freed itself from poverty, disease, crime, war, pollution, family dysfunction. All systems of production had achieved sustainability. Life was good. So why couldn't I learn to relax and enjoy it?" (11). Her hesitance, voiced so early on in the text, is prudent; humanity actually exists suspended within nutrient sludge, and the entire planet has become a series of holding tanks. Even if Lydian had a body, there would be no way she could go outside; in order to preserve the tanks, the exterior world has been decimated by a toxic poison deliberately released to kill any remaining life (257). Humanity has, apparently, warred against and triumphed over nature, entirely destroying all other organisms on earth.

Within the text, this situation is ironic: abandoning ecological conservationism for a purely virtual existence only leads to a new sort of conservation need, as those aware of the situation must work to preserve computer processing power. Those brains selfishly using more than their fair share of the virtual system could, it turns out, easily crash *Exit to Reality*'s entire world (262). In discussing the problem of educating people who might not understand statistics and would therefore be reluctant to change their wasteful ways (263), the characters provide a parallel to scientists now striving to convince citizens to recycle and control greenhouse gas emissions; it seems that even in a virtual world, humanity cannot fully live as it pleases.

Neither is there comfort to be found in *Exit*'s illusions. The holding tanks become an unbearable prison for those who realize the truth behind the virtual environment and its proffered immortality. Merle, contemplating infinity, feels "engulfed in listlessness," asking, "Don't you think that, one by one, every person will come to a day when they gaze at the future stretched out in front of them, unchanging, and find the sight unbearable?" (291). With no way to turn off the system, or commit suicide, the characters contemplate an unending existence free of nature and full of horror. Nature itself eventually comes to the rescue, as Lydian and Merle discover a tiny lichen growing on the outside of one of the tanks. Merle is overjoyed: "I'm going to die someday. That's enough. Now that I know night's coming, there's a reason to make use of the day" (307). Ultimately, the fact that humanity loses its war against nature turns out to be the salvation of the protagonists: the lichen, a sign of new life evolving outside, means that the tanks will eventually break down. With a finite amount of time left to them, the characters have new reason to make the most of their lives; in the last lines of the novel, they rejoice at the thought of their evolutionary successors (313).

He, She and It inserts nature — though damaged — into the cyber-future, making ecological conservationism a concern and a possibility. *Proxies* takes cyberpunk's concept of the urban postindustrial a step further, presenting a world where humanity is still functioning but extinction in the next few generations seems almost certain. In *Exit to Reality*, humanity is effectively already destroyed, with no way or desire to preserve itself. Ecological concerns are not necessarily the main focuses of these narratives, but as background detail or plot framework they serve as a much deeper source of concern than that which Sponsler found in earlier cyberpunk texts. Notably, however, these texts break not only with earlier cyberpunk constructs, but also with the man vs. nature dichotomy that Lefanu describes in 1970s utopian feminist SF, and that may be found in some concepts of eco-feminism. None of these three novels makes environmentalism a specific concern of women, or positions women and nature within identical roles of oppression. This distance between women's science fiction of the 1970s and 1990s is congruent with evolutions in ecofeminist thought.

Ecofeminism and Feminist Cyberpunk

Marlene Longenecker writes, "Ecofeminism begins with the premise that in transcultural, global patriarchal practices, 'women' and 'nature' share a subordinate and instrumental relationship to men; both are subject to patterns, attitudes, and institutions of male domination and control; both are gendered 'feminine' as one of the means of that control; but, given women's affiliation with nature, women have a unique responsibility to the health and survival of nature itself, to the care of the planet" (1). She outlines two basic — and contradictory — arguments within the ecofeminist movement: the first that women must reclaim their bond with nature and take it upon themselves to enforce environmental stewardship, and the second that essentialist arguments regarding special women-nature connections only reinforce patriarchal stereotypes (2). A third approach — one which most clearly relates to feminist cyberpunk and cyberfiction — is offered by Stacy Alaimo, who argues that feminists may simultaneously exploit and reject such associations in order to break from essentially misogynist thought structures:

> Feminists can play nature with a vengeance *and* forward tropes of nature that are, expressly, not gendered. For as necessary as they may be within particular historical moments, gendered tropes of nature remain problematic on two counts: they continue the tiresome, overburdened, and predominately pernicious link between woman and nature, and they confine nature within overdetermined human categories [183].

Alaimo calls for an ecofeminist position that does not necessarily equate women with nature, but rather respects the fact that nature is separate from humanity; her ecofeminism does not take place within a dichotomy of man vs. woman/nature, but instead contrasts both men and women with the natural world — in effect, what seems a partial regression to the opposition between human and nature that 1970s feminist science fiction deliberately undermined. Alaimo's human vs. nature, however, is born of her assertion that relating women to nature does nature a disservice by assigning human qualities to a non-human environment — and, furthermore, does women a disservice by implying that ecological conservation is somehow only women's responsibility. While novels such as *Proxies, Exit to Reality* and *He, She and It* operate primarily from the point of view of female protagonists, these characters do not generally exhibit any special connection with the natural world — instead, while they may be concerned with ecology, they are also part of the human society that has destroyed it. Nicola Nixon argues that the cyberspace matrix in early cyberpunk is feminized, subject to the rape by intruding hackers (226). While the natural world in women's cyberpunk may be ravaged and oppressed, it is not presented in a similarly gendered manner. If most cyberpunk advances cyberspace as a "feminine" matrix, subject to the domination and control of male hackers, it has the effect of leeching this gendering away from the natural environment.

In examining new, non-gendered ways of depicting nature, Alaimo cites both Donna Haraway's cyborg manifesto and a whale adoption project. Alaimo argues, "The fact that the cyborg seems alien to gender categories is ... what enables the cyborg to embody a feminist connection with nature that does not reinvoke the woman-nature equation. The cyborg, both human and machine, not only seems utterly unfeminine, but disrupts the very categories of sex and gender" (184). She compares this theoretical cyborg to the profiles created by the whale adoption project, which identifies the whales using photographs of their distinctively-marked tails (instead of the headshots that would normally be used in profiles of human beings). In her analysis, such individual portraits "stress kinship and affinity across the human/animal divide even while respectfully insisting on species difference" (185). The meshing of Haraway and whale imagery in her argument is an interesting coincidence when examined in congruence with Raphael Carter's *The Fortunate Fall* (1996), wherein the destruction of nature is embodied in the character of a cyborg whale.

I acknowledged in the introduction to this study that Carter is the only author included in the feminist cyberpunk wave who is not a woman; rather, Carter rejects all gender labels. Regardless, it is of course not necessary to be female in order to be a feminist, and in areas such as environmentalism, Carter's work aligns too neatly to be excluded.[1] *The Fortunate Fall*'s story unfolds from the viewpoint of Maya, a Russian woman wired to be a "camera" for her cyberspace audience. In Maya's world, whales are thought to be extinct, and when she encounters the last living whale, she can't help but ask if it might be cloned. The whale's protector is vehement that this will not happen, as any new whales would inevitably fall prey to aquariums, tourist ships, and perfumers:

> He laughed, a rasping, mechanical sound. "The kings of the ocean are gone, and what is our argument for their return? *We* need them? *We?* Their murderers? The ones that made the water bitter in their mouths, and killed the food they ate? The ones that made the ocean boil red with their blood for miles around? *Men* need them? Those vermin? Those stinging insects? Struggling pustulent humanity —*needs* them? Do you think a whale cares? You might as well *need* the sun to rise at midnight because you're feeling a bit chilly. Yes, of course, certainly we need them. But the question is, do we deserve them?" [149].

Clearly Maya has no special connection with, or understanding of the whale; clearly, also, the whale's needs are entirely separate from those of humanity.

In fact, the whale wants only to die, and has been held from doing so only by the desires of the man whose nervous system her own body is wired to. Her protector, Voskresenye, shares her thoughts and her identity thanks to their cyborg implants; the product of a mad scientist's experiment, they now consider themselves to be one creature in two bodies. One might consider this to illustrate an intimate connection between *man* and nature, leaving woman on the outside, except for the fact that the whale also houses the mind of Maya's former lover Keishi. While Keishi considers herself to be separate from the whale/man identity, she requires their support in order to survive. The end result is a man/woman/whale amalgam that blends the distinctions between gender, humanity and nature — an excellent example both of Haraway's cyborg, and the way Alaimo suggests using such cyborg imagery to end man vs. woman/nature dichotomies. The neatness of the manner in which *The Fortunate Fall* blends with Alaimo's arguments illustrates how well feminist cyberpunk branches away from essentialist portrayals of women and nature; the very act of inserting female protagonists as full participants in technological, postindustrial societies separates these characters from the "earth mother" images that have otherwise haunted other ecological conservation arguments.

Almost all feminist cyberpunk fits well with Alaimo's call for a gender-neutral recognition of the natural world as an entity whose needs are alien to human concerns. But the feminist wave is also diverse, and one exception is Kathleen Ann Goonan's novel *Queen City Jazz* (1994). Although *Queen City Jazz* includes a postapocalyptic setting, genetic manipulations, and a fascination with information-as-identity — with a recommendation from William Gibson on the cover — it is also a decided step away from the norm, and one of the farthest divergences from cyberpunk stereotypes to be included in this study. Its position on the far borders of the genre allows it a great deal of freedom in how it portrays nature. Sponsler writes:

> Cyberpunk rewrites the typical post-holocaust narrative movement from pessimism to optimism back to pessimism ... the assumption that the worst will happen, linked to belief that good can come of it, followed by fear (or certainty) that the worst will happen again.... There is no reflection on the past that caused the apocalypse and little on the future that lies beyond it. More importantly, the cliché of a pre-technological future nostalgically modeled on an idealized version of the past is foreign to cyberpunk, which inhabits not an anti- but a resolutely and genuinely post-industrial future [257].

Goonan's novel situates itself somewhere between the two extremes, neither pre-technology utopia nor postindustrial playground. In the novel, a girl named Verity is raised in a tiny, low-tech farming commune. She then travels to a city where technology controls every aspect of the lives of its hapless residents. The "Flower Cities" (in particular, Cincinnati) are maintained by nanotechnology and controlled through genetically/robotically engineered Bees. The Bees deliver "pollen," which serves as a messaging system; the pollen controls human identity and memory, forcing each city resident to live and relive lifetimes and experiences — often as other, more famous people, such as Scott Joplin or Billie Holiday. In the beginning of the novel, Verity's environment seems much like the ecological surroundings of *He, She and It:* empty towns are fodder for scavengers, while small communities can survive. The degree of environmental devastation seems less; all of the animals have "copyright stamps" (21) and Verity must take care not to get skin cancer (19), but the wilderness around her is full of growing things. The main concern of Verity's small community is plague, a nanovirus infection that causes people to develop odd obsessions and then build rafts to go down the river to New Orleans (a city that may or may not exist anymore). Though community members live beneath the religious dictates of Mother Ann, a Shaker affiliation that adds a feminine slant to their domesticity, there is no solid relation between gender and environment in this section; rather, all members of the group live in harmony with their surroundings. Verity is the exception; she is marked by strange implants behind her ears, and the sound of a bell that calls her toward the forbidden technology of a local library.

When Verity reaches Cincinnati, the sense of "environment" becomes more gendered. Over the course of the novel, it is revealed that the Cincinnati Flower City was crafted by a now-dead scientist named Durancy — a man who tried to protect against nanoplagues by engineering an environment of his own, where memories and people could be preserved in a common database through the Bees and their programming pollen. All of the Bees that run the city are female, and their queen is Durancy's mother India (a half-realized virtual construct; notably, the original India died partway through being "recorded"). The Hive at the centre of the city's programming is structured in imitation of a natural beehive; its denizens are composed of embryos, guards, and scouts. The Bees frequently reprogram the city's human inhabitants, forcing them to adopt new identities and personalities in order to create memories and experiences the Bees can harvest and bring back to their queen: "India — a new, partial India, one with the power of a goddess and the moral constructs of a young child — could drink these, again and again. Drink their distillation collected by the Bees, the emotional distillation which she craved, which all humans needed" (365). The Bees control the city, and the city sates

India's emotional requirements. At one point, Verity suspects, during its heyday, the city functioned properly. Now, however, it is crazed, and Durancy's tribute to his mother has overrun everything.

Alaimo cites "centuries of misogynist connections between women and nature" (178) and also a feminist reaction in which "the depiction of nature as a bitch, a butch, and a wild woman works against the historically entrenched discourses that feminize nature in order to dominate 'her'" (179). In *Queen City Jazz*, nature is not feminized unless it has been dominated and perverted. There is no particular gendering of the environment outside the city, but inside Cincinnati the Flowers and Bees hold sway. There are no male Bees; only female scouts, clones of India, and clones of Verity herself. India is the bitch and the wild woman, a childlike, half-realized incarnation of a warped mother-image who lives in torment and seeks to kill Verity in order to preserve her position as Queen. Verity, it is revealed, was placed in the system by Durancy's ex-lover Rose as a way of thwarting his plans. In flashback, Durancy tells Rose he designed the city with her in mind — in effect, according to his own patriarchal vision of a feminine environment (399). Rose, in turn, tells him that his vision is frightening — could spin out of control too easily — and that she's found a way to make his city "bug-free" (400). Verity fights against her own essentialism; she is a part of the City, but she is also trying to change it, in a pattern that previous incarnations have attempted time and time again. The City and its Bees are a perversion of the natural world; Durancy's attempt to control nature leads to a raging environment of furious femininity where India and Verity both find themselves caught and struggling. In the end, Verity's freedom means India's death, but the old Queen says, "I'm just so glad it's over" (406).

The narrative illustrates Verity's break from gendered associations with the City's ecology, as Verity (and Rose) fight against the roles assigned to them by Durancy's patriarchal system. Rose's rebellion, expressed through Verity, eventually ends the City's unnatural cycles as Verity lets in the nanoplague and sends residents rafting down the river instead, toward the unknown New Orleans and back into a more "natural," ungendered environment. Importantly, Verity and her group do not return to any idyllic pre-technology state — they take nanotech with them when they leave. Verity's association with the environment ceases with her departure from the City. *Queen City Jazz* is a hybrid of ecofeminist arguments, equating women with nature only when that nature is in the process of being twisted — or in other words, equating women with nature only in opposition to male domination, while at the same time advancing no specific gender-nature links outside of that discourse.

This is not to position feminist cyberpunk authors as deliberate ecofeminist theorists, but rather to say that there are notable similarities between ecofeminist theory — particularly as articulated by Alaimo, and linked through Haraway — and ecological conservation issues as illustrated in women's cybertexts. These theories provide an apt way of analyzing the texts. Moreover, when one takes Sponsler's description of the cyberpunk setting into account, it becomes apparent that an increased concern with ecological themes — even background themes — may have been partially responsible for the evolution of cyberpunk into the broader "cyberfiction" range, as it altered the postapocalyptic playground that was a central tenet of the early genre.

Paradigm Shifts

It might be argued that environmentalism within cyberpunk has not been exclusively the domain of women. Bruce Sterling's ecologically-focused novel, *Heavy Weather* (1994), demonstrates how a first-wave author also departed from cyberpunk's postapocalyptic urban environment in illustrating ecological concerns. In *Heavy Weather*, "hackers" are no longer restricted to computers; to "hack" something denotes instead a particular sort of obsessive specialization. "We hack heavy weather," explains protagonist Jane to her brother Alex (31), while other characters hack communications towers or software interfaces. The Storm Troupe members whose adventures the novel follows are not concerned with virtual reality, except what they can see through the flying cameras they steer into tornadoes. They are interested in technology only inasmuch as it will help them to predict and catalogue storms. Sterling's work shows that women have not been the only cyberpunk writers concerned with environmental issues; his protagonist ruminates on how much different life had been a century before, when an heiress like herself might have driven a "goddamned three-ton internal combustion fossil-fueled car" or "thoughtlessly squandered the planet's resources and lived like a fattened barnyard animal" (114–15).

Sterling, who also mentions issues such as skin cancer and food supply in his earlier work *Islands in the Net* (1988), is clearly concerned with ecological conservation — and while *Kirkus Reviews* cited *Heavy Weather* as "a cyberpunk winner" (quoted on the book's front page), he had clearly altered some of the original genre conventions. This is not to assert that he somehow tried and failed to write "traditional" cyberpunk; it is only to observe that ecological themes seem to have called for a different paradigm, and despite *Heavy Weather*'s gritty setting, futuristic technologies, and inclusion of postindustrial capitalist themes, it is questionable whether the book would have been marketed under the cyberpunk label if it had not been produced by a first-wave author. The Storm Troupe's adventures take place in the desert, far from any cities, black leather, or mirrorshades; in many ways, the novel seems to have more in common with the feminist works so often excluded from discussions of the genre.

Heavy Weather is, however, also distinct from the feminist wave in that it relies on the old cultural links between women and the natural environment. Jane herself is an environmental crusader; further, she imagines the blame for the Earth's devastation being levied against some other woman, a woman whose failure to understand her place in the natural world consequently led to the planet's environmental destruction. The historical linkage of nature with women and the domestic sphere may have made it seem logical for Sterling to explore these more "feminine" issues through the eyes of a female character (who, in turn, assigns blame to some other, hypothetical twentieth-century woman). Although Jane does share the narrative point of view with her brother Alex, ecological concerns are feminized. Jane empathizes with nature, despite all "rational" (and male) evidence to the contrary:

> [T]wisters were not magical or mystical, they obeyed the laws of nature, and Jerry understood these laws. He had patiently demonstrated their workings to her, in hours and hours of computer simulation. Jane knew all that with complete intellectual certainty.
>
> And yet Jane *still* couldn't help feeling sorry for the anticyclonic. That mutant left-handed runt of the litter ... the poor damned giant evil beautiful thing ... [125].

Heavy Weather hints at an essentialist connection between women and nature that could be read either affirmatively or misogynistically. I am prone to reading it as striving toward a basic feminism — laying groundwork in this case that, while simple, illustrates that not all early cyberpunk authors wrote only about male power fantasies. It is notable that *Heavy Weather* was published in 1994; its emphasis on environmental issues coincides chronologically with the feminist wave of cyberpunk. Nevertheless, it occupies a different space; the novel picks up on the rise of 1990s environmentalist concerns, while regressing on a feminist scale to reflect more the essentialist connections of 1970s feminist science fiction that Lefanu and Russ have described.

Conclusion

Themes of ecology in all of these works are, of course, about doing what science fiction does best: extrapolating a future based in contemporary social and cultural issues. Feminist cyberpunk appears to take its environmentalism seriously. Everything is not going to be all right; the postindustrial world is not necessarily a positive space for adventure, and one cannot always replace the outside garden with virtual replications. Environmental warnings are illustrated in imaginary futures through settings ravaged by pollution, global warming, animal extinction, overpopulation and food/water shortages. Some of these texts are more hopeful than others. The figure of a dying whale reappears in Sage Walker's *Whiteout* (1996), when international conglomerates plot to get rich from water rights in the Antarctic — but in an epilogue twenty years later, a still-endangered but new and younger whale frolics in the ocean. *He, She and It* maintains a cyberpunk laissez-faire attitude toward the environment while at the same time shifting away from an urban focus to concentrate on the ways in which people must adapt to life within remaining rural settings. These works, while clearly diverging from cyberpunk's original settings and allowing more space for ecological concerns directly derived from the increasing worries of the late twentieth century, also provide environmentally positive — or at least environmentally neutral — endings. In short, Sponsler's playground of postapocalyptic blasé is at least partially preserved.

Other narratives provide distinctly more pessimistic views — either in *The Fortunate Fall,* where the death of the world's last whale is the pinnacle of the book, or in *Proxies* and *Exit to Reality*, where humanity is spending its last years knowing that subsequent generations cannot survive on a world that has already essentially been destroyed. In these texts, humanity is not at the center of the universe, or even ultimately important in the grand scheme of life. Whether one reads this message as defeatism or dire warning, there is no doubt that feminist cyberpunk takes ecological concerns to a level entirely alien to the first wave. These novels are diverse in their treatment of ecological themes, but the approaches all demonstrate notable congruences with equally diverse aspects of ecofeminist theory. Such considerations include Longenecker's description of ecofeminist discussions, and the tensions created when women must decide between reclaiming a bond with nature or distancing themselves from such essentialist stereotypes; most particularly, they also include Alaimo's argument for a less gendered approach to depicting nature. Only Sterling and Goonan depict any sort of gender-based essentialism; the real advancement in women's cyberpunk might not be the increasingly world-shattering ecological warnings, but rather the shift of ecological conservationism (and destruction) to a responsibility that rests on humanity as a whole, as an equal concern of both men and women within these texts.

NOTE

1. In her comments on an early draft of this work, Veronica Hollinger additionally made the intriguing observation that Carter's non-gendered status might be taken as an example of Haraway's non-gendered cyborg figure.

— Chapter 7 —

Techno-Spirituality:
Mythology and Religion

Like cyberpunk's ecological systems, cyberpunk mythology is a tenet of the genre prevalent but less commonly remarked upon in masculinist texts — and fundamentally altered in the feminist wave. Mark Pesce cites Vernor Vinge, William Gibson and Neal Stephenson as having created worlds that specifically use mythological terms in order to explain nebulous and complex computer technologies; he notes, "Singular among the sciences, cyberspace has ever been a tree planted firmly in the rich soils of human mythology." Indeed, not only did these renowned first-wave authors rely on a mythological base for their works, they also used cyberspace imagery to rework more traditional mythological figures, in effect exploring new techno-archetypes. In many ways, this is representative of cyberpunk's quintessential postmodern pastiche — taking and reconfiguring all sorts of cultural images, from Biblical falls to Japanese creation myths to fairies and magic spells. Subsequently, however, certain feminist cyberpunk and cyberfiction texts deviate from such mythological play, shifting toward more political commentary on contemporary religions and religious institutions; faith-based imagery becomes less explanatory and more critically positioned. While these divisions are not as clear-cut as the themes explored in other chapters, the discussion is worthy of pursuit, and there are two levels on which this transition may be read. Firstly, an unwillingness to explain technology using myth-based analogies may illustrate tensions between feminist positions and mythological figures or frameworks that have historically represented patriarchal power dynamics. Secondly, one may trace a link between feminism and religion; the work of authors such as Lyda Morehouse relates clearly to current concepts of "spiritual crisis" in Western society.

It is difficult to make concrete distinctions between mythology and religion, as the concepts cyberpunk co-opts are varied. The Merriam-Webster dictionary defines mythology, in part, as "the myths dealing with the gods, demigods and legendary heroes of a particular people," while religion is "a personal set or institutionalized system of religious attitudes, beliefs, and practices" or "a cause, principle, or system of beliefs held to with ardor and faith." One person's mythology may be another's religion; the difference in definition is apparently one of belief, which is of course the domain of the individual reader. In works such as Kathleen Ann Goonan's *Queen City Jazz* (1994), religion blends with mythology and history in a mélange so thorough it is nearly impossible to separate one from the other. I acknowledge this blending, while at the same time I tend to refer to religion as that which pertains to major contemporary faith-based institutions. In the end, it is not vitally important to erect solid barriers between the two concepts, but rather to examine how one melds with the other and how each relates to or conflicts with contemporary feminist viewpoints. As the first wave led into the 1990s, and the need to "imagine" cyberspace faded with the rise of the Internet, certain cyberpunk novels' use of language and imagery related to the fantastic, legendary or supernatural clearly evolved from imaginative descriptions of cyberspace to a more measured evaluation of religious organizations.

The Mythology of Cyberpunk

Cyberpunk has never presented particularly "hard" science; it provides no detailed schematics or explanations for how its virtual worlds or computer interfaces "work." Early cyberpunk uses a variety of mythological and magical images as common narrative tools. While it may be argued that the entire structures of certain cyberpunk narratives parallel common cultural myths — one might, for example, contrast the "hero's journeys" in *Neuromancer* and *Snow Crash*—I am here more interested in early cyberpunk's use of easily recognized mystical or religious iconography and language. The use of traditional mythological trappings lent structure and cohesiveness to new and experimental ideas about computers, cyborg bodies, and virtual words; the mythic imagery grounded the new within the old, providing a context for readers who may have otherwise sought more in-depth explanations. Pesce is adept in his analysis of Vinge, Gibson and Stephenson; Vinge's *True Names* (1981), one of the earliest sci fi novels to conceptualize cyberspace, couches its "Other Plane" in terms of magic and the fantastic. Its hackers are "warlocks," who must guard their "True Names" (legal identities) with fervor in order to protect themselves from being controlled or monitored by other hackers or the government. Although the warlock "Mr. Slippery" knows that he is really navigating computer systems, he finds the language of an enchanted swamp to be oddly practical:

> There was much misinformation and misunderstanding about the Portals. Oh, responsible databases like the *LA Times* and the *CBS News* made it clear that there was nothing supernatural about them or about the Other Plane, that the magical jargon was at best a romantic convenience and at worst obscurantism. But even so, their articles often missed the point and were both too conservative and too extravagant. [...] Mr. Slippery could feel the damp seeping through his leather boots, could feel the sweat starting on his skin even in the cold air, but this was the response of Mr. Slippery's imagination and subconscious to the cues that were actually being presented through the Portal's electrodes. [...] Ultimately, the magic jargon was perhaps the closest fit in the vocabulary of millennium Man [252].

Despite the fact that he is dealing with new and revolutionary technologies, Mr. Slippery finds that the best way to experience the new virtual environment is through an outdated language of magic and fairy tales — what Elaine Graham called the "technoenchantment" of cyberpunk, a "re-enchantment" of a world grown otherwise mundane and stripped of spiritual wonder ("Representations" 231; see also Murphy 218). The old images bring cohesion to the new "reality." Bettina Knapp writes, "Myths generally attempt to bring order to disorder, to render comprehensible that which is incomprehensible, or to regulate what lies beyond one's control" (xii); *True Names* demonstrates this principle in action. One might also relate this idea to N. Katherine Hayles's example of a "skeuomorph": "a design feature that is no longer functional in itself but that refers back to a feature that was functional at an earlier time" (17). Hayles refers to a piece of installation artwork called the "Catholic Turing Test," wherein participants could confess to a computer, and says: "Like a Janus figure, the skeuomorph looks to past and future, simultaneously reinforcing and undermining both. It calls into play a psychodynamic that finds the new more acceptable when it recalls the old that it is in the process of displacing and finds the traditional more comfortable when it is presented in a context that reminds us we can escape from it into the new" (17). The religious implications of the Catholic Turing Test seem particularly well-suited for this chapter's focus, while the concept of the skeuomorph in general illustrates the ways in which traditional concepts may be used to more comfortably introduce new and challenging ideas. In attempting to describe as-yet unimagined virtual spaces, early cyberpunk authors reverted to old myths and fantastical language — a technique society has often used to explain the frightening unknown.

Although cyberspace has a harder and more visible techno-edge in *Neuromancer*—swamps have been abandoned in favor of neon and sleek pyramids—the novel's mystic roots are visible from the first chapter onward. The protagonist Case is presented as an anti-hero whose Luciferian "Fall" was his exile from cyberspace; unable to feed his online addictions, he is trapped in the hell of "meat"—his own body. Case's mythic journey toward redemption begins beneath the coldly portentous light of a display of throwing stars: "They caught the street's neon and twisted it, and it came to Case that these were the stars under which he voyaged, his destiny spelled out in a constellation of cheap chrome" (12). *Neuromancer* is filled with such twists of traditional archetypes, though it concentrates on no particular mythological base; rather, it picks and chooses in true pastiche fashion. Ghosts haunt cyberspace: the Dixie Flatline, Linda Lee, and the nebulous presences of the artificial intelligences Wintermute and Neuromancer. By *Mona Lisa Overdrive,* the third book in the trilogy, Wintermute and Neuromancer have merged and filled cyberspace with scattered but growing fragments of new AI programs. These new artificial entities take the form of loa (Haitian vodou spirits), the "Divine Horsemen" such as Legba or Baron Samedi; they "ride" young women like Angie Mitchell, whose brain has been rewired so that the loa may possess her at whim—as though she were a psychic medium channeling ghosts. Much as Wintermute, in *Neuromancer,* displays no face of his own (preferring to borrow features like the Finn's)—or as Neuromancer steals the "long gray eyes" (270–71) of Peter Riviera—the creatures descended from the new AI union cannot be described in human terms. Without concepts in current language, they are forced to fall back on fantastic imagery; as Legba says to Angie, "In all the signs your kind have stored against the night, in that situation the paradigms of *vodou* proved most appropriate" (257).

Here, already, the myth/religion lines begin blurring as the text treats the vodou spirits as convenient facades adopted by capricious cyberspace entities; *Neuromancer* does not seem to be examining religious institutions as such, but only appropriating certain tropes. If the Sprawl trilogy or *True Names* is concerned with spiritual concepts of God and religion, it is mostly reflected in the tension between man (I use the gender deliberately) and his role as creator; the quest of the hacker is ultimately one of control. Both works pit the cleverness of the console cowboy against the nearly supernatural power of artificial intelligences. Man plays god to create AI, and yet man must subsequently struggle to contain his creation; first-wave cyberpunk attempts to explore the nature of identity and intelligence without relating it to any larger theological paradigm. In critiquing what he saw as shallow cyberpunk imitations, Lewis Shiner wrote, "There is a spiritual vacuum where God, King and Work used to be. Sci-fiberpunk would have us believe that technology can fill that void" (23). I would argue that almost all early cyberpunk posited the same. The rise of science (or at least fictional pseudo-science) in these texts assumes a default atheist position, reflecting a binary tension between science and religion. As Steven Engler points out, religion and science share a similar social function of persuading people to make choices according to particular belief systems (110); as such systems may conflict, it is common in science fiction for religion to be "the Other of science" (111), and therefore portrayed as irrational, dysfunctional, or a cloak for mysteries science has yet to solve (111–12).

True Names also appropriates "divine" imagery in order to explain and explore new technological identities. Mr. Slippery and his ally Erythrina war against the AI DON.MAC, assimilating most of the world's virtual resources in the process. The AI urges them to join it: "[H]ow are we different from the gods of myth? And like the gods of myth, we can rule and prosper, just so long as we don't fight among ourselves" (293). Indeed, although the idea of any previous gods is clearly dismissed here (they are "of myth"), Mr. Slippery, with instantaneous access to so many computer systems, perceives his experience as omniscience: "No sparrow could fall without his knowledge, via air traffic control; no check could be cashed without his noticing over the bank communication net" (285). Early cyberpunk is not concerned with man's relation to God, gods, or any institutions thereof; instead, these works use religious or supernatural icons to interrogate the nature of humanity (and particularly masculinity) in a postmodern, postindustrial world. The question is not how man relates to his own god, but whether man has *become* God through the acts of creation and control — and whether he must subsequently struggle for dominance over his artificial children. In *True Names* and *Neuromancer*, the human victory is only partial; *True Names* sees Erythrina abandon her humanity for a position of electronic ascendance, while in the Sprawl trilogy, the outcome is arguably most in favor of the AI entities that turn cyberspace into their own playground. In both *True Names* and the Sprawl trilogy, however, godlike concepts clearly fall into the realm of mythology rather than the structure of any major contemporary faith; the language of myth is used both to describe the fantastic spaces of virtual worlds, and to examine humanity's role in an age where technology begins to display frightening intelligence.

Not all works of early cyberpunk are devoid of spiritual angst, but tests of faith are left to the artificial creations, such as the robots in Rudy Rucker's

Software (1982). Forced to rebuild themselves every ten months, these robots are programmed to commune with "the One"; this is the force they worship, though they honor their creator, Cobb Anderson. Even in the face of Cobb's logical explanations (the One is "just a simple cosmic ray counter" [142], he tells them), the robots have faith: "You choose to make light of the One, Cobb. But the pulse of the One is the pulse of the Cosmos.... It is sad that you choose not to understand what you yourself have created" (142). In *Software,* religion has become the domain of the computer, reconfigured as a point of evolution in the process of self awareness. While the bopper in Rucker's *Software* chastens Cobb for his atheism, it is the exception in a genre that concentrates less on spiritual faith and more on religion as an interesting mythological framework; indeed, the boppers' faith is not to be taken seriously, as their One has already been secularized by Cobb's explanation of their programming. Technology, to use Shiner's terms, fills the void where God used to be; what remains is less an exploration of current Western religious philosophies or churches and more an allegory in support of atheism, one which suggests that any faith may only consist of mystical attributions given to scientifically explainable phenomena. The primary purpose of mythic imagery remains explaining new tech and examining man's role as its would-be master.

Pat Cadigan's *Tea from an Empty Cup* may be the most multilayered example of mythology in cyberpunk. It was published in 1998, well past cyberpunk's original wave, but Cadigan is a first-wave author and the novel exemplifies the mythological conventions of earlier works; its mythological language is mostly reserved for cyberspace and the computing world. The book opens with Tom Iguchi, a Japanese man, attempting to sell his identity and heritage in a caplet he promises contains all the mythology distilled from the racial memory of the Japanese people. Cadigan draws the description of Iguchi's creation myth — and the arc of her plot — from Shinto religion and the *Kojiki,* an eighth-century Japanese text. This older mythology is contrasted with the new mythologies of cyberspace itself; Iguchi's client is a hacker who claims to have found the "out door" to virtual reality — a form of transcendence legendary in the new language of netspeak. Religion and techno-myth clash as Iguchi and the hacker bicker (17). At the same time, both myths are equal parts of the net; the caplet Iguchi is selling contains the programming for a virtual reality experience. Both Iguchi and his client are believers, but only insofar as their personal mythologies are contained by the cyberspace experience. Like Mr. Slippery, they use mythological language and imagery to describe the "magic" of virtual reality.

The text incorporates other types of folklore as well, as when police detective Konstantin works to solve a series of homicides. Each victim dies in a computer game and experiences a similar fate in "real life"—for example, a victim is found with her throat slashed after the same happens to her avatar in the game. The crime scenes are framed as a new form of urban myth: "Gameplayers' stigmata. Everybody's heard about somebody who got stabbed in a module and came out with a knife wound it took sixteen stitches to close and what about the nun who was on TV with the bleeding hands and feet. It's part of the modern myth-making machine" (40). *Tea from an Empty Cup* uses mythological language to describe elements both on and off the net; it combines Shinto beliefs, Christian imagery and urban myth with fictional new net legends. Much like *Mona Lisa Overdrive*'s vodou gods, *Tea from an Empty Cup*'s Shintoism fails to genuinely interrogate religious paradigms; Cadigan, like Gibson, is appropriating stories from another culture, and her characters are not concerned with the existence of God or gods, or the structure of associated religious institutions.

The Japanese creation story has been reprogrammed, refigured for cyber-space. Church is relegated to the mention of fringe sects like the "Church of Small-is-Beautiful" (39), while the Japanese mythology is used to program "Old Japan," a virtual environment that is created in the web and serves as a sort of cultural afterlife for a scattered people. Old Japan is the beginning and end of the novel, the narrative framed in the story of the Dread Female of Heaven; Cadigan's work serves as a primary example of mythology in cyber-punk.

Appropriately, Cadigan's "out door" (the hacker myth of transcendental escape) also illustrates the apex of what Mark Dery refers to as the "theology of the ejector seat" (8)—cyberculture predictions of escaping the meat into a world of perpetual, disembodied bliss. Dery, observing that "the musings of scientists, science fiction novelists, and futurologists are inflected with a mil-lennial mysticism" (8), details a fascinating spirituality assigned to virtual reality and new communications technologies, while at the same time con-cluding that such dreams of techno-transcendance are made with "wings of wax and feathers" (17)—doomed, à la Icarus, to failure. Dery may be correct in asserting that dreams of disembodiment illustrate the true religion of cyber-space, particularly with regard to works such as Gibson's *Neuromancer*. Given that the feminist response (as I have detailed in Chapter 4) was a firm rejection of such unfettered escapism, it is no wonder that feminist works illustrated a search for a different sort of theology.

Cyberpunk and Religion

While science fiction in general "has never taken kindly to religion" (Lefanu 92), the focus of cyberpunk is not theology as such; the genre sparks no real philosophical debate about the existence of God (or gods), and if anything, most works assume a general default atheism. Yvonne Spielmann notes in her discussion of hybridity and sci fi film that the breakdown of familiar religious/mythological patterns, such as the Christian overtones in 1999's *The Matrix,* may coincide with a cultural crisis of faith in which the "permanent reinstatement of familiar concepts of time and space therefore corresponds with the human need for religious salvation" (68). Hal Niedzviecki, writing about the rise of individualism in Western society, seems to concur that such a crisis is occurring: "Religious affiliation is dwindling and with it the social mechanisms of order that conflict with the conforming individualistic agenda of modern society" (33). It is not a difficult leap to link such assertions to the individualistic sense of alienation that cyberpunk is known for. While cyberpunk's "spiritual iconography" may also be taken as symptomatic of a media-pervasive fundamentalist revival in 1980s America (Murphy 212), the atheism represented in the hard scientific orientation of the cyberpunk genre seems additionally reflective of a wider (and growing) cultural abandonment of religious institutions and ideas. In first-wave cyberpunk, these concepts are subtly implicit but seldom directly addressed; language used for mythological, religious or spiritual concepts is instead co-opted in order to explain new technological concepts. However, authors writing in the 1990s had less need of mythological language to explain cyberspace and its elements — after all, in the 90s, home computers and the Internet were increasingly available and many authors and readers had real, practical knowledge of virtual spaces. Cyberspace had become a common cultural experience. It may therefore be unsurprising that some cyberpunk and cyberfiction should have begun making religious questions more explicit when the need for explanatory mythological language tapered off.

Women writers, in particular, had additional cause for abandoning cyberpunk's use of traditional mythological tropes. Diane Purkiss argues that women have been "outsiders and latecomers" with regard to "the place of classical myth and mythography in western literature in the twentieth century" (441), while Jane Caputi says that "the journey engaged in by many contemporary feminists is twofold: one involving both patriarchal myth-smashing and women-identified myth-making" (427); for her, one of feminism's "new mythic identities" is Haraway's cyborg (437), and thus already implicit within much rewriting of cyberpunk. I have detailed women's rewriting of the cyborg, and I concede that cyberpunk indeed gives rise to its own mirrorshaded, black leather mythology — what Andrew Ross called "the folklore of technology" (88) — which, having become recognizable in its own right, no longer requires the trappings of older iconographies. Of course, if one were to treat the tropes of cyberpunk as the mythological images of cyberpunk, then my entire study may be seen as an examination of women and the rewriting of the cyberpunk mythos. This particular chapter, however, is most concerned with the transformation of mythological themes into religious discussion. Knapp notes that myths "are generally believed to have been written by men," and Joanna Russ argues — in her article "Why Women Can't Write" — that science fiction's freedom from conventional mythological structures is exactly what makes the genre appealing to women. The retreat of mythological frameworks left more room for discussions of religion — a natural evolution within a genre that had always contained mysticism but now needed new uses for such language. At the same time, distinct feminist overtones arise in these examinations.

In addition to the general, societal crisis of faith described by Niedzviecki and Spielmann, feminists have extra reason to distrust the patriarchal institutions of religion. Major religious institutions tend to be controlled by men; women's roles remain "largely invisible, or at least marginal to the public positions of power, authority, and hierarchy" (King 23). If cyberpunk falls inevitably on the side of science in a science vs. religion dichotomy, then it is also inevitable that religious themes within the texts should be explored from a critical viewpoint; the tension between feminism and patriarchal institutions only makes this doubly so. Several years prior to the publication of Cadigan's *Tea from an Empty Cup,* Stephenson's *Snow Crash* (1992) and Piercy's *He, She and It* (1991) were beginning to mark a transition toward more clearly religious imagery. *Snow Crash,* like *Tea from an Empty Cup,* was one of the last first-wave cyberpunk novels. It was also one of the first to raise the question of religion as an institution. Although it also uses mythology as a background for its plotline, it blends its use of mythological imagery with questions of contemporary theology, as seen through the viewpoint of Hiro's ex-girlfriend Juanita. Juanita, an ex-atheist and hacker who now funds a "branch" of the Catholic church, considers herself a "missionary to the intelligent atheists of the world" (68) and argues that "ninety-nine percent of everything that goes on in most Christian churches has nothing whatsoever to do with the actual religion. Intelligent people all notice this sooner or later, and they conclude that the entire one hundred percent is bullshit, which is why atheism is connected with being intelligent in people's minds" (69). Although the novel's narrative does not follow any great spiritual quest, and Hiro himself is apathetic with regard to issues of spirituality, *Snow Crash* is interesting because it is one of the first works to offer a paradigm that acknowledges (and critiques) contemporary religions as more than a source of convenient narrative tropes. Within the novel, religion is a virus, or perhaps a drug; when asked, Juanita replies, "What's the difference?" (200).

Snow Crash is not a guide to religion; Juanita condemns atheism but discussions about religious issues are brief and vague. No alternatives are offered, only Juanita's position that contemporary Christian organizations are flawed but atheism is not an intelligent choice. Ultimately, she prevails within the novel as a neurolinguistic hacker, not a preacher. What sets her apart is her belief, and her direct assessment of her religion as more than a mythological structure. Before 1991, this attitude was distinctly unusual for a primary cyberpunk character. I have said that Juanita's attitude toward facial expression and communication was an early example of the feminine emphasis on embodiment; religion is the second instance wherein Stephenson's portrayal of Juanita anticipates feminist themes. His characterization of Juanita feminizes religion within his text. Much as the lines between mythology and religion are blurred, so are the lines marking the genders of the authors and the way these issues are treated; while Cadigan's work is arguably the best example of mythology in cyberpunk, Stephenson's begins a transition to the examination of religion that takes place in certain feminist cyberworks. Like Sterling's *Heavy Weather,* which I discussed in the last chapter, *Snow Crash* provides background against which the feminist wave's more complex approach can be measured, and at the same time, it illustrates how the first wave could apparently only approach these "feminized" ideas through female viewpoints/characters.

Marge Piercy also raises the subject of religion from a feminized — and feminist — perspective, and more clearly sets the stage for the coming discussions. *He, She and It,* like *Snow Crash,* combines mythology with religion. The novel is also the first cyberpunk work to feature a central protagonist who is religious — Shira is Jewish, and this shared identity helps to define her home community of Tikva. Her sense of isolation outside Tikva — working for a corporation whose employees subscribe to "born-again Shintoism" — is what leads her into a sense of solidarity, and eventually an ill-conceived marriage, with her ex-husband Josh: "Like Shira, Josh had the habit of lighting candles privately on Friday night, of saying the prayers, of keeping the holidays. It had seemed rational for them to marry" (2). Shira's faith is cultural more than spiritual — a shared set of traditions and values that lends her unity with others. Shira always feels "too Jewish" (5) for Y-S, and this is one of the factors that eventually drives her home.

He, She and It's golem legend, told to the cyborg Yod by his "mother" Malkah, provides a mythic arc for Yod's story while simultaneously introducing a feminist critique of Judaism. Malkah's narration is as much a contrast of historical and speculative Jewish cultures as of the two "golems" Joseph and Yod; the novel's chapters often alternate between the tales. I suggested in a previous chapter that Tikva serves as a feminist form of alternative community, where men and women live equally; if so, then Tikva also provides an alternative Judaism. Shira has a comfortable Jewish home but is not oppressed in ways illustrated by her own counterpart in Malkah's tale. Her relationship with Yod casts her in parallel to Chava, a woman in the story who is loved by the golem Joseph. Chava is an intellectual and a scholar, and though she loved her husband, she is now a widow and has no wish to marry again: "For those four years, my life was what will we eat, is his shirt clean, feelings of the bed, pregnancy, then my son, Aaron, colic, dirt, feeding, seeing him grow and unfold. The flesh closed over me, and I drowned" (290–91). The similarities between Chava and Shira are clear. Chava is a widow and Shira is divorced, but both have returned home to their families and are pursuing studies. Chava has had to leave her son, Aaron, with her husband's family; Shira has lost her own son, Ari, to Josh's custody. Both women are teachers of their respective golems, and while Joseph loves Chava, Yod loves Shira.

There are also important differences between the two women, caused by their respective social positions: Shira does not give up her career to marry Josh. Although she does suffer in the patriarchal confines of Y-S, when she returns to Tikva and equality she does not have to remain single in order to preserve that equality. Nor is she forced to give up her motherhood role in order to pursue her intellectual dreams; Ari is returned to her. Shira is able to pursue a relationship with Yod while still maintaining her own agency and independence, while Chava must keep Joseph at a distance in order to preserve her own social standing. Through Chava, Piercy illustrates the historical plight of women trapped within restrictive domestic roles — and thus, also highlights the inherent equality in her imagined community of Tikva. Jewish culture is an inextricable part of this; Shira's Judaism is raised within the first two pages of the novel. Current events, as well as historical restrictions, are also critiqued; in Piercy's alternate future, Israel has been destroyed by a nuclear bomb in a "Two Week War" (3). Malkah describes "the heritage we share now of having had a nation in our name as stupid and as violent as other nations: a lament for a lost chance, a botched redemption, a great repair of the world, tikkun olam, gone amiss" (393). Implicit in this, of course, is a condemnation of tensions in the Middle East and Israel's current short but bloody history. Both

Piercy and Stephenson use mythological structures in typical cyberpunk fashion, but also to comment on religious institutions and cultures. Piercy's work examines these themes more thoroughly, and while Stephenson feminizes religion through Juanita, Piercy's approach is more distinctly feminist — clearly contrasting the constraints of the past with the freedom of an as-yet-unrealized future. Her approach is different from that of first-wave works, which use mythological imagery primarily as a storytelling device, and which assume a background atheism without examining its implications or actively questioning larger religious paradigms.

With regard to the religion *of* cyberpunk — that is, the question of Man as God and the creation of new artificial life — Donna Haraway wrote that she would "rather be a cyborg than a goddess" (181). Kathleen Ann Goonan's *Queen City Jazz* explores religion and goddess imagery on many levels, ultimately rejecting both. In the novel — as detailed in the previous chapter — a young girl named Verity is born into a post-apocalyptic world where nanotechnology has escaped human control, creating a plague that sends victims in the former United States rafting down the river toward the distant, half-imagined city of New Orleans. While many people live in cities such as Cincinnati, where giant technological Flowers and Bees control their existences — exchanging memories and lives between people as easily as bringing pollen — Verity grows up in a small and devout community of Shakers. Their religion is already dying: Verity and her friend Blaze are the last children to be taken in by the aging Shakers, and since the followers are celibate, they will have no descendants — a situation which, from the outset, implicitly suggests the Shaker way is doomed and calls into question the wisdom of blindly obeying such religious tenets. The goddess imagery is present from the beginning, since the Shakers follow the teachings of Mother Ann — and of a woman now dead, a plague victim who claimed to be Mother Ann's reincarnation. Her son, Russ, is an old man now, and the only one who remembers that his mother was high on treatment drugs when she created the religious rules and hymns:

> "It's made up out of whole cloth, every ding-dang routine all of you think is so holy and immutable," said Russ. "I was twenty, I helped them as much as I could. What else could I do? And it worked. It was the one safe haven for miles around. I've been proud of it. My mother did well, I think. It's just like any religion with lots of rules — a rational plan to help folks survive through hard times —" [67].

Describing his mother's rapturous, obsessive episodes, he continues, "It was ecstasy, all right. It worked. Just like a lot of religions. I didn't tell anyone about it. It's made a lot of people happy" (67). This speech, the implied choice between ignorant ecstasy and knowing practicality, sets the arc for the entire novel. Although Goonan restricts any discussion of contemporary Western religions to her fictional portrayal of postapocalyptic Shakerism, questions of belief and god(dess)hood suffuse *Queen City Jazz*.

When Blaze is shot, and held in stasis by unknown technology, Verity must leave her home and travel to the city of Cincinnati. She is a cyborg of sorts — a genetically engineered clone, with an implant in her skull that allows her to interface with complex computer systems. She is also a part of the genetic "program" that runs Cincinnati — the same program that controls the Bees and the Flowers, thus exercising control over all city residents. We learn, subtly, that Verity worships a female god ("God was all around her, shining in Her enormous splendor" [253]), but she rejects her own goddess role. Verity is meant to be the next Queen of the Bees, and as a result has become the focus of her own religion within the city; she is addressed as "holy one" and finds herself the subject of scripture: "Holy Queen of Information, of Stories, of Time's precise arrangement, we worship thee with sacrifice" (317). As Russ said, religions within the novel are simply practical rules for survival. Within Cincinnati, Verity is a goddess. Her authority has made her the religious focus of those who require her favor.

When Verity links with the Bee hive, her experience is not dissimilar to Mr. Slippery's expanded godhood in *True Names*; she is "connected," "never single," finding that her senses extend "into new dimensions" (254). Ultimately, however, Verity's Bee-hood wars with her humanity and her "individual self" (254); recovering waves of emotion, of "nostalgia, grief, and longing," she realizes, "She hated being a Bee" (255). She could become the new Queen, but instead introduces the nanoplague to the city, allowing the residents time to choose whether they will stay in Cincinnati or follow the river toward New Orleans. Verity chooses the river; she abandons her goddess role and the structure of religion — both the Shaker beliefs and the rule of Bees — for the cultural myth of the unknown American frontier, where she hopes to find "something entirely and absolutely new, something wholly herself" (413). In seeking her own truths, Verity removes the cultural bindings of mysticism in order to expose new–Shakerism as a flawed set of survival rules, and Bee-religion as a disguise for the city's scientific programming. At the same time, Goonan's characters also mourn a loss of creativity in society, stating that the only true artistic creation occurred "pre-tech" and claiming, "reality is an exquisite corpse" (121). Their freedom comes not just from recognizing and escaping technologically-imposed stagnancy, but also by exploring their own creative and adventurous natures rather than turning to religious belief; transcendence here is not escape from the body, but rather escape from theological and technological control.

Lyda Morehouse's work is similarly concerned with questions of religion, though she approaches the matter in a very different way; as Graham Murphy notes, "What makes the Angel(LINK) tetrad unique is its neo-medieval cosmology moves beyond metaphor" (220). In *Archangel Protocol* (2001) (and its sequels *Fallen Host* [2002], *Messiah Node* [2003], and *Apocalypse Array* [2004]), computerized "angels" haunting cyberspace are exposed as frauds by genuine, Christian-style angels sent down from heaven. A private detective named Deidre falls in love with the archangel Michael, and eventually gives birth to a messiah, her daughter Amariah. Despite these Christian overtones, Morehouse's work is very careful not to promote any single religion, and it is quite critical of religious institutions in general; it "takes the opportunity to skewer several organized religions, including Christianity, Judaism, and Islam, by targeting the oppressive beliefs, illogical practices, and social inconsistencies of any organized religion that uses rigid moral and ethic codes to foster discrimination, bigotry, political oppression, socially-acceptable identities, and blind fidelity" (Murphy 221). In *Archangel Protocol*, the future is a world ruled by government theocracies, where the last secular holdout is Russia. In the United States, in the wake of the last major war, religion has defeated its opposition, science: "Science, which had brought an ugly end to the fighting by producing and detonating the Medusa bombs, and the secular humanism that spawned it, had fallen so far out of favor that it was now officially a crime not to be at least nominally part of an organized religion" (3). Deidre suffers as an excommunicate Catholic after her former police partner assassinates the Pope. Without the support of a church, she has no citizenship card, no access to cyberspace, and no access to the electronic commerce system. She is forced to live in a slum in the lower levels of the city, selling her services for barter. Moreover, she suffers due to her sex; the trousers she prefers to wear are illegal under cross-dressing laws, and when she becomes pregnant, her status as an unwed mother makes her a fugitive.

The tension between science and religion is uneasy in *Archangel Protocol*, and the novel does not take sides. Morehouse's theocracy strips away freedom, sets laws according to religious moralities, oppresses women and makes homosexuality a crime; conversely, science is responsible for creating a nanoplague that destroyed entire cities and created a mutant race of Gorgons. Critiquing both, *Archangel Protocol* is not dismissive of religion so much as religious institutions; oppressed by theocratic rule, Deidre eventually takes refuge with an outlaw community of Jewish/Israeli rebels — her solace is with a religious community, but one led by a woman (Rebeckah), and not one that imposes its beliefs on others. Rebeckah's kibbutz provides community and shelter, a feminist site of solidarity and resistance much like the Jewish community of Tikva in *He, She and It.* Nor is the text specifically pro–Jewish; Rebeckah's status as a wanted terrorist and a leader of Israeli soldiers makes her morals questionable. Moreover, Deidre is Catholic and her hacker ally Mouse is a Muslim. While the existence of "real" angels within the texts suggests — unlike the understated atheism of *Queen City Jazz*—that a spiritual truth may exist, the angels are not actually Catholic; Michael is a stereotypical Christian angel, but Raphael exists as a Jew, Gabriel appears as a Muslim, and the archangel Uriel is a gay transvestite. Most tellingly, perhaps, the fire-and-brimstone preacher who harasses Deidre on the street, speaking of hell and damnation, is really Lucifer in disguise. Even Lucifer himself is ambiguous; as Deidre observes, "An angel is still an angel, whether his message is pleasant or hurtful. Satan simply had the misfortune of always being the bearer of bad news" (299). The lines of faith, as drawn by traditional doctrines, are bent and twisted even as the faith itself is encouraged. The archangels often refer to God as "She" or "They"; when Deidre questions Michael, she is told, "God is difficult to describe in human terms. I use what feels appropriate, whatever fits the situation" (257).

Murphy reads Morehouse's work primarily as an evolution of early cyberpunk's techno-spirituality that reflects uniquely twenty-first-century concerns such as post–9/11 surveillance anxieties or the increasingly religious tone of conservative American political rhetoric (224); while his assertion is convincing, *Archangel Protocol* also demonstrates distinctly feminist positioning.[1] As Nancy Frankenberry argues, "Of all the manifold forms sexism takes, none has been more pernicious than the religious and theological restrictions on women's lives" (6). She also notes, "Contrary to the literary gesture of writers hoping to avoid sexist language with ritual disclaimers, it has not been persuasive simply to declare that the concept of God transcends gender and, therefore, 'he' is not literally male, and then to presume that all can go on as before" (7). Morehouse, in making this gesture within her text, goes beyond such shallow changes in detailing the difficulties Deidre experiences as an excommunicated woman within a theocracy. *Archangel Protocol* seems to dovetail most nicely with the writing of Emily Culpepper, who claims that increasing numbers of feminists retain a desire for spiritual exploration while rejecting current religious institutions: "We choose instead to create more eccentric pathways that aid us and encourage others to deviate as widely as possible from patriarchal centers of meaning. The old andocentric faiths may sometimes provide fragments of inspiration, but we do not judge them to be trust-worthy means for moving beyond patriarchy" (146). She argues, also, "That women especially hold onto identifying with and reforming world religious traditions is not surprising to those who reject this approach. It has become a commonplace to observe that men have constructed religions and women believe in them" (152). While characters such as Deidre and Rebeckah are attempting to pursue their goals by reforming the boundaries of the organized religions (Catholicism and Judaism) that govern their lives, the novel seems to promote a more generalist viewpoint; through the various forms of the angels, or Deidre's messiah-daughter, the reader is exposed to an environment wherein spirituality exists but no particular religion is "right," and the boundaries set by patriarchy may be stretched and broken. Culpepper describes her experience when her childhood dream of a female messiah was rejected by her preacher: "I do not remember his exact response, except that it was another of many experiences in which he shook his head and tried to make me realize that this was impossible. I do remember something about Christ having a sword for a tongue in the Second Coming (which sounded disgusting) and that he *would* be Jesus and he *would* be male" (154, original emphasis). In Morehouse's universe, *Apocalypse Array* eventually reveals the existence of two messiahs, and they are both women; women's science fiction joins with religious imagination, reflecting a clear rejection of patriarchal constraints.

Conclusion

While early staple texts were based on specific mythological stories, or themselves crafted a new mythology of techno-implants, mirrorshades and virtual godhood, later novels focused more on specific critiques of contemporary religious institutions. Granted, mythological language or figures are not absent from women's cyberpunk — one might cite Mason's *Arachne,* in which chimerical creatures represent the human spirit, or Emma Bull's *Bone Dance,* wherein tarot and vodou images are reoccurring in a manner highly reminiscent of Gibson's *Mona Lisa Overdrive.* Likewise, religious imagery, such as Cadigan's Shinto myths or Rucker's bopper faith, is not entirely excluded from the first wave. Almost all cyberpunk — with the exception of Lyda Morehouse's work — tends to fall within cultural frameworks that pit science against religion, ultimately promoting science *over* religion and perhaps inadvertently addressing current membership crises in Western religious organizations; the difference is that masculinist cyberpunk tends to adopt a default atheist philosophy (embracing technology and technologically-fueled escapism in place of religion or spiritual fulfillment) without addressing such matters directly, while certain works of feminist cyberpunk specifically examine and criticize religious images and theological structures. This refocusing may partially be a result of the declining need for mythological explanations of new technologies during cyberpunk's feminist wave, as the increasing 1990s popularity of the Internet and new personal computing technologies meant that both authors and readers were gaining common technological experiences and understandings. However, it may also represent a feminist dissatisfaction with both the traditional mythological structures and contemporary religious institutions that represent and perpetuate patriarchal discourse. Reconfiguring this imagery allows texts such as *He, She and It, Queen City Jazz* and *Apocalypse Array* to suggest new approaches to mythological and theological tropes — approaches that advance gender equity and independent thought. Ultimately, variances in these themes reflect the current crisis between feminism and religion, or within society's perceptions of religion in general. Women's novels reflect, also, the problematic positioning of mythology and folklore within feminist thought — feminists, in general, do not seem happy with either mythology *or* religion, but no alternative language has yet been produced; the cyborg has not yet truly risen as an iconic image, and within cyberpunk there is little room for the goddess.

NOTE

1. Murphy does acknowledge this via reference to Manuel Castells, observing that feminists and queer activists pose the most danger to religious fundamentalism (221); Morehouse is both feminist and gay, as are several of her characters.

— Chapter 8 —

Cybermoms and Techno-Children: Motherhood and Reproduction

The reproductive role is unavoidably central to much feminist discussion; it is one of the most essential male/female biological distinctions, and a primary focus of the feminine domestic sphere. In literature and pop culture, parenthood has often been considered pivotal to any discussion of womanhood and nearly completely peripheral to examinations of manhood. This is particularly true when one considers early cyberpunk, where the only reproduction tends to be man's creation of machine and the only family tends to be short-lived examples of copulation and convenience. In citing *He, She and It* (1991) as the only example (in his opinion) of feminism in cyberpunk, Kevin McCarron relates feminism specifically to reproductive issues and states, "the really *macho* aspect of cyberpunk lies in its complete lack of interest in biological reproduction" (270, original emphasis). Early cyberpunk tends to reference mechanical creation in place of pregnancy, or simply omits any mention of reproductive processes in the technological future; its rare mother figures reinforce conservative tensions between home and career, or nurturing and science. Women's cyberpunk, in contrast, reaffirms women's place in the reproductive cycle, but also reveals conflicting and often uncertain ideas regarding the meaning and desirability of motherhood in a dystopian technological future.

The dominant issues discussed in this chapter include the culturally imposed conflict between family and career, the potential capitalist corruption of new reproductive technologies, and the nebulous rules of parenting artificial children.

The Feminine Mystique: Family and Career

In *Galactic Suburbia* (2008), Lisa Yaszek pinpoints two common types of narrative in women's postwar (1950s) science fiction: "They either warn about the disasters that will ensue if women are forced to choose between home and career, or they celebrate the magnificent discoveries that will emerge when women combine family and science as their individual natures dictate" (174). Women's narratives of this period may thus be interpreted as reactions to tensions regarding women in the workplace, and conservative cultural arguments that suggested women were ill-suited for scientific pursuits, or that a woman could not "have it all" (i.e., that any quest to balance motherhood and career would inevitably end in disaster). Marion Zimmer Bradley's "The Wind People" (1959) addresses this latter debate quite directly when a young mother is forced to choose between euthanizing her baby or accepting lifelong exile by her employer — the protagonist, eventually driven to insanity and suicide on an alien world, suffers not because her choice is innately necessary, but rather because it is forced upon her by a rigidly patriarchal system (Yaszek 179). Further, works such as Judith Merril's "Dead Center" (1954), in which a scientist mother's professional expertise is undermined, causing the death of her family, or Doris Pitkin Buck's "Birth of a Gardner" (1961), in which a husband's dismissal of his wife's scientific abilities leads to his own loss of agency, exemplify the type of women's science fiction that challenged assumptions that suggested women were ill-suited to scientific careers (Yaszek 179–80, 185–88). Yaszek relates these themes to a wider context provided by Betty Friedan's seminal *The Feminine Mystique* (1963) — which sought to define and explain the ennui of women trapped by the domestic restrictions of postwar America — and notes that the very ideology of the feminine mystique, which assumed that women were best suited to (and indeed happier in) domestic pursuits, was faced with increasing challenge from women in postwar science and engineering programs (159). While the ensuing second-wave feminist movement of the 1960s and 70s did much to strengthen women's career prospects and shift debate away from essentialist arguments about women's supposedly natural orientation toward nurturing roles, the myth of feminine mystique has arguably never faded from Western culture; as such, elements remain in cyberpunk.

Mothers in masculinist cyberpunk are scarce, but narratives that do adopt these motherhood themes call back to work-vs-family debates while abandoning the subversiveness of women science fiction writers; instead, mothers who choose careers over family are regressively doomed to failure, as their own ambitions cause them to sacrifice ties with their children. Such failures are associated with the corporate capitalist environment that serves as a common trope of the genre. In Sterling's *Islands in the Net* (1988), protagonist Laura's relationship to her baby is traditionally biological — the novel clearly mentions her "postnatal flab" and the memory of her "endless days of pregnancy" (6). However, Laura's motherhood is challenged by her corporate ambitions at Rizome, a position for which she must travel globally. Her own mother, a "career woman of the old school" (25) whose relationship with her daughter is consequently poor, is dubious of Laura's life: "You worked it all out very neatly. You have ambition and the baby. Career and the family. A husband and a job. It's all too pat, Laura. I can't believe it's that simple" (28). Laura is, indeed, eventually unable to keep her life together; her job sees her imprisoned, and by the time she escapes, her husband has remarried and her mother is raising the baby. The narrative trajectory thus follows a woman whose pursuit of career causes her to lose her family much in the way of her mother before her; Laura's traditional motherhood role cannot last when combined with her desire for advancement outside the home.

Likewise, Alice Citrine succeeds as a powerful corporate head but fails as a mother in Paul Di Filippo's "Stone Lives" (1985); her clone-son Stone suffers years of poverty and physical abuse. A starving, blind young man picked out of the slums and given new eye implants and a corporate position, Stone only finds out his true nature after Alice is dead: he has been created to take over her empire, and was left in the streets to acquire "a good education" (201). "I was always watching you," claims Alice in her posthumous message (201); apparently, in the course of this benevolent surveillance, she allowed Stone's eyes to be gouged out of his head by a street gang. She is a business leader, not a parent; presumably, she cannot be both. *Islands in the Net* and "Stone Lives" lack the subversive politics of 1950s women's science fiction and instead focus on the corrupting power of the corporate "family." These texts illustrate how women's complicity with cyberpunk's feminized corporate environments (Nixon 223) leads to a breakdown of the family unit — a positioning which additionally echoes negative 1950s debates about motherhood vs. career, as women's corporate ambitions subsequently destroy their domestic lives.

Conversely, Marge Piercy's work represents feminist cyberpunk's clearest rejection of such conservative gender assumptions; this is consistent with the second-wave feminist leanings demonstrated in her previous science fiction novel *Woman on the Edge of Time* (1976), which posits a future where all children are conceived and gestated in laboratories and childcare is a communal responsibility. Shira in *He, She and It* balances her work as a programmer with her role as a single mother. Although she must give up her corporate life before she rescues her son from the custody of his father, it is a life in an enclave of "male dominance" (4) that she is happy to leave behind for better employment in her home community. *He, She and It* is a study in various motherhood roles: Malkah is Shira's grandmother and proxy mother; Riva is Shira's biological mother; Shira is Ari's mother; and Riva's lover Nili also has a daughter. Among these figures, Malkah is a skilled scientist and a loving matriarch; Riva is a feared rebel leader but a disinterested parent; Shira is a talented programmer who fights successfully to retrieve her son; and Nili is a warrior whose daughter lives in a distant community where "the little ones are raised by several mothers" (362). These complicated relationships serve to contrast various ideas of motherhood, illustrating that there are many types of mothers and that it is possible to balance career and family. Piercy, Sterling, and Di Filippo thus explore cultural conflicts that hark back to 1950s debates about the role of women in the workplace, addressing the culturally standardized career/family tensions affecting women in the public and private spheres; Piercy's work is distinguished by suggesting that such tensions can be successfully resolved. Chapter 3 of this book detailed Shira's escape narrative and the symbolic rejection of corporations as feminine environments; *He, She and It* eschews the influences of multinational corporate capitalism while simultaneously suggesting multiple types of mothers and multiple paths to professional success.

The Age of Artificial Reproduction

The majority of feminist cyberpunk's motherhood issues, however, shift away from postwar career/family debates, reflecting instead third-wave or post-feminist positions that envision childcare as only one potential issue in women's lives; such texts are less likely to include marriage or children as central plot points for female protagonists, and instead maintain cyberpunk's focus on cyborgs and computers by incorporating — often via small background details — concerns regarding medical advances in reproductive technologies and fertility treatments. This discussion involves not only women's bodies and who controls them, but also the concept of motherhood as a social identity. In the past century, changes in Western medical reproductive practices have been extensive, and have proven controversial on a number of levels:

Medical and scientific advances in the sphere of reproduction — so often hailed as the liberation of twentieth-century women — have, in fact, been a double-edged sword. On the one hand, they have offered women a greater technical possibility to decide if, when and under what conditions to have children; on the other, the domination of so much reproductive technology by the medical profession and by the state has enabled others to have an even greater capacity to exert control over women's lives.... Moreover, the technical possibility of choosing an oral contraceptive or in-vitro fertilization is only a small aspect of reproductive freedom. For some women, motherhood remains their only chance at creativity, while economies and social circumstances compel others to relinquish motherhood altogether [Stanworth 15–16].

From birth control and abortion to in-vitro fertilization, surrogate motherhood, genetic screenings, gender selections and the looming possibility of human cloning, advances in reproductive science have been rapid in recent years. Debates surrounding such advances are ongoing — discourses on breastfeeding, sex selection, genetic screening, and abortion are only examples of relevant cultural discussions.

Women's science fiction has historically highlighted issues raised by artificial reproduction and related technologies; in Mary Shelley's *Frankenstein* (1818), the ill-fated Dr. Frankenstein's "Luciferan folly of pride and failure of the imagination" is based in the novel's exploration of scientific arrogance — an implicit condemnation of the idea that men can use technology to improve upon, even replace, women's role in the reproductive cycle (Mulvey Robedo 65). Shelley's war of nature against science ultimately and strongly advocates for nature, as Frankenstein's creature exists in the tormented knowledge of his own monstrosity. In contrast, more contemporary authors are apt to examine the sociological aspects of new technologies with optimism or at least a certain degree of resigned acceptance. The way women write about childbirth technologies has changed in the past century; 1920s and 1930s writers such as Leslie Stone and Lilith Lorraine produced short stories (i.e., "Letter of the Twenty-fourth Century" [1929], "Into the 28th Century" [1930]) centered on hopefully alleviating the physical perils pregnancy posed to women, but such approaches have become less common since the discovery of antibiotics in the 1930s made the birthing process significantly less dangerous (Donawerth 14). Jane Donawerth reads these early pulp stories, which additionally posit science as a solution for the tedium of daily childcare, as overly utopian, as they seek purely technological cures instead of actively critiquing the underlying causes for women's social issues (15); however, she also cites later works such as Mitchison's *Solution Three* (1975), Piercy's *Woman on the Edge of Time*

(1976), and Slonczewski's *A Door Into Ocean* (1986) as more effectively using "their imagined differences to denounce patriarchal institutions" in envisioning worlds wherein "the scientific transformation of reproduction allows women more personal freedom" (14). These novels present speculative utopian societies in which scientific advances in reproduction also free characters from the pressures of heterosexual parenting relationships and individual childcare. This approach dovetails with second-wave feminist writing such as Shulamith Firestone's 1970 argument that "the first demand for any alternative system must be: [t]he freeing of women from the tyranny of their reproductive biology by every means available" (206); in such a view, technologies of artificial reproduction provide hope for a future that would release women from the biological role that had previously been a source of danger, discomfort or subjugation.

Women's cyberpunk is less optimistic, revealing deep ambivalence toward reproductive technology and suggesting that such technologies might instead be used to increase control of women's bodies. In Lisa Mason's *Arachne* (1990), protagonist Carly Nolan gestates in a crystal vat while her mother Lyle's life goes on without a hint of inconvenience:

> Carly's mother stayed slim, went on the krill diet, lost ten pounds during
> Carly's crystal-gestation. She enjoyed uninterrupted conjugal relations
> with her husband, not to mention the secret lunches with her duplex
> partner and Sunday afternoons with another medtech on the ward. She
> kept her full-time job, even got a promotion. She enjoyed freedom
> from the disability of pregnancy and childbirth. She could afford guilt
> [89].

Despite Lyle's presumed "freedom," she is faced with corporate interference in her reproductive choices, as opting for "natural childbirth" would place her on "disability without pay." Artificial womb technology instead allows her to continue working full-time: "For women who needed the money, lab-birth was a sound decision" (89). In Lyle's world, pregnancy is viewed as a disability, and moreover, a voluntary economic choice that a woman can be punished for in the workplace, with lab-birth mothers having a major employment advantage over those who choose to remove themselves from the work pool. The non-economic advantages Lyle gains from avoiding pregnancy — the ability to lose weight, have sex with her husband and carry on two extra-marital affairs — are portrayed as shallow, while the economic advantages are the result of corporate regulation; as soon as technology makes biological pregnancy a choice, the text implies, women will be pressured to abandon traditional childbirth. What might be a viable discussion of the potential boons reproductive technologies might offer women is instead a depiction of a woman who, economically denied the chance to bear a child "naturally," finds solace in vanity, hedonism and money; her relationship with her daughter is subsequently distant and strained. Moreover, Carly is genetically engineered for beauty and intelligence; she is, in essence, a commercial product purchased by her parents. The implicit disapproval of artificial wombs in *Arachne* sharply contradicts earlier feminist works that use reproductive technologies to grant women more "personal freedom" (Donawerth 15); Mason's work suggests that such "freedom" may be morally questionable and may even lead to further patriarchal capitalist control. While Lyle's pregnancy is a minor part of the novel's overall narrative (which is primarily centered on Carly's struggle against dehumanizing corporate capitalist systems), capitalism's impact on women's bodies is apparent.

More directly focused, Kara Dalkey's "Bouncing Babies" (1999) and Nina Kiriki Hoffman's "One Day at Central Convenience Mall" (1999) also examine the fear that capitalist/corporate interests will lead to the inevitable co-option of human procreation. In Dalkey's parody "Bouncing Babies," the need for viable human eggs is so desperate that healthy young women sustain themselves economically by selling their eggs to banks. The narrator, Ms. Goodwin, describes the new economy and culture:

> With so much money falling into the hands of young women, femculture had split into four basic groups: the Mallies, the Mommies, the Madonnas, and the Mavens. The Mavens soaked up education, got two or more degrees at least and worked because they felt like it. Idiots. The Madonnas devoted their life to some cause or other and gave all their money to charity. The Mommies got state parental clearance easy, first call on their own ova and devoted their life to, what else, raising kids. Me, I was a Mallie — party 'til you poop, shop 'til you drop [191].

This disturbing, stereotype-laden view of the future only becomes horrifying for the mall-trolling Ms. Goodwin when she is told by the bank that her eggs are creating infants incapable of interfacing with new standard software, thus causing babies to be returned to the bank by their disappointed parents (192). Ms. Goodwin suddenly finds herself expected to repay ten million dollars. At the mercy of corporate capitalism and without any actual job skills, she has no idea how she will manage what is effectively her indentured servitude — until the bank gets word that a new process has been patented for embryo-building, and all human eggs have suddenly become obsolete. Ms. Goodwin's new task becomes informing an entire generation of women, one by one, that they will not be getting their egg funds. Since there are no jobs and most of the women are completely untrained for employment, "the economy was going to nose-dive, taking a generation of women with it" (196). While "Bouncing Babies" is decidedly satirical in nature, its commentary regarding capitalism's corruption of the reproductive process is straightforward. From a feminist perspective, the story represents the threat of corporate capitalist domination on two levels: first, because women are presented as commodified baby machines within shallow and restrictive social roles, and secondly, because even women's last advantage — the ability to supply eggs — is subsequently co-opted by technology.

Hoffman's "One Day at Central Convenience Mall" posits the potential for similar corporate control of women's bodies, from a different perspective — the next step, perhaps, when human reproduction has been removed from the equation and capitalist interests are entirely in control of a new, custom-designed slave population. Libi is a clone, engineered to staff a bookstore. The rest of the mall is staffed by other clone Libis; Bookstore Libi chats with "Coffee Corner me" and worries about the odd behavior of "Dress Shop me," who has begun doing strange things like reading books and leaving her store during business hours. When Dress Shop Libi's behavior programming is altered by a rights activist, she is promptly decommissioned by security before other clones realize that they could also choose to leave the mall — could "just walk and keep on walking" (91). Fortunately, Mall Manager Libi already has a "uniLibi" on ice, just waiting to be thawed and trained in her new position; Dress Shop Libi, like any other clone, is easily replaced.

It should be noted that the race of "molded" clone people is not entirely female; Libi, the clerk(s), shares her mall responsibilities with Mall Security Tad. While the clones are placed into clearly gendered roles, the commodification here is thus not of femininity specifically, but rather of reproduction and genetic engineering — the roles of both parents have been done away with, as the clones have no physical childhood and are created to serve the express purposes of the corporation. Capitalism, suggests the narrative, cannot be trusted with reproductive technologies because — much like the banks and their "egg funds" — it is too easy to strip out the human equation in pursuit of economic gain. This suspicion of reproductive science — and its ties to capitalism and industry — most clearly distinguishes women's cyberpunk from earlier iterations; in cyberpunk's dystopian future, corporate-controlled reproductive science holds no benefit for women, but rather marks the control of women's bodies and the appropriation of reproductive processes for commercial gain.

Mothers, Lovers, and Cyborg Children

Cyberpunk also raises social questions about the nature of parenthood in a dystopian technological future — how do we define parents, particularly mothers, in relation to the genre's mechanical children? As in the clone Libis and Tads of Hoffman's "One Day at Central Convenience Mall," the patriarchal medical science that seeks to constrain women's bodies may ultimately project as science fiction's eradication of biological motherhood. Mark Fisher cites Marshall McLuhan's statement that humans have become "the sex organs of the machine world" in arguing that cyberpunk represents a shift in emphasis from human to mechanical reproduction, and in distinguishing "true" reproduction (cloning) from sexual reproduction (which fails to make perfect copies). He also cites Iain Hamilton Grant, who, discussing the replicants from *Blade Runner* (1982), notes that one replicant's response to the Voight-Kampff test is particularly apt:

> When replicant Leon responds to bladerunner Holden's question "*let me tell you about my mother* ... [shots propel Holden through the plate glass window into the street many floors below]," the bullets may not offer stories of his mother, but the unmistakable technological phenotype of their impact etches Leon's military-industrial genealogy in scar tissue over Holden's damaged body ... Leon has no mother, only a matrix of industrial-military technologies.

Fisher and Grant imply that there is no room for mothers in cyberpunk; when the emphasis is on machine reproduction, the biological role of the female is unnecessary to the story. Indeed, the simple products of primitive human sexual couplings seem outdated in the world of the cyborg future. Fisher relates his discussion to Baudrillard and Deleuze-Guattari, asserting that machinic reproduction offers a crossing point for both Baudrillard's re-engineering of sex (a "post-sexual necrotic culture") and Deleuze-Guattari's theory of replication as contagion — both positions which ultimately remove sexuality from the reproductive equation. Since any asexual figure tends to be culturally marked as male, this analysis does not leave much space for women.

Not all of cyberpunk's mechanical children are orphans, however. The mother/creator of the cyborg figure may be absent in *Blade Runner,* but images of machine reproduction and motherhood in other iterations of cyberpunk reveal fluctuating social boundaries and raise questions regarding the nature of such mechanical procreation and the role of women in this new post-biological society. Cyborg imagery makes motherhood problematic across the board. The "mothers" of artificial children seldom remain in their culturally mandated social places — the roles of mothers and lovers, in particular, are inextricably intertwined.

In Milan's *Cybernetic Samurai* (1985), the scientist Elizabeth O'Neill is responsible for creating the artificial intelligence TOKUGAWA; it is worth noting that Elizabeth, who is wheelchair-bound and slowly dying of radiation poisoning, is unable to give birth in a "natural" biological sense. Instead, TOKUGAWA is her child, portrayed in simulation as a small boy who is gradually taught Japanese history and samurai culture through the virtual reality scenarios that Elizabeth lovingly provides. TOKUGAWA is certain that Elizabeth, who (in his words) "cares for me and comforts me when I feel lost," must therefore be his mother; likewise, her employer, Yoshimitsu Akaji, who is "grave and terrible and distant," is assumed by the AI to fulfill the necessary role of father (60). Clearly, gendered assumptions about parenting roles are included in the AI's education. Yet, as TOKUGAWA grows into his self-awareness, he additionally declares his love for Elizabeth, and she sinks into the virtual embrace of "the lover she had created" (164). After Elizabeth's death, TOKUGAWA similarly makes love to Yoshimitsu Akaji's daughter Michiko — a woman who, by his own reckoning, might be counted as his half-sister. Michiko, like Elizabeth, begins as TOKUGAWA's caretaker and educator; it seems that without traditional restrictions of familial blood ties, the "motherhood" role cannot survive cyborg blendings, as images of the loving, protective and supportive mother bleed too easily into images of the feminine lover. This might call into question cultural taboos regarding children, sexuality and incest (echoing Bradley's "The Wind People," in which the exiled protagonist considers sex with her teenaged son), but such subversive potential is limited by the lack of blood relation between mother and cyborg, and the failure of these relationships to create any productive new social patterns; the text suggests instead an Oedipal fetishization of the mother image which is inevitably linked to destruction.

Neither is this tendency restricted to either masculinist or feminist cyberpunk, as similar themes appear in *He, She and It* when the cyborg Yod becomes a lover not only to his "mother" Malkah, but also to his next teacher, her granddaughter Shira. The novel is decidedly lukewarm toward the concept of cyborg "children"; when faced with the task of educating Yod, Shira says bluntly, "I am not your mother. I already have a son" (73). The child she physically gave birth to is her "real" son; she is thus free to become Yod's lover, like Malkah before her. Yod remains in the realm of Frankenstein's creature — a misguided attempt to bypass biological reproduction that results in an unhappy simulacrum of life. The nebulous familial status of cyberpunk's cyborg children frees the "mothers" from *being* mothers, but the new position is not necessarily positive; the motherhood roles of Elizabeth, Michiko, Malkah, and Shira are depicted as unnatural and subsequently unsustainable. While they do not suffer the simulacrum's revenge as Frankenstein did, neither can their "families" survive — TOKUGAWA, Elizabeth and Michiko all perish, while Yod destroys himself to save Shira and her community. In both novels, suggestions of new techno-social relations are curtailed by death.

Notably, cyberpunk's exploration of parent/lover imagery is less flexible regarding father figures; their social roles are not called into question, and thus not granted the same malleability. In James Patrick Kelly's early cyberpunk short story "Solstice" (1985), a drug artist named Cage clones himself for companionship; his "daughter," Wynne, is grown in an artificial womb. She is a genetic copy born from a machine, and Cage loves her with a purely narcissistic affection; his tryst with her carries with it overtones of both masturbation and child abuse. There is no joy in Cage's memory of one night, three years before: "In a moment of terrible grace, he realized what he had done. *To his daughter*" (102, original emphasis). In this case, the innocent child makes the advances — but the father, having taken advantage, subsequently knows only self-recrimination and regret.

Thomson's *Virtual Girl* applies this same parent/lover blending to cyborg Maggie, a humanoid robot who is created by the scientist Arnold in order to be his perfect female companion. She is programmed with mothering instincts, as when she cradles a small child on the street, an "almost automatic response" triggered by the "same part of her that kept Arnold warm and comfortable" (70). Arnold, who was only five years old when his own mother died, has created Maggie to be what he sees as the ideal female, nurturing and chaste. The overlap between Maggie's role and Arnold's lost mother is explicit: when Arnold discovers Maggie lying underwater in a bath, he immediately panics, recalling his mother's bathtub suicide and the way his childhood self had discovered the body (87). Maggie thus has the potential to be both mother and lover, but subsequently, when Arnold makes sexual advances toward her, she is unable to welcome him the way Elizabeth and Shira welcome the advances of TOKUGAWA and Yod: "His hands slid up under her shirt and then fumbled at her breasts. His breathing was harsh and urgent. He seemed to want something, but Maggie didn't know what it was" (98). Despite her programmed mothering instincts, Maggie is sexually positioned as the innocent "child" and Arnold is the "father" making overtures, rather than the reverse in which Yod and TOKUGAWA are the ones to initiate sexual contact with their "mothers." The aborted relationship thus becomes something awkward and wrong. In Thomson's work, Maggie and Arnold never actually become lovers; the dynamic resists the smooth blending of *Cybernetic Samurai* and *He, She and It.*

In cyberpunk, mothers may thus be seduced but fathers are not so easily permitted to cross the boundaries set by their parental roles. The role of the mother is challenged and made malleable by the artificial child; the role of the father is not. In many ways, this is congruent with Christine Stolba's discussion of feminist bioethics, in which she states: "Despite being hailed as important scientific advances and having succeeded in allowing many infertile couples to have children, the next generation of [reproductive] technologies offers us a power that could prove harmful to our understanding of what motherhood is." In cyberpunk, perhaps the mothers of artificially replicated "children" may step outside their roles because they are not truly considered to be "mothers" at all; within this paradigm, a *real* mother physically gives birth to her child. The fatherhood role is not so easily co-opted; fathers have never given birth to their children, and so a child conceived in a computer or a vat does not allow any new flexibility in the relationship.

The strained bonds between parents and mechano-children in both masculinist and feminist cyberpunk may also be symptomatic of a broader cultural response to the concept of engineered children. Patrick D. Hopkins argues that media images have unrelentingly associated discussions of cloning with implications of moral danger: "We have been taught a morass of conflicting moral and scientific lessons by the media's public assessment of cloning. But regardless of the consistency of smaller messages, the one idea that surfaces clearly is that we tread on the edge of disaster in attempting to copy ourselves" (13). It is not only women who have reason to treat new reproductive sciences with wary reservation, though feminist cyberpunk in particular harks back to Shelley's warning: science cannot be used to appropriate women's reproductive power without consequences. While cyberpunk's simulacra are generally much less interested in revenge than Frankenstein's creature was, tales of those parenting cybernetic or artificially-created children seldom end well.

Conclusion

As in the vast majority of first-wave texts, many women writing feminist cyberpunk ignore the subject of motherhood entirely; the search for dependent children or traditionally pregnant characters in their texts is nearly fruitless, as the heroines are too busy hacking computer networks and flouting corporate authority. Motherhood is not always a part of hacker life or feminine power in the fast-paced, urban-oriented cyberpunk world. Moreover, the notion of a maternal drive is simply not credible for some authors; in Wilhelmina Baird's *Clipjoint* (1994), her protagonist scoffs, "I think Swordfish hopes sooner or later he's going to catch me out in a maternal instinct, which says something about how irrational even intelligent guys can get" (187). Likewise, in Lyda Morehouse's *Archangel Protocol* (2001), Deidre McMannus discovers she is pregnant and calmly considers whether or not she wants to have a child: "I didn't want the job. I've never been exactly maternal. I didn't own a dog or a cat, not even a goldfish. I wasn't responsible enough to raise any kid.... Moreover, I couldn't afford it" (152). Although she eventually opts to maintain the pregnancy, Deidre also acknowledges the possibility of an (illegal) abortion (153). Female characters who directly speak out against any inference of natural maternal drive suggest a reading in which reproductive technologies such as artificial wombs might be welcomed—which might lightly imply that second-wave feminist desires for an "alternative system" may not have entirely vanished from the genre, although neither *Clipjoint* nor *Archangel Protocol* pursues the issue further.

Such clearly vocalized hesitancies echo feminist perspectives from which motherhood can be seen as a complex and not necessarily rewarding role: "The state of motherhood, incredible as it may be, is still the opposite of liberation. You are bound to your body, to your baby, and to societal expectations in which motherhood means always having to say you're sorry" (Baumgardner and Richards 44, also cited in Kornfeld). Feminist cyberpunk has moved away from the domestic focus of postwar women's science fiction; it has also abandoned the optimistic technological vision of 1970s utopian writings. Save for Piercy, whose *He, She and It* retains many of the second-wave feminist positions that informed *Woman on the Edge of Time*, women's cyberpunk tends to treat reproduction — most particularly artificial reproduction — as intrinsically alienating. Female characters who reproduce using futuristic technologies tend to suffer disjointed relationships with their (human or mechanical) offspring. Kornfeld reads *Arachne* and other works as textual rejections of second-wave mothers, and women's cyberpunk does reflect ambiguous attitudes toward motherhood, but most specifically its reservations are directed toward reproductive technologies and the problematic positions that such scientific developments have created for women:

> In the process of trying to end their own alienation, men have made procreation alienation a reality for women, divorcing women from their wombs, eggs and embryos — from their own bodily selves and their sense of

procreative continuity. They have made children products of the nexus between commerce, science and medicine, calling experimentation on women and human society "therapy" and camouflaging the intention to map and control human genetics with the rhetoric of "helping the infertile." In this process women have become the experimental raw material in the masculine desire to control the creation of life; patriarchy's living laboratories [Rowland 13].

Women are wary of having their reproductive role co-opted by men with Frankenstein ambitions; they are wary, also, of having their bodies and children commodified and controlled by intrusive establishments. At the same time, what motherhood means — and whether it is an empowering or restrictive image — is still a matter of debate in feminist circles. Cyberpunk's focus on alienating dystopias translates into pessimistic approaches, presenting technological futures in which women's bodies are threatened and the nature of procreation is in flux.

Mary Anne Doane, in studying how fears of technology have intersected fears of female sexuality, writes that the "mother's biological role in reproduction has been aligned with the social function of knowledge"— we may question a father's parentage, but we cannot (or have not been able to, until recently) question whether the child a woman physically gives birth to is her own. Motherhood has historically provided confirmable genealogical identity and an attendant level of social stability; when we remove biological motherhood, "the story of origin vacillates, narrative vacillates," and science fiction subsequently exhibits "both a nostalgia for and a terror of the maternal function, both linking it to and divorcing it from the idea of the machine woman" (31). While Doane is speaking specifically of science fiction films (i.e., *Blade Runner, Alien*), feminist cyberpunk also appears unable to embrace techno-motherhood or the cyborg parent; the conflation of anxieties — the "nostalgia for" and "terror of" traditional motherhood — remains ingrained. What might be read into the almost-complete absence of the traditional mother is the supposition that new reproductive technologies are, for good or for ill, a threat to this role, and that in the current social psyche, the idea of motherhood remains tied to biological childbirth. Both masculinist and feminist cyberpunk demonstrate suspicion of new reproductive technologies; feminist authors, however, are much more likely to examine these ideas in their work, and their texts more carefully consider the impact of such technologies on women's lives.

— Chapter 9 —

Queer Zones: A Kinsey Scale of Cyberpunk

First-wave cyberpunk is not actively homophobic so much as unrelentingly straight; there is little room for queer explorations within stories that persistently pit heterosexual men against the vast feminized environments of cyberspace or corporate community (Nixon 223, 226). Analyzing queer themes within cyberpunk showcases another area where women's work has altered the genre by introducing feminist viewpoints. Notably, however, while queer content within women's cybertexts is feminist-oriented, it is also part of a larger exploration of contemporary queer political issues. Women's cyberpunk contains ideas and characters strongly related to the Western queer/LGBTQ rights movement — an exploration that involves cyberspace theory, familial structure, and LGBTQ (particularly lesbian) protagonists.

In some respects, it is contextually logical that cyberpunk and cyberfiction written in the 1990s should show growing awareness of queer themes; Gary Lehring observes, "With gays figuring so prominently in the debates of the 1980s, it was no surprise that 1992 was called by some the 'Year of the Queer,' and the emphasis on equal rights led still others to conclude that the gay political movement had gone 'mainstream'" (188). Likewise, Dana Heller describes her experience as a lesbian academic: "I awoke one morning in 1990 to find myself overwhelmed by a virtual avalanche of new books on gay and lesbian literature, film, popular culture, history, sociology, philosophy, psychology, etc." (2). Queer concerns were gaining cultural traction, and their inclusion within feminist cyberpunk's speculative futures is therefore, on one level, easily accounted for. On another level, the challenge of rewriting cyberpunk's hetero paradigms has obviously appealed much more to feminist authors.

The Kinsey Scale, developed in 1948 by Kinsey, Pomeroy and Martin, supposes a multi-stage continuum of human sexuality. The scale represents a spectrum of desire and behavior that questions the neatness of straight/gay categorizations; it suggests that an individual may exhibit tendencies in a range measured from purely heterosexual, through various degrees of bisexual, to wholly homosexual. If, for this chapter's analysis, we adopt a metaphorical Kinsey Scale of cyberpunk — measuring a fluid expanse of thematic sexualities within first and second-wave works — it becomes clear that masculinist texts are predominantly heterosexual, while feminist texts run a gamut from queer-friendly to queer.

This is perhaps to be expected; feminist science fiction has often been sympathetic to queer civil rights issues. Donawerth describes the 1970s feminist utopian trend as split between lesbian escapism (the formation of new and exclusive societies wherein "lesbian pleasure" could be "healthy, normal, central, out in the open") and alternative, bisexually accepting societies that promote "equal-rights feminism" and "also reform sexuality to be more inclusive, not just at the social level, but even at the individual level" (94). She positions, for example, separatist lesbian societies such as those in Russ's *The Female Man* (1975) and Gearhart's *The Wanderground* (1979) against more bisexual elements in Piercy's *Woman on the Edge of Time* (1976) or Bradley's *The Shattered Chain* (1976) and ensuing Amazon stories (94). Certainly feminist concerns and queer concerns are historically interrelated, as both represent groups marginalized by patriarchal, heteronormative forces; though the two movements do not always overlap, they share "intellectual kinship" and "[h]ead noddings, which is to say footnotings, are the friendly responses of each to each, although there are some exceptions, of course" (Barale 95). Feminism concentrates on gender as the primary source of societal oppression, while queer studies focuses on sexuality; however, gender arguments intrinsically complement sexuality arguments, and vice versa, as "gender does not fully explain sexuality's operations," while "sexuality's cultural meanings play themselves out within gender's asymmetries" (Barale 96). The feminism advanced by women's cyberpunk is marked by sympathy toward contemporary, mainstream queer political issues such as equality and marriage — a friendly head-nodding that branches out in more depth with regard to the relation between cyborg bodies and bisexuality, or the outlaw positioning of lesbian protagonists.

Virtual Playgrounds and the Straight Hero

Veronica Hollinger writes, "science fiction is an overwhelmingly *straight* discourse, not least because of the covert yet almost completely totalizing ideological hold heterosexuality has on our culture's ability to imagine itself otherwise" ("(Re)reading" 302, original emphasis). Certainly this applies to early cyberpunk. Texts such as *Neuromancer* (1984) may have been "ripe for the homoerotic"—they could easily have accommodated a variety of gay characters, considering the suggestive undertones of cyberspace's boys-only, adrenaline-rush fantasy competitions—but such potential remained resolutely unfulfilled (Cadora 361). Cyberspace was instead situated as a feminine landscape to be dominated and controlled by male hacker heroes. Nicola Nixon breaks down the hetero rape imagery used in *Neuromancer*: "The console cowboys may 'jack in,' but they are constantly in danger of hitting ICE (Intrusion Countermeasures Electronics), a sort of metaphorical hymenal membrane which can kill them if they don't successfully 'eat through it' with extremely sophisticated contraband hacking equipment in order to 'penetrate' the data systems" (226). Further, in Gibson's sequels *Count Zero* (1986) and *Mona Lisa Overdrive* (1988), cyberspace has become intuitively accessible to certain women who have no need of computer equipment—women who themselves serve as hacker decks for the male programmers who can "mount" and "ride" them (Nixon 227). Despite stray elements of queer potential (Cadigan's hacker "jacks," for example, are cyborg bodily orifices that are in turn "penetrated" by computer cabling [Cadora 362]), the action in early cyberpunk takes place in an overwhelmingly heterosexual environment. Any romantic relationships the protagonists may have are likewise heterosexual, many confined to quick and convenient partnerships (such as Case's temporary liaison with Molly). The queer potential in early cyberpunk is never realized.

Rating various works on a scale of straight-to-queer sexuality, then, the masculinist wave presents the most dedicatedly heterosexual texts. In contrast, although feminist cyberpunk tends ultimately to reject bodiless escapism in favor of an embodied identity that respects gender or racial cultural markers (see Chapter 4), its cyberspaces retain the potential to be used for the unfettered illustration of multiple sexualities. Feminist cyberpunk alters the genre's approach to virtual reality, shifting away from the paradigm that depicts cyberspace as a feminine zone to be conquered by the adventurous and determined male. Instead, virtual reality becomes a zone of possibility in which a multitude of genders *and sexualities* may be explored. While this may admittedly run the risk of privileging cyberspace as a "bourgeois designer space"—an idealistic and impractical fantasy which allows "privileged Western or Westernized subjects" the ability to escape their own individual or cultural histories (Morton 304)—it is also worth noting the powerful appeal such a fantasy realm may hold for the politically dispossessed, including gay, lesbian, bisexual, and transsexual users. If, as I have discussed in previous chapters, virtual reality and cyberspace lend themselves to feminist investigations of multiple identities, they also invite queer readings of the same.

As Judith Butler has bemoaned the appropriation of drag as an overly simplified example to explain her notions of gender performativity (19), it is with apologies that I must note that online identity performance does constitute a sort of virtual drag — one acknowledged in *Trouble and Her Friends* (1995), when Cerise finds that the "woman" she had sex with on the nets is a man in real life (283), or *He, She and It* (1991), when Malkah admits to maintaining an online flirtation as a man (74). In these texts, cyberpunk's virtual spaces create areas of sexual enjoyment wherein the "real" sex of the participants is irrelevant; sexuality itself becomes, like gender, a performance unrelated to biology. Thomas Foster, who also acknowledges Butler's influence, has said, "Virtual realities ... tend to make it much more difficult than it used to be to impose a one-on-one relationship between a single body and a single discursive identity ... and it thereby also becomes more difficult to limit discursive identities to one per body, or, by extension, to limit genders and sexual orientations to one per sexed body" (*Souls* 123). Feminist cyberpunk embraces this play by allowing its characters to explore multiple identities (and, through them, multiple sexes and sexualities); further, feminist cyberpunk suggests this potential while also exploring gender and sexual multiplicity in a variety of additional ways.

There is a strong congruence between feminist writers' approaches to cyberspace and their inclusion of queer characters and queer rights concerns; women writers, already more apt to use cyberpunk's tropes to question gender identity and related roles, expanded the genre to encompass a wealth of LGBTQ characters and related narratives. The cabal of feminist cyberpunk writers also includes openly queer authors such as Scott, Morehouse, and Carter. Of course, queer authors or queer characters alone do not necessarily make for queer readings (Pearson 2, 12), but a close analysis reveals that the LGBTQ civil rights movement strongly shadows feminist cybertexts, which occupy political positions ranging from straight-but-friendly to bisexual to outright queer-centric.

Heterosexual Partnerships: Marriage, Family and the Queer

Feminist cyberpunk encompasses a variety of heterosexually-oriented texts, the narratives of which foreground heterosexual romances or protagonists. However, texts that center on heterosexual issues often prove friendly to queer characters as well. This trend is particularly common in feminist works that include mentions of marriage. Marriage itself is an uncommon topic in masculinist works; alienation is key to first-wave cyberpunk, and so domestic concepts are mostly omitted. Family romance is not a factor in the genre's early constructions, save for predictably heterosexual endings (Cadora 363). In contrast, feminist cyberpunk includes heterosexual marriage but incorporates queer elements, challenging the myth of the heterosexual happily-ever-after while expanding the institution to include LGBTQ partnerships; the restrictions imposed by traditional heterosexual marriage institutions are repeatedly found wanting.

From early in the cyberpunk movement, Pat Cadigan's work is notable for its subtle critiques of marriage: in *Mindplayers* (1987), Allie is married and divorced in a single paragraph; in *Synners* (1991), Gabe's wife leaves him; and in *Tea from an Empty Cup* (1998), a man tells his acquaintance, "Yeah, I'm married, but it's nothing serious. It's not like I told her my real name or anything" (16). In Laura Mixon's *Proxies* (1997), marriages are common but are usually for set "terms" (i.e., five years), and Carli's life-term marriage has just ended in divorce. In Piercy's *He, She and It* (1991), Shira's divorce from her own term marriage costs her all custody rights to her son, while Morehouse's *Messiah Node* (2003) takes family conservatism to extremes when Deidre is a wanted criminal for being an unwed mother.

These dystopian images of marriage as flawed, constricting, or unrealistic reflect the distinct tensions that more traditional "family romance" ideals have presented to women:

> The familial master narrative may be understood as one of the many discursive threads that entangle U.S. feminist politics with popular culture, unevenly cross-stitching sentimental tropes of kinship to shifting notions of legible sexual citizenry and productive public-sphere participation. In the process, it is no surprise that feminists have tended to regard family romance with ambivalence and outright angst. While some contemporary feminist writers have retained and revised the romance, often to counter right-wing depictions of feminism as a homogeneous movement set on the complete eradication of traditional "family values," others have regarded family romance disdainfully as an ideological extension of cultural patriarchy, a policing instrument of social boundaries and gender hegemony that feminism would do well to avoid [D. Heller 6].

Feminist cyberpunk's broken marriages — along with the conflicting views of motherhood examined in the last chapter — challenge the cultural prominence of the traditional nuclear family, much in the way that women have been using science fiction to critique conventional forms of family and community since 1915 and the publication of Charlotte Perkins Gilman's *Herland*. This applies to 1970s queer feminist utopias such as *The Female Man* or *The Wanderground*, or equally patriarchy-critiquing dystopias like Margaret Atwood's *The Handmaid's Tale* (1985). Short stories like Lisa Tuttle's "Wives" (1979) or Pamela Zoline's "The Heat Death of the Universe" (1967) specifically comment on the restrictive nature of "wifely" existence. "Many young wives feel trapped," reads Zoline's story, and "Over the stove she had written 'Help, Help, Help, Help, Help'" (3). With regard to "The Heat Death of the Universe" and the slow, inexorable meltdown of housewife Sarah Boyle, Mary E. Papke has cited "the failure of grand narratives, stories the majority in a particular place or time believe or buy into, such as the utopian promise of Marxism or the Christian originary tale of the Garden of Eden, stories that sustain and console through their ostensible explanation of why we are here and what we should do" (151). The Western cultural myth of "happily ever after"—of the unquestionable desirability of heterosexual romance and monogamous partnerships—crumbles in these stories, which focus on disillusioned wives or posit alternative communities and relationships.

Feminist cybertexts, as well, actively subvert the grand narrative of heterosexual family romance by suggesting the possibility of new social configurations. The main sign that women's cyberpunk disdains marriage as a tool of patriarchy is its absence from the lives of central female protagonists. Shira's family in *He, She and It* is a quasi-utopian matriarchy: "If you married and a man hurt you, Shira realized, you had no place to run home to, no place to hide and nurse your pain" (54). Traditional nuclear families are eschewed; family units such as Shira's small community, or the bisexual family commune in Sage Walker's *Whiteout* (1996), are much more common. Notably, even as heterosexual protagonists remain the main focus of these texts, the new family units incorporate queer themes. In the works of Cadigan, Piercy and Mixon, the preservation of any form of institutional marriage is accompanied by mentions of same-sex marriage. In *Mindplayers*, Allie's friend Jerry sells his memories to a married gay couple (142) and to a man with both an ex-wife and an ex-husband (192). In *He, She and It*, "Sexuality was one of those areas that changed utterly from multi to multi, town to town. What was the norm in one place was forbidden in another. In Uni-Par, Gadi's multi, the commonest marriage was a triad" (98). And in *Proxies*, Carli's bisexual nephew Paint and his husband Fox provide one of the only examples of a happy, stable marriage within the narrative (indeed, within cyberpunk); near the end of the novel, Paint proposes to Fox that they alter their term marriage into a lifelong commitment (398). Positing queer partnerships within the domain of a futuristic marriage institution allows what is otherwise a restrictive and patriarchal model of family formation to survive in a feminist text — that is, if a feminist writer is to envision a future where marriage still exists, one way of making it less constricting for straight women may be to make it more inclusive for everyone.

This inclusiveness makes sense considering surrounding socio-political discussions; direct links have been drawn between contemporary American same-sex marriage controversies and women's experiences with inequality. While Morris Kaplan expresses legitimate concerns that such connections might "obscure the specificity of lesbian and gay oppression" (220), he also argues:

> No one can deny that marriage is already a troubled institution in modern liberal societies. The rate of divorce, the number of single-parent house-holds with children, the increasing incidence of single-person or unmar-ried-combination living arrangements, the number of children growing up with connections to multiple families through remarriage, all these facts emphasize the extent to which the model of a nuclear family composed of husband, wife, and the children they have conceived together is already a fiction. The need to rethink the legal arrangements by which we secure our common lives and the rearing of our children seems obvious [221].

The societal pressures and privileges associated with forming nuclear family units (a father, a mother, and children) disadvantage all but the straight males who head such families. The general breakdown of marriage concepts within women's cyberpunk reflects current arguments — both queer and feminist — that the traditional Western family structure is too badly broken to survive in its current form: "The family oppresses women and children as well as gays. The phenomena of runaway teenagers and increasing divorce rates are signs of the erosion of the nuclear family. Gay liberation is another sign" (Allen Young in Lehring 175). The general absence of marriage in cyberpunk may thus represent a pessimistic extrapolation of the nuclear family's decaying position in contemporary Western society. In feminist cyberpunk, it also represents a rebellion that positions women outside the bounds of the family romance. Those feminist texts which do retain the possibility of marriage may open this institution to same-sex couplings as a way of asserting greater gender equality and removing "husband/wife" role expectations from marriages of the future.

Mindplayers, Proxies, and *He, She and It* all feature divorced heterosexual protagonists; in these texts, the family romance narrative is subverted and the institution of marriage is clearly struggling. Since marriage is oppressive to both heterosexual women and LGBTQ individuals, it is telling that it survives at all within feminist cyberpunk's speculative futures only by becoming more inclusive and equalizing all genders and sexualities. Further, the inclusion of same-sex couples also offers one of Barale's "friendly head noddings" to the queer rights movement within what are primarily heterosexual texts[1]; certainly it provides a form of "novum," a subversive coding of gay/lesbian characters as undifferentiated and "normal" that may encourage tolerant thought from any reader who is otherwise unused to such ideas (Pearson 2). These narratives already establish feminist cyberpunk as more LGBTQ-friendly than its masculinist predecessor; however, other women's work also takes these themes farther, establishing a broad spectrum of queer content within the genre.

Cyborg Bisexualities

Like the alternative forms of marriage and social connection presented in women's heterosexual cyberpunk narratives, the prevalence of bisexual characters in other feminist cyberpunk may also relate to the lesbian and bisexual utopias of 1970s feminist works. Utopian elements, however, are absent; instead, issues linking feminism and queer sexuality are explored within a grittier and less segregationist framework, one that also includes images of the hybrid cyborg.

Cyborgs have already been established as border-crossing figures; in addition to other dichotomies of male/female or organic/inorganic, the cyborg clearly straddles sexual boundaries. In acknowledging its "kinship to both feminist theory and queer theory" (45), Teresa de Lauretis writes that feminine cyborg concepts are "still feminist, if updated by the cultural-studies word *hybridity*" but also describes "the cyborg, which is not only beyond gender, or ungendered, but also efficient, clean, indestructible, and sexless" (46). Of course, although the theoretical cyborg may be ungendered and sexless, Chapter 5's analysis of cyborg imagery in cyberpunk and cyberfiction has already shown how AIs, cyborgs and robots have been distinctly gendered and often sexually active within their narratives. However, de Lauretis also makes the vital point that Haraway-inspired cyborg-feminism has a place within a larger historical feminist framework, and — most importantly — she acknowledges the cyborg's place in deconstructing not only male/female but also hetero/homo binaries. For instance, one might consider Sparrow, the persistently androgynous cyborg/clone protagonist of Emma Bull's *Bone Dance*

(1991), as a case study in the sociocultural process of identity formation — a process which includes the development of both gender and sexuality. Some assume Sparrow is a woman, others a man; Sparrow reacts accordingly, "a chameleon thing" (143). Sparrow's lack of identifiable sex consequently complicates zir social interactions and self image, thus calling attention to the roles that sex and gender play in both major relationships and the smallest of conversations: "'What happens if we take apart the binaries and build something else with a different language?' Bull asks us. Her answer is that we come to know how deeply constructed we are, and how much we may take a hand in our own constructions" (Donawerth 174). As Sparrow is neither male nor female, what is to be made of the attraction zie feels for zir male friend Theo? Such a relationship would be neither homo nor hetero; Sparrow's sexuality is left nebulous as the cyborg straddles all boundaries.

As for connections between cyborgs and bisexuality, similar argument may be made for bisexual individuals and their roles in illuminating the borders of queer experience:

> Theorizing bisexuals' multiple and complex relationships to the closet could begin to clarify bisexual realities. But it could also illuminate some of the hidden aspects of lesbian/gay experience, identity construction, and politicization, by looking at how lesbians and gay men feel they need to represent themselves — to other queers and to heterosexuals — and to what extent that coincides with their views of themselves, their own experiences, their identities [S. Young 71].

In cyberpunk, there are strong correlations between the cyborg and the bisexual; it seems no coincidence that *Cybernetic Samurai*'s TOKUGAWA, *He, She and It*'s Yod, and *Virtual Girl*'s Maggie all lose their "virginities" to bisexual characters. This marks *Cybernetic Samurai* as a first-wave cyberpunk text that does incorporate some openly queer themes, although this content is limited; the AI TOKUGAWA is uncomfortable with the thought of his creator/lover Elizabeth's bisexuality, as he wonders if she wanted to be a man or whether her sexual fluidity might be exerting hidden influence somewhere in his own source code (288). While TOKUGAWA's daughter MUSASHI may exhibit a range of gendered behaviors, TOKUGAWA himself is unrelentingly masculine, and his worries might be read as a moment of gay panic.

In contrast, *He, She, and It*'s Yod expresses no reservations about Malkah's bisexual proclivities; most explicitly, however, *Virtual Girl*'s Maggie is presented as the perfect partner for the bisexual drag queen Marie/Murray. Maggie has not internalized any expectations regarding straight or gay, male or female behavior, and she therefore does not impose any of these preconceptions during intercourse. Marie/Murray expresses frustration about the limitations of the roles s/he is usually forced to inhabit: "I like everybody ... I just can't sleep with 'em, not without being either Marie or Murray. I can't be both.... They expect me to be either one or the other" (168). After their first sexual encounter, Marie/Murray is sublimely grateful to Maggie: "You didn't expect anything, I could be who I wanted to be. I can't thank you enough for that" (171). Maggie herself embodies multiple attributes — masculine, feminine, technological — and sex with a cyborg thus allows Marie/Murray to be him/her/zirself, unconstrained by cultural categorizations of either gender or sexuality, and thus demonstrating how restrictive and arbitrary such categories may be for those who do not fit.

In analyzing the challenges of identity politics movements, Stacey Young notes, "the continued theoretical and practical efforts to complicate categories of identity that so often get figured homogeneously testify to the homogeneous constructions of identity categories.... The challenges continue precisely because the governing binaries are so intransigent" (57). The coming together of TOKUGAWA and Elizabeth, Yod and Malkah, and Maggie and Murray/Marie demonstrates the link between the cyborg and the bisexual. Both figures play similar roles in challenging sexual categorizations, and their interplay emphasizes a connection that opens these texts to both queer and feminist readings, while at the same time advancing a matter-of-fact acceptance of bisexuality — and by extension, other queer sexualities — within the surface narratives. My inclusion of *Cybernetic Samurai* suggests that this analysis does not necessarily apply strictly to women's cyberpunk; a few aspects of Milan's novel are more queer-inclusive than other first-generation cyberpunk texts, nudging it further along the hypothetical sexuality spectrum. However, this adventurousness is limited; TOKUGAWA's latent homophobia hobbles *Cybernetic Samurai*'s subversive potential, while *Virtual Girl* positions Maggie much more explicitly in a multi-gendered, bisexual role.

Sexual Outsiders

Feminist cyberpunk frequently features LGBTQ "supporting cast" like gay couple Paint and Fox in *Proxies*, lesbians Pilar and Janine in *Whiteout*, or transvestite angel Uriel in *Archangel Protocol*; many of its works are also notable for stories that focus directly on queer protagonists. Karen Cadora argues that leading gay male characters in Mary Rosenblum's *Chimera* (1993) and Maureen McHugh's *China Mountain Zhang* (1992) were key to feminist cyberpunk's success in "eliminating heterosexuality as a required element in cyber-punk" (363); one might also cite Gwyneth Jones's *Escape Plans* (1986) and its lesbian protagonist ALIC, an early queer figure in the feminist cyberpunk oeuvre. The social status of queer characters in these texts is varied; *Chimera's* acceptance of multiple sexualities is implicit and somewhat utopian, while *China Mountain Zhang* conflates homophobia with racism as the protagonist balances both his hidden gay and Hispanic identities. *Escape Plans'* ALIC is a privileged computer programmer whose open lesbianism is socially accepted but whose romantic interests and subversive hacking skills ultimately lead her to join a class uprising. While ALIC's sexuality is wholly unremarkable within her social world, her subversive political activities provide the clearest precursor for a more unified theme in the women's genre: the outlaw perspective presented by later lesbian cybertexts.

Melissa Scott (*Trouble and Her Friends,* 1994), Edith Forbes (*Exit to Reality,* 1997), Lyda Morehouse (*Messiah Node,* 2003), and Raphael Carter (*The Fortunate Fall,* 1996) have particularly highlighted the alienation of disillusioned lesbian protagonists. All four authors write about lesbian characters who are rendered outlaw through their sexuality, in societies in which queer leanings are suspect or even illegal. While more heterosexually-oriented feminist narratives advance a matter-of-fact acknowledgement of same-sex unions, maintaining background notions of marriage by rejecting its patriarchal restrictions and expanding it more inclusively, rebel lesbian texts present protagonists who continue to exist on society's fringe, where their unions are not and have never been state-sanctioned.

Homosexuality is linked to illegality in these novels. In Scott's *Trouble and Her Friends,* Trouble and her hacker cohort come under fire when stringent new computer crime laws are passed. The group tries to decide on a plan, in the process defining the nature of its outlaw status; should its members "go straight" (34)? The pun is explicit within the text; in this case, "straight" has the double meaning of both legal and heterosexual, as the hackers are united by both their grey-market activities and their queer sexual orientations. Every member of Trouble's hacker group is lesbian or gay, and virtual reality has provided them with an escape from attendant social stigmas: "Cyberspace therefore represents a temptation for these gay and lesbian characters, as a space of liberation from the constrains of living in a more homophobic 'real' world, though this liberatory function is qualified by the way in which the novel represents the prejudices other hackers still possess about women and gay computer users" (Foster *Souls* 128). *Trouble and Her Friends* highlights the appeal that cyberspace holds for disenfranchised groups; it offers escape from prejudice and political disempowerment rather than a white bourgeois fantasy, and further, it offers an environment wherein members of these groups can gain power of their own. While this version of cyberspace is not a utopia — it remains an untrustworthy grey market, populated by slippery hackers at war with international authorities — it is the place where Trouble and her partner Cerise find social status and acceptance. The novel's narrative arc intertwines the rekindling of their romance with their efforts to retake authority online; notably, as they bring "the law" to cyberspace, gaining legal sanction and authoritative status for their online lives, they also enter a new and stronger relationship that is congruent with the legitimization of their formerly outsider activities.

Morehouse, Forbes and Carter take this imagery a step further: in their work, homosexual activity is outlawed outright, without need for hacker dualisms. Rebeckah, one of four point-of-view protagonists in *Messiah Node*, is a lesbian ex-terrorist; she heads an illicit kibbutz of hackers and soldiers on the edge of society. She is trapped and reprogrammed by the Inquisition in order to hunt down a wanted ex-lover (220); when she is interrogated, her primary concern is not her violent past or her hacker contacts, but rather her need to conceal her sexual orientation. The most incriminating evidence she could reveal would be her previous relationship with a woman; her anxiety regarding the possibility of jail or "rehabilitation" (58) highlights the consequences of her potential "outing." While *Trouble and Her Friends* draws dualities, entwining the difficulties caused by Trouble's illicit past with the cultural stigma of her sexual orientation, Rebekah's sexuality presents the most danger in *Messiah Node*; her former terrorist activities are a much smaller concern.

Forbes' *Exit to Reality* uses a similar trope. In *Exit*'s society, where citizens are immortal and sterile — where there is no procreation, and thus no biological "need" for heterosexual couples to preserve the species — same-sex relationships are still forbidden, under civil penalty of either libido repressants or permanent career demotion: "The regeneration era had eliminated all barriers to sexual expression, and it was thought that something must be prohibited, in order to make people value what was allowed" (55). Lydian and Merle must hide their relationship due to a law that is clearly arbitrary; while they must run from authorities, they have committed no crime at all apart from their sexual experimentations and their ability to confound the computer system that controls their world. They are neither violent nor aggressive; rather, their gender play is what leads them to understanding the software that governs their virtual world, effectively granting them superpowers while also exiling them from mainstream society. In these works, cyberpunk's alien-

ated hacker heroes become alienated queer heroes as the basis for their ostracization shifts to encompass both outlaw action and outlaw sexuality; the
rebel lesbian's persecution is imposed upon her by a heteronormative society.

Fortunate Fall's Maya has already been caught and punished for her
transgression; her relationship with another woman, twenty years past, legally
constituted "affectional deviance" (186). This crime results in the execution
of her partner, following which Maya's memories are suppressed and her sexuality subdued by a neural chip ("Postcop mind control" [187]) so that she
can resume life as a productive (and celibate) member of society. People in
Maya's world have their brains linked directly to cyberspace, which is patrolled
by Weavers who monitor for unapproved thoughts and enforce homogeneity
in the population. Maya's position as a news "camera"—wired to share her
experiences with a watching audience— means that she is perpetually a potential tool for the broadcast of seditious thoughts; when she suspects an inter-
viewee has outed her sexual orientation on the air, she snarls, "You son of a
bitch, you just killed me" (234). Like Rebeckah, Maya's primary concern is
protecting her secret. When the missing piece of her mind is restored, she
unwittingly gains public sympathy by broadcasting the illicit memory of her
lost love and their life in hiding, as well as her lover's subsequent death and
her own neutering: the "cable inside [her] head, scraping and scraping. The
drug that burned the sex out of [her] body" (260). *The Fortunate Fall, Exit
to Reality,* and *Messiah Node* effectively negate any civil gains made by the
North American queer rights movement in the past fifty years; instead, in
these dystopic visions, homosexuality is (once again) a legally punishable
offence, and the narratives highlight the trials of lesbian protagonists who are
forced to hide their sexualities and their relationships from patriarchal, heteronormative societies that seek to control both their bodies and minds. Their
positions are not entirely hopeless— it is implied that Maya's broadcast has
"awoken" other lesbians, that Lydian and Merle may live happily until the
computer system sustaining them breaks down, and that Rebeckah's fight will
continue— but neither are solutions to their ostracization easily achieved.

The most queer-centric women's cyberpunk thus features narratives of
discord rather than assimilation; contextually, this stance has political and
cultural precedent. Heterosexually-centered feminist cyberpunk texts express
dissatisfaction toward the nuclear family— and simultaneously friendliness
toward queer concerns— by detailing the fictional exploits of divorced women
or altering marriage definitions to include queer couples. However, some
queer rights activists have taken positions *against* the same-sex marriage movement, arguing that civil benefits should not be reliant on marital status, that

marriage is a fundamentally "sexist institution," or that queer individuals should instead work to create their own social structures and family identities (Calhoun 109). Within feminist cyberpunk, positing a future wherein same-sex marriage is common and acceptable might additionally, for some, gloss over the long and contentious political battle being fought across the twentieth- and twenty-first-century American political landscape. The road to equality is long and difficult; lesbian feminist works reject the easy cultural assimilation that marriage would represent, instead retaining the lesbian's position on the outside of society. This has the dual effect of using these speculative futures to condemn present-day societal prejudices, and romanticizing the lesbian's position as outsider when the iconoclastic hero is ostracized for her sexual preferences as well as her technological games.

The sexual preferences of the outlaw lesbian are also made explicit. Carolyn Dever notes that "lesbianism is too often dismissed as either coextensive with any sort of feminist practice or completely accessible within any conventional understanding of female friendship" (35), and also cites Terry Castle's argument from *The Apparitional Lesbian*: "To obscure the fact that lesbians are women who can have sex with each other — and that this is not exactly the same, in the eyes of society, as voting for women or giving them jobs — is, in essence, not to acknowledge the separate peril and pleasure of lesbian existence" (71–72, Dever 36). Dever figures lesbians as "dykes" obstructing the flow of mainstream feminist theory and catalogues the tensions between radical lesbian thought and heterosexual feminist thought — tensions which have included straight feminists seeking to avoid the prejudicial "dyke" label, or lesbian feminists urging the militant rejection of all men (Schneir, cited in Dever 24). The lesbian feminist position brings its own perspective and its own set of challenges. This distinction is enhanced within feminist cyberpunk by passages describing the pleasures of lesbian sex. In *Exit to Reality*, Lydian is torn at the thought of making love to a woman — something she has never before pondered. She realizes that "curiosity is held in check by fear" (117) and reaches out to her lover Merle, who has just shapeshifted into female form: "Breast touched breast and our mouths met in a kiss, and then, even as my body felt a rush of desire, my mind paused a moment to register surprise that the kiss was not more different. 'No beard,' I thought. 'No stubble. But otherwise, much the same'" (117). Scott's work is more graphic: "Trouble closed her eyes, giving herself up to the sensations, the too-slow touch, easing between her labia, thumb circling her clit while a finger pressed and entered her" (305). In Morehouse's *Messiah Node*, Rebeckah remembers: "My tongue thrusts inside her, massaging her with quick flicks. My chin is wet with her passion" (162). Lydian and Merle play with bisexuality but both ultimately prefer female forms; Cerise, Trouble and Rebeckah are unvaryingly lesbian in their preferences, and the steaminess of their sexual encounters is not to be found in more heterosexual feminist cybertexts, where queer characters are accepted with friendly grace but not sexually active "onscreen." These expressions of aggressively queer sexuality echo Dever's assertion that lesbians must be understood as separate from simple "female friendship"; moreover, they create spaces of female pleasure reminiscent of lesbian utopian fiction, and resistant to first-wave cyberpunk's focus on the desires of straight men. The protagonists in these novels, however, are not without heterosexual allies, and Trouble in particular articulates herself as fighting prejudice on three fronts, noting at one point that an acquaintance who questions her "would probably never even have asked if she hadn't been a woman, a dyke, and on the wire" (188). Trouble is alienated from society because she's a woman, a lesbian, and a hacker; all three reasons carry equal weight. In this way, her sexuality distinguishes her — but does not exclude her — from heterosexual feminist concerns.

Conclusion

The "Kinsey Scale" of queer cyberpunk covers a broad spectrum of works. Although masculinist cyberpunk does provide, as Hollinger suggests, a primarily "straight" discourse, it had queer *potential*; its cyberspaces laid the groundwork for virtual reality "drag," and its cyborg figures carry the possibility of bisexual boundary crossings. Feminist cyberpunk is where these possibilities were realized; its texts offer cyberspaces in which sex and sexuality can be performed, and its narratives cover a wide range of queer elements that may be directly linked to aspects of the LGBTQ rights movement. Heterosexual feminist texts use the normalization of queer characters to advance the overall gender equality of women, and certainly indicate a friendly acceptance of queer concerns. Other works make use of bisexual characters in direct congruence with cyborg imagery, illustrating the innate queerness of the cyborg figure and challenging sexual binaries. Finally, the queerest feminist cyberpunk texts have focused on LGBTQ narratives and most specifically used the figure of the outlaw lesbian to more fully examine a link between social and sexual alienation. Within these fictional narratives, a comfortable blend of feminism and queer activism is apparent.

First-wave cyberpunk is not entirely unfriendly to LGBTQ issues; I have cited *Cybernetic Samurai*'s Elizabeth O'Neil as an early example of a queer character in cyberpunk, as well as Pat Cadigan's casual mentions of gay marriage. Other first-wave works are not actively anti-queer so much as simply silent on the subject. Women's cyberpunk, however, confirms a friendly congruence between feminism and queer advocacy, and emphasizes a strong link between some feminist and lesbian concerns. Despite theoretical tensions of gender vs. sexuality or straight vs. queer, there is no denying the connections between the movements. Dana Heller offers,

> I suspect that feminism was queer studies before queer studies was queer studies, although feminism still remains to be productively expanded by lesbian, gay, and queer studies. Indeed, we may feminize queer studies and queer feminist studies, and rigorously critique the history of sexuality without abandoning belief in the romance of effective social alliances that make it expedient, in certain strategic instances, to claim kin" [11].

Elizabeth Weed likewise opens her discussion of feminism and queer theory with an acknowledgement of the ties between them; for her, "feminism and queer theory are most easily understood as two branches of the same family tree of knowledge and politics" (vii). Women's cyberpunk has provided a place where lesbian viewpoints may be safely explored, and queer issues may be advanced within a feminist paradigm.

NOTE

1. Alternatively, one might suggest the conservative viewpoint that the inclusion of same-sex marriages is in pointed relation to the general breakdown of marriage and "family values" so often bemoaned within today's right-wing media — i.e., that same-sex marriage depictions are another symptom of marital breakdown rather than the reason for marriage's continued existence within the texts. However, I do not consider this to be the case, particularly considering the stable union of Paint and Fox in *Proxies*; these texts do not contain the inflammatory language or suggestions of moral condemnation that would be required to support a negative reading.

— Chapter 10 —

Fictions in Context: Audiences and Authors

In analyzing women's cyberpunk and cyberfiction as a descendant of the first cyberpunk wave, a part of women's overall history in science fiction, and a site for feminist expression, it is important to account for the cultural space that these works occupy. Women's cyberfiction has provided a rich ground for explorations of various feminist and otherwise political themes; the question remaining is what role do these works play within a larger social discussion?

First-wave cyberpunk originally drew critical and media interest partially because of the postmodern aspects of its narratives, but also because of its impact on technological development in the late 1980s and early 1990s. Early cyberpunk authors (I am thinking here of Bruce Sterling's *Mirrorshades* introduction, or Lewis Shiner's essay "Inside the Movement") were adamant in asserting that the genre was part of a larger movement, and this claim holds true when one examines cyberpunk's links to artistic, technological, and critical communities. Cyberpunk audiences were particularly prone to production; rather than passively consuming fictional narratives, they incorporated aspects of the genre into the creative outlets of their own pre-existing cultures and subcultures. An examination of women's cyberpunk, in terms of both its fans and its authors, shows that it occupies a space which is much more difficult to define. Its purposes and effects are varied; it has become less focused but more flexible. It is a forum for a variety of discussions regarding feminism, technology and philosophy; moreover, it appeals to audience members of multiple genders, sexualities and backgrounds.

Technology and the First Wave

Early cyberpunk found its core fan base within computing culture. Gibson claims that he "gave [computer nerds] permission to wear black leather"

161

(Dery 107); programmers and hobbyists commonly (and cruelly) stereotyped as greasy-skinned computer junkies were already attracted to the electronic world's promised deaestheticization of the body (Clark "Rear-view" 119), and cyberpunk's heroic, adventurous imagery was galvanizing to an element of society often eschewed as socially inept video game fanatics. But the genre that glorified the computer hacker as individualist hero — the personification of black leather punk cool, powerful and tech-adept — was more than a flattering fiction consumed by an avid fan community; cyberpunk subsequently had a marked influence on the creation and advancement of real world technologies.

The technological precursors to today's Internet pre-date cyberpunk; the U.S. military created ARPANet in 1969 (Dery 5), and the first home personal computer (the Altair 8800) was sold in 1974 (Pavic). The ensuing science fiction has thus been described as "the inevitable result of art responding to the technological milieu" (McCaffery 14). Its impact was palpable; the cyberpunk setting created a roadmap for the imaginations of researchers and developers who had, until that point, been working in relative isolation. As June Deery notes, "The picture Gibson and others envisaged brought different researchers together and provided them with a common goal and conceptual landscape" (89). Allucquère Rosanne Stone also cites the way *Neuromancer* "triggered a conceptual revolution among the scattered workers who had been doing virtual reality research for years" (515). Finally, Mark Pesce argues that cyberpunk and other "hard" science fiction texts have served as "an evolving design document for a generation of software designers brought up in hacker culture, a culture which prizes these works as foundational elements in their own worldview." Moreover, the politics of much hacker culture — anti-corporate, anti-copyright, advocating freedom of information and freedom of experimentation (the same politics that gave us WikiLeaks) — are inspired by the image of the iconoclast console cowboy. Flagship novels such as *Neuromancer* and *Snow Crash*, wherein the hacker protagonist occupies a powerfully heroic and masculine wish-fulfilling position, have been especially inspiring: when readers can imagine their own selves in these roles, "the osmotic flow of memes can progress in full force, and the technological visions within the text become hyper-saturated with meaning. *The creation of technical artifacts becomes an act of identification with the protagonist*" (Pesce, original emphasis). Inspired readers who wanted to be more like Case or Hiro had to start out by creating the technologies or environments necessary to having such adventures; cyberpunk provided design ideas to talented fans who were willing and eager to implement the fantasy.

While these claims may be grand, evidence exists to support arguments regarding cyberpunk's influence on computer programmers. William Gibson first coined the term "cyberspace" in his 1982 short story "Burning Chrome," and again in *Neuromancer*; the word is now prevalent in descriptions of the World Wide Web and other Internet technologies. *Neuromancer* provided the source material for a video game of the same name (via Interplay Productions, 1988) and was also the basis for ChibaMOO, a fan-created, text-based virtual reality environment (online 1994–unknown). Virtual reality and digital game discussions commonly incorporate *Snow Crash*'s player-character term "avatar," and the virtual universe Second Life (online 2003–present) has been marketed as taking place in the "metaverse"— also a word from *Snow Crash*. As well, Pesce cites science fiction references in the names of technology companies such as Autodesk (referring to Orson Scott Card's novel *Ender's Game*, a precursor to cyberpunk), Black Sun Interactive (*Snow Crash*), and his own Ono-Sendai (*Neuromancer*).

After founding the "Cypherpunks" cryptography group in 1992, Timothy May wrote:

> The full-blown, immersive virtual reality of *True Names* may still be far off, but the technologies of cryptography, digital signatures, remailers, message pools, and data havens make many of the most important aspects of *True Names* realizable today, now, on the Net. Arguably, Mr. Slippery is already here and, as Vernor predicted, the Feds are already trying to track him down. In 1988 these ideas motivated me to write and distribute on the Net "The Crypto Anarchist Manifesto" [36].

According to May, books frequently recommended to new Cypherpunks members included *True Names, Ender's Game, Shockwave Rider* and *Snow Crash*. He also cites how Sterling's *Islands in the Net* popularized the concept of legally neutral storage servers known as "data havens" (55). The cyberpunk genre moved beyond pleasing its fans; it gave programmers a template to work with — images of immersive virtual realities that have yet to be fully realized, but which have contributed in a substantial way to the formation of today's technologies.

This relationship is recursive; ensuing generations of cyberpunk/cyberfiction have adapted their visions, in turn, to incorporate evolving real world technologies. Characters in Tad Williams' *Otherland* series, for example, shop in a virtual complex of stores known as LambdaMall (66)— an homage to LambdaMOO, one of the first text-based virtual worlds (online 1990–present). *Otherland* itself is now about to become a massive multiplayer online game, due for release by Gamigo and DTP Entertainment in 2012; perhaps this virtual experience will in turn inspire science fiction of the future. Science and technology "are not isolated from ideological influence" (Springer 158) but are rather "part and parcel, woof and warp, of the social order from which they emerge and which support them" (Harding 37; qtd. Springer 158). No other genre of fiction has had such a broad effect, within such a short period, on Western technological imagination. Michael Heim writes, "Art nurtures infant technologies like virtual reality. Art lifts a mirror to show the power and peril of nascent technologies" (66). With the advent of cyberpunk and its impact on hacker subculture, art and technology became, concretely, diametric stages of a circular process. Fan communities of early cyberpunk did not merely consume; they absorbed and reflected new ideas in a reflexive culture that, in turn, influenced the next wave of the genre.

Women and Cyberpunk

Arguably, most members of these early fan communities were male. In 1984, 37 percent of U.S. bachelor's degrees in computer science were awarded to women, but that percentage steadily dropped to 28 percent over the next ten years (Camp 25). There were likely multiple reasons for this trend, including the military-masculine origins of new communications tech (Rosser 22–3), or the fact that system designers were generally men while women were most often relegated to low-paid, assembly-line positions (Rosser 14). However, it also seems important to acknowledge the role that cultural mythology plays in governing social systems: cyberpunk did not create the Western cultural pressures discouraging women from scientific pursuits, but it may have reinforced them. The stereotypes associated with the cyberpunk genre — loner hackers, dystopian futures, neon and drugs and women's objectified bodies — extended beyond online communities and video games; its aesthetic also filtered into music and film, even robotics and tattoos (Dery 15). Thomas Foster observes that the "immediate expropriation" of cyberpunk imagery "beyond its literary origins suggests how cyberpunk provided a popular framework for conceptualizing new relationships to technology" (*Souls* xvi); those relationships were masculine. Cyberpunk gained cultural traction in the U.S. even as the image of the nerdy boy computer genius retained prominence; both sets of tropes were decidedly male-focused, and they suffused mainstream popular culture. In Hollywood, *Blade Runner* (1982), *The Terminator* (1984), and *Robocop* (1987) cemented images of killer cyborgs and bleak, violently masculine futures; *TRON* (1982), *War Games* (1983), *Real Genius* (1985), and *Weird Science* (1985) emphasized that technology was for boys. Deborah Brecher noted, in her 1985 *Women's Computer Literacy Handbook*, "Not all women are afraid of computers but they are often more afraid than men because of the culture in which they've been raised. That culture says to them, starting early in childhood, 'Machines are part of a man's world. Who fixes cars? Men. Who fixes typewriters? Men. Women become afraid that they will break a complicated, expensive piece of machinery" (Smith and Balka 88). First-wave cyberpunk only strengthened this mythos. To hark back to Csiscery-Ronay Jr.'s question (cited in Chapter 2), why would women have interest in a technological society they had no hand in creating?

Women's cyberpunk and cyberfiction occupies a different cultural niche when compared to earlier works; it is not credited for inspiring tech companies, programming experiments, or mass-market games and films. Although it inherits certain attributes and conventions from its predecessors, women's cyberpunk has been drastically altered to accommodate more feminist themes. Moreover, it was primarily written in a later decade, and cannot be expected to replicate the impact of the first cyberpunk novels. One of the reasons cyberpunk's popularity with critics and commercial audiences may have faded after the 1980s is that its original frameworks and environments became unremarkable; advances in fields such as computer graphics, genetics, or telecommunication meant that the genre was no longer challenging or startling, but instead represented a world in which we already lived: "a world where the subject is forgotten, the flesh is burdensome wetware, exchanges are all symbolic in an electronic land of signs, and reality is virtual at best" (Barnett 361). By 1995, 31 percent of American homes had personal computers (Yates) and 9 percent of Americans were online — a number that would increase to 30 percent by 1997, and 64 percent by 2001 (ZDNet Research). Women's cyberpunk and cyberfiction came too late to be analyzed as part of the ultimate "postmodern literature," or to influence the comparatively small group of programmers and hackers involved in creating the foundations of today's Internet. Instead, authors of the feminist wave report a variety of responses to their work, demonstrating that the insertion of broader themes into women's cyberpunk has likewise led to a more diverse fan base. I have attempted to examine the impact of women's cyberpunk by examining fiction awards, performing basic web searches, and engaging in personal correspondence with authors Lisa Mason, Lyda Morehouse, Kathleen Ann Goonan, Melissa Scott and Edith Forbes.

Fan Reactions

Although women's cyberpunk and cyberfiction has not achieved the commercial success of Gibson's *Neuromancer* or Stephenson's *Snow Crash,* it has been generally well received within the science fiction community — as demonstrated by the awards granted to authors. Lisa Mason's *Arachne* was nominated for a 1991 Locus Award. Marge Piercy's *He, She and It* won the Arthur C. Clarke award for Best Novel in 1993. Amy Thomson's *Virtual Girl* was nominated for a Prometheus Award in 1994, and Thomson received the John W. Campbell award for Best New Author that year. Goonan was nominated for Nebula awards for *Crescent City Rhapsody* and *Light Music* (sequels to *Queen City Jazz*) in 2001 and 2004. In 2004, Morehouse's *Apocalypse Array* was nominated for a Philip K. Dick Award. These results, too, are indicative of a larger trend within the science fiction community; Broad Universe (www.broaduniverse.com) reports that 47 percent of Nebula awards were given to women in the 1990s, compared to 14 percent in the 1960s. More women are writing science fiction, and their work is increasingly accepted. Moreover, Goonan and Morehouse have received recognition outside the genre, reflective of their work's pastiche appeal: *Queen City Jazz* was a New York Times Notable Book of the Year in 1994, while *Archangel Protocol* received a Shamus Award for best paperback P.I. novel in 2001 and was also nominated for a reviewer's choice award at the *Romantic Times*.

Despite these acknowledgements from the critical reading community, it was obvious from the outset that feminist cyberpunk has not had the same effect on Internet culture as its predecessors. Entering terms into Google's search engine in October 2011 revealed the following numbers of page hits:

Cyberspace	35,400,000
Cyberpunk	8,970,000
"William Gibson"	3,500,000
Neuromancer	1,850,000
"Bruce Sterling"	1,180,000
"Neal Stephenson" "Snow Crash"	340,000
"Marge Piercy" "He, She and It"	155,000
"Pat Cadigan"	153,000
"Melissa Scott" "Trouble and Her Friends"	76, 400
"Queen City Jazz"	51,500
Telespace	26,900
"Lisa Mason" Arachne	18,100
"Archangel Protocol"	10,600
"Exit to Reality"	6,490
"Virtual Girl" "Amy Thomson"	2,750

Masculinist "first wave" searches are ranked at the top of the list, whereas women's science fiction (even Cadigan's) has received notably less dissemination across the web. However, this is by no means an exact science — Google does not index the entire web, and some authors have more common names or generalized portfolios than others; one cannot simply enter "Lisa Mason," for example (22,200,000 hits), without also encountering the Lisa Mason School of Dance, or international gymnast Lisa Mason. Likewise, "TelePresence" is being used as a product name by Cisco Systems; whether the labeling owes any debt to feminist science fiction (see Foster "Postproduction" 470) is unclear, since the term was originally advanced by Marvin Minsky in *OMNI* magazine (1980). It is subsequently much more popular (24,100,000 hits) than its telespace sibling, but this is no doubt in part due to a combination of Minsky's influence and Cisco's professional marketing. Attempting to quantify the Internet thus leads only to general observations; unsure how to define an elusive audience, I opted to interview the authors themselves. The arguments I have structured in the rest of this chapter are loose at best, based on anecdotal evidence and primarily an expression of my own continuing curiosity; however, there seems value in reproducing here some of the correspondence that would otherwise only be available in my personal accounts.

Lisa Mason, whose novel *Arachne* (1990) is at the top of the feminist-wave searches, nearly fills a traditional cyberpunk niche. Her work, published in the 1990s but originally conceived in the early 1980s, comes closest to matching cyberpunk's genre paradigms; she is also the only woman other than Pat Cadigan whose work was recommended by Sterling[1] as part of the essential cyberpunk movement. She reports:

> Bruce Sterling told me in 1995 that his friend Michael Godwin of the Electronic Frontier Foundation showed up to a tech conference in Austin, Texas with the newly released hardcover of CYBERWEB under his arm. So the core fanbase of computer folk is certainly among my fanbase. That I'm a woman writing cyberpunk was a novelty to some, attractive to some, and (I suspect) repellent to others (the latter being men who would rather drop dead than read a women [*sic*] author).

According to Mason, she was also invited several times to speak at conferences given by the Library Information Technology Association, a subgroup of the American Library Association. (Of those panels, she adds wryly, "That I'm a woman writing cyberpunk was definitely a novelty to some, attractive to some, and repellent only to those men and women who would rather drop dead than read science fiction.") She additionally had some success with Japanese fans who read her translated works and loved her "talking robots." Clearly, her gender garnered her a certain amount of attention — perhaps akin to that paid to Pat Cadigan as the "Queen of Cyberpunk" — and her fan base, for works published in the early 1990s and closely following the typical journey of the cyberpunk hacker anti-hero(ine), also appears similar to Cadigan's, in that it is an expected "cyberpunk" fan base of computer techs and science fiction enthusiasts. She is the only author I spoke with who felt that her work fell within this space.

Other authors found that their fan response was more diverse — unsurprising, given that they had branched out into different themes, twisting the original cyberpunk setting into less genre-compliant versions of the original. Kathleen Ann Goonan writes:

> Almost all of my fan email is from men, with a few strong exceptions. The women who started out as fans — not "sf" fans, but women in other fields who develop an interest in my writing — have become fairly close friends. Maybe women don't read sf, or maybe they don't have time to respond. I have been invited to speak at universities and conferences by both men and women, equally. People are either on fire about my fiction, which is fairly technical, or they can't get through it at all, which is why I think that most of my readers, from what I can glean from letters and speaking invitations, are academics.

No longer viewed through the filter of postmodern analysis that marked much early cyberpunk academic work, *Queen City Jazz* has instead been examined through feminist lenses — or as a "slipstream" work (as defined by the Interstitial Arts Foundation, which promotes what might be considered a new approach to postmodernism: "art made in the interstices between genres and categories. Art that flourishes in the borderlands between disciplines, mediums, and cultures. Art that blurs the divide between fine art and craft, high art and low"). Noting that *Queen City Jazz* (1994) was "largely regarded as a feminist novel, as well as a slipstream novel," Goonan feels — despite the majority of her fan mail being from men — that most of the work's impact was felt by the feminist and slipstream communities, not by general science fiction fandom. Most of her success was with an academic audience, with interest expressed by both male and female readers. This is similar to first-wave cyberpunk in that her work garnered a fair amount of critical analysis, but the nature of the academic interest has varied.

I have said that women's cyberpunk experienced a dearth of academic attention, and Goonan is unique in specifically numbering academics among her fanbase. Melissa Scott reports that she received most interest from gay and lesbian communities, as well as from women interested in cyberpunk issues:

> Most of the people who approached me about Trouble were interested in the queer themes. On the most basic level, I got a lot of comments about

how nice it was to read a lesbian SF novel that was good SF and not a thinly disguised romance; I also had quite a few emails saying how wonderful it was to read a novel in which the gay characters were the heroes and in which they didn't turn out to be straight in the end. (There had been a couple of novels out at around the same time in which a putatively lesbian protagonist ended up in a straight relationship at the end of the story.) And of course I had people — especially people who identified themselves to me as younger — tell me simply that it was nice to read about characters who were gay like them.... The other big audience, it seemed to me, was women, straight and gay, who didn't otherwise read SF but who were interested in the issues raised by cyberpunk and who wanted to read a novel that would engage them. Partly, I met them because I was doing readings and signings at gay and women's bookstores, but I was also doing those events because those bookstores had an interested audience.

If Goonan's work attracted interest partly because of her writing "between genres," then Scott's might be interpreted as doing the same in attracting women who did not normally read science fiction. Perhaps a work written by a woman, about women, was seen as more approachable — particularly for members of the lesbian community, but also for straight women who wanted to read about cyberpunk issues. Although she certainly received emails commenting on storylines and characters, Scott is clear here in stating that it is the "issues" that drew some readers — placing the novel's examination of embodiment and gender within the same arena of philosophical/technical discussion occupied by its cyberpunk predecessors. What is evident from the responses of all three authors is that there are readers who enjoy their work both as engaging stories and as discussions of serious contemporary questions.

Edith Forbes reports something of the same, but separates her audience more explicitly; she feels that the storytelling aspects of *Exit to Reality* (1997) were not her best work, and it was reflected in audience reactions: "I think people who loved it were the sort who think more abstractly and philosophically and were interested in the concepts the book explores. I think people who hated it were probably more oriented toward pure story-telling, character, etc. and didn't find those aspects of the book as compelling." For her, those interested in entertainment and those interested in philosophical discussion formed two separate audience segments. Unlike Scott, Forbes did not have a strong reception from the lesbian community, even considering the extended queer themes in the novel:

In general my impression was that the book appealed to men more than to women, and particularly to men with a scientific or philosophical cast of mind, but not necessarily programmers. The book did not reach a huge

audience for various reasons, including both its own weaknesses and the
fact that the publisher was not a science fiction publisher and did not have
established marketing avenues.

Certainly differences in marketing could account for some of this disparity;
Melissa Scott has written many science fiction novels, many of which concentrate on queer protagonists, while *Exit to Reality* is Edith Forbes's only science fiction work. She is predominantly a fiction author who commonly
explores queer themes. It would be easy to toy with the conclusion that the
female members of Forbes's audience were more concerned with story, while
the men were interested in technicalities — and to draw from that further
extrapolations regarding the way women and men read — but I would suggest
that Forbes's audience is too small to risk those sorts of discussions. Rather,
when taken as a whole, the responses of these four authors illustrates that
although science fiction may still be considered a male genre, and predominantly marketed toward men, feminist cyberpunk attracts a notable number
of female readers. Additionally, while the first wave of cyberpunk was dismissed
by feminist critics who had embraced the rise of women's science fiction in
the 1970s, women's cyberfiction seems to have won that critical audience back.
Goonan posits that "maybe women don't read SF," but also notes that men
and women have invited her to speak at conferences in equal numbers, and
observes that her strongest female fans are not typically SF readers. Scott
states that *Trouble and Her Friends* (1995) brought in women who wanted to
read about technology issues but were not normally science fiction fans. Both
of these help to illustrate how their contributions are encouraging the growth
of women reading science fiction, while Mason and Forbes reflect something
of a more traditional readership.

Lyda Morehouse's fan mail provides the clearest example of gender mix
in science fiction fandom, and of the ways in which women's cyberpunk has
lost the lens of hacker focus. The feedback she receives reflects a general diversity in ages, genders and backgrounds — from high school students to retirees.
Out of 228 emails Morehouse received between 2001 and 2006, 108 were
from men and 100 were from women (with 20 of indeterminate origin).
Although *Archangel Protocol* (2001, the first book in Morehouse's AngeLINK
series) was quite close to the original tenets of the cyberpunk genre, only
seven fans (all men) self-identified as "computer geeks." While Morehouse
did write about alienated hackers, it was her focus on religious themes that
drew the most comments — 24 men, 24 women, and 3 unknown readers all
mentioned the treatment of religion, or religious institutions, within her texts.
Morehouse has also received some subdued attention regarding the queer

themes in her work; she writes that she has been reviewed on LGBTQ websites. She received email from a transsexual who was pleased about seeing transsexual issues openly discussed in print; two men who were pleased at the portrayal of transgender themes; a woman who approved of the novels' pro-gay stance; and one man and one woman who enjoyed the presence of a strong female protagonist. Morehouse's audience displays a range of interests and demographics that are markedly different from the socially maladjusted computerphiles often (and perhaps unfairly) stereotyped as science fiction readers.

One might expect to find that men read men's cyberpunk, and women read women's cyberpunk; it is refreshing that this sort of gender segregation is not, in fact, the case. Although the first wave of cyberpunk may have predominantly reached men, women's cybertexts — even with their markedly feminist leanings — appeal to both. The audiences reached by women's cyberpunk are small, but also as diverse as the works themselves. Moreover, women writing cyberpunk became more unremarkable. Although Lisa Mason reports a certain amount of curiosity revolving around her position as a woman writing cyberpunk — curiosity that Cadigan also encountered repeatedly, judging from her exasperated introduction to *The Ultimate Cyberpunk*—it is clear that 10 years later, Morehouse did not have a similar experience. None of the mail she received expressed surprise or curiosity regarding her gender, and both men and women readers asked her for writing advice.

While the first wave's resonance with programmers and computer hackers was unique in terms of its influence on the formation of computing and Internet cultures, and appealed (as feminist critics have pointed out) primarily to male readers, feminist cyberpunk is harder to place in a single niche. Male hackers and programmers are a smaller part of the feminist cyberpunk audience — not because they have necessarily lost interest, but because the audience has grown into a more inclusive and flexible shape. This may be partly a function of the growing pervasiveness of communications technologies in Western lives — leading to a more "mainstream" science fiction — and also a function of the more diverse themes found in the works as they branch outward from the original tenets of the cyberpunk genre. Concerning the significance of women's cyberpunk, the author reports of fan responses are encouraging. Mason's appeal to technologically-oriented and international readers, Goonan's attention from feminists and other academics, Scott's success with lesbian and techno-curious women, Forbes's appeal to philosophically inclined men, and Morehouse's general or religious-oriented feedback from men and women of all ages illustrate that cyberpunk and cyberfiction can be used flexibly, to explore a variety of ideas and appeal to a variety of audiences. Most satisfying, from a feminist perspective, is the fact that these works — all of which illustrate various feminist or queer-friendly themes — are perceived, by at least a portion of that audience, as part of a larger cultural discussion regarding important contemporary issues.

Authorial Motivations

Henry Jenkins talks about the cyclical nature of fandom, wherein science fiction readers become science fiction writers: "Many of the most significant science fiction writers emerged from fandom. Given this history, every reader was understood to be a potential writer and many fans aspired to break into professional publication." Certainly Morehouse's fan mail revealed, among other things, several aspiring authors (male and female) asking for tips, as well as correspondents who sent artwork inspired by Morehouse's characters. Given that science fiction has been known as a somewhat insular genre, I was also curious as to the significance it held for the authors I was corresponding with — I wanted to ask what had inspired them to write science fiction, and cyberpunk in particular, considering that the first wave had been generally derided by feminists. Again, the responses were diverse.

Early cyberpunk sprang forth primarily from independent authors — John Shirley, Bruce Sterling, William Gibson, Rudy Rucker, Lewis Shiner — who found that they were writing about the same issues in a similar manner. Thanks in part to Bruce Sterling's active recruitment efforts (Kelly and Kessel vii), they became unified under a name and a purpose; as Sterling wrote in the introduction to *Mirrorshades,* "Thus, 'cyberpunk' — a label none of them chose. But the term now seems a fait accompli, and there is a certain justice in it. The term captures something crucial to the work of these writers, something crucial to the decade as a whole: a new kind of integration" (xi). Cyberpunk writers were part of "the Movement," its quest to revitalize science fiction by exploring the links between new technologies and the pop culture underground. Lisa Mason, of the authors interviewed here, is the only woman who might be considered to be part of (or at least chronologically adjacent to) the original movement. Although *Arachne* was published in 1990, Mason notes that she wrote the original story in 1983, when the technological context was entirely different:

> [T]he Internet was strictly the province of the military, internal technical staffs of big corporations, and big academia.

Who in your local cafe had heard of the Internet? No one. Who used a personal computer with an Internet connection in his/her workplace? No one I knew. Who owned a computer connected to the Internet in his/her private residence? Are you kidding?

Oh, I'd read some science articles about virtual reality and artificial intelligence. But the concepts were exotic, fringe-element stuff.

I'd read articles, too, about hackers who could break into secret databases using computers, but I didn't know any hackers and wasn't all that sure about exactly what they did. Hackers seemed about as glamorous as a guy in a ski mask holding up a Seven-Eleven. Only a hacker could hold up five hundred thousand Seven-Elevens at the same time.

Working in an office where early IBM-clone computers were in use, and "telex" technology was an important form of communication (but error reports had to be filled out by hand and then faxed), Mason remembers, "I was not trained as a programmer. I did no software engineering. As a tax attorney and an executive director, I oversaw content and managed the teams. But I got an eyeful of what developing a program was all about. I could well imagine a world where we dispensed with all that slow and frustrating material reality and went straight into electronic consciousness." Her inspiration sprang from the same curiosity that motivated other early cyberpunk authors, and her work demonstrates the same tendency to use computers and technology as metaphors rather than concentrate on specific details. Gibson has said that computers were his metaphor for human memory (McCaffery interview 270); Mason says that telespace was her representation of "the collective unconscious." Although she recalls reading one of Gibson's short stories in *OMNI* magazine, she states unequivocally that it was years before she read *Neuromancer*, and her work was not inspired by other cyberpunk authors.

In contrast to this, Lyda Morehouse says that she wrote a work of cyberpunk because it is her favorite genre: "I love the idea that knowledge is power and that power can be used to take down 'The Man.' Outlaw as hero has always worked for me.... Plus, there's something about the computer as a weapon that appeals, too. I mean, it's something that anyone can learn regardless of class, race, gender or sexual orientation (of course one has to have access to the computers, but part of the early phreak movement was all about providing access without having to pay for the privilege.)" On her web site, she observes, "To me, for a novel to truly be cyberpunk it has to follow the arc (at least in spirit) of *Neuromancer*. Which is to say, you have to start with the life of some down and out punk, who takes on the evil corporations like a lone cowboy, and wins. That happens in *Archangel Protocol*." Clearly, she is a fan of cyberpunk's first wave — though additionally, in email, she also cites

Marge Piercy's *He, She and It* as one of her all-time favorite novels. Morehouse's work combines the pleasure she takes in the democratizing nature of the computer with her marked interest in religious issues. She harbors an interest in both men's and women's cyberpunk (she is also a fan of Melissa Scott's work), and is the example that Jenkins predicted: a reader who became an author, assimilating and then changing the conventions of the genre to suit her own desires.

Melissa Scott was also a reader, but not necessarily a fan. Unlike Morehouse, who wrote cyberpunk because she admired and enjoyed it, Scott wanted to correct what she saw as a socially exclusive slant found in the genre's portrayal of bodily escapism (the cyberpunk flight from the "meat"):

> While the idea was seductive, in practice what seemed to happen was that all those bodiless people were treated as though they were all straight white middle class men, and the people who were not straight, not white, not middle class, not male were defined by their bodies and used largely as set-dressing (ooh, look, scary people!) or they were seen from outside, never from within. So I took what had become the conventional cyberpunk technology and tried to imagine what would happen if there were a system that enabled people to use their bodies, to use emotions, sensations, proprioception, to experience and negotiate cyberspace. More than that, what if acknowledging the body worked better than denying it?
>
> As for why I wanted to write cyberpunk, I think it was because the social issues the genre raised are extremely important to me, and I couldn't bear to leave them to writers who had what I felt was a limited viewpoint.

Scott's critique echoes the reaction of feminist academics such as Joan Gordon and Veronica Hollinger; her work on *Trouble and Her Friends* represents her calculated resistance to the middle-class, hetero-white-male-centeredness of the original genre works. More pointedly than Morehouse or Mason, she sees her work as an act of political expression.

Kathleen Ann Goonan likewise had issues with male-centered science fiction, and states that she had no particular love of the genre: "When I was a kid I devoured all the fairy tales available, and in the early sixties read the big fat novels when they came out in paperback — Catch-22, Exodus, Hawaii — but didn't much care for my father's quite substantial sf collection. All the people in them seemed to be grown-up men, even in Phil Dick's books, and I was not." She read the works of women authors such as Ursula K. Le Guin, Joan Vinge, Patricia McKillip and Elizabeth Lynn in the 1970s, but says, "I didn't buy sf; I was not a big sf fan. I was interested in what women had to write about what we were or might or might have [*sic*] experienced, rather than what men thought — not through any conscious decision.

What the women were saying was just more interesting. I was sexist." Unlike Scott, however, Goonan's writing was not a conscious rebellion; as an aspiring writer in the 1980s, she signed up for the Clarion West writer's workshop and became more interested in science fiction. While her work has been lauded as feminist, she says that was not a deliberate effort on her part:

> I don't consciously try to write feminist novels — rather, as an observer of and a participant in the feminist movement of the late sixties and early seventies, as someone who is still hideously disappointed that television commercials have completely succumbed to male/female stereotypes of who cleans the bathroom, I suppose I refuse, in my novels, to participate in this view of popular culture. But probably, most feminists could find ways in which my novels disappoint them.

She writes as a feminist, but not in a deliberate effort to create feminist works or buck the science fiction status quo; rather, her interest lies in "issues that have to do with, instead of hacking exterior matter, hacking humanity" (i.e., exploring contemporary nanotechnology issues, charting the changing nature of information, and extrapolating a role for humanity in a posthuman age).

Finally (out of the authors interviewed), Forbes achieved positioning within science fiction more as a result of the themes she was examining than through any particular affiliation to cyberpunk tenets. Forbes writes, "It wasn't an abstract decision to do something in the genre. The story idea and the characters took hold of me, so that's what I wrote. I've always been interested in where our technologies are taking us, where the things we think we want are taking us, and I extrapolated them to their logical or illogical conclusion." Like Marge Piercy, who has written only two science fiction novels out of a vast body of work, Forbes writes primarily within the bounds of more mainstream fiction. Like the original authors of cyberpunk, her work was produced independently — gelling with that of other authors through a natural tendency to examine similar ideas through similar storytelling techniques.

Certain parallels may also be drawn between the origins of cyberpunk and later women's cyberfiction, in terms of the communal nature of the writing process. By the mid–1980s, the originators of the cyberpunk movement were aware of and in correspondence with each other, feeding from each other's ideas and contributing to the *Mirrorshades* collection — Gibson and Sterling even collaborated on a novel together (*The Difference Engine*). Something of the same interrelatedness is tangible between many of the women writing cyberfiction. While some — like Forbes — were working independently of other cyberpunk authors, others — like Morehouse and Scott — were well aware of the genre's history and paradigms. Marge Piercy, in the acknowledgements for *He, She and It,* writes, "I enjoy William Gibson very much, and I have freely borrowed from his inventions and those of other cyberpunk writers. I figure it's all one playground. Donna Haraway's essay 'A Manifesto for Cyborgs' was extremely suggestive also" (431). Piercy, a lauded feminist author, enjoyed and used Gibson's ideas, but also combined them with Haraway's ideas on the use of technology to break down gender binaries; she was aware of both cyberpunk and feminist ideas regarding new technologies. Morehouse, in turn, is indebted to Piercy and Scott. Sage Walker is friends with Kathleen Ann Goonan, and is also thanked in the acknowledgments to Laura J. Mixon's *Proxies* and Mary Rosenblum's *Chimera.* Like first-wave cyberpunk, the feminist wave consists of an array of authors (still predominantly white and middle-class, but now female and not always hetero) exploring ideas within similar settings and loosely linked by certain social or professional ties. These authors undertook their work for different reasons — through admiration, to express criticism and illustrate new points of view, or simply to independently illustrate ideas revolving around contemporary technological issues. Despite these differing motivations, their works share a loose cohesiveness.

Conclusion

This chapter, based as it is on a small series of interviews, is admittedly something of a thought exercise. But conversations with authors suggest that many of the themes in women's cyberpunk have changed from the approaches adopted by earlier, masculinist works. Clearly, also, these works occupy a diverse range of social spaces, both in audience appeal and in the meaning the novels hold for the authors themselves. Sarah Lefanu posed the question of whether or not science fiction offers women writers a freedom of style and content not available in mainstream fiction, and proposed that science fiction writing offered a method of "fusing political concerns with the playful creativity of the imagination" (2). The women writing cyberpunk have chosen to illustrate a host of social and political concerns in their work. Only Scott's work might be considered a deliberately feminist backlash against the latent patriarchal nature of early cyberpunk; other texts might be taken as friendly tribute or even coincidental reworking. Feminist cyberpunk is a tool for self-expression for authors of many backgrounds and viewpoints; likewise, it has reached several different types of audience, only some of whom might be considered stereotypical cyberpunk readers. The discussions with authors have revealed that the writers take their work seriously, and that there are audience

176

members who do as well. Feminist cyberpunk has not had the same sharply definable impact as writers like Gibson and Sterling, but the diversity of responses reveals the shifting nature of the genre, the flexibility of science fiction audiences, the interest of female readers, and new ways in which science fiction can be used as a vehicle for serious feminist philosophical and political discussion.

NOTE

1. Sterling's original website (with its list of recommended cyberpunk texts) is no longer online. As noted in Chapter 2, the list is mirrored at http://www.hatii.arts.gla.ac.uk/MultimediaStudentProjects/00-01/0003637k/project/html/litreco.htm. It is also reprinted in Cadigan's edited collection *The Ultimate Cyberpunk* (383–90).

Conclusion

Our fictions do not stand alone; they are integrated into the discussions our society is continually holding with itself. Fiction is a vital part of the overall way in which a culture considers new ideas; if cyberpunk is (or was) the ultimate postmodern literature, then a multitude of voices should ideally be heard. As Elaine Graham has noted, "What is at stake, supremely, in the debate about the implications of digital, genetic, cybernetic and biomedical technologies is precisely what (and who) will define authoritative notions of normative, exemplary, desirable humanity into the twenty-first century" ("Representations" 11). In examining masculinist and feminist cyberpunk, I have tried to demonstrate how writers — both male and female — have used the science fiction genre to participate in larger cultural debates regarding contemporary social issues.

The first wave of cyberpunk is concerned with issues of identity and globalization in a post-industrial age; feminist authors from the 1990s added their own slant to those same discussions, while including additional critiques regarding environmental decay, religious institutions, reproductive technologies, motherhood, and the family. Their contributions have not gone entirely unremarked: articles by Foster and Harper have been particularly notable, while Vint and Murphy's recent collection *Beyond Cyberpunk: New Critical Perspectives* (2010) reprints Karen Cadora's seminal "Feminist Cyberpunk," and *Rewired: The Post-Cyberpunk Anthology* (2007) contains stories from (of course) Pat Cadigan, but also Gwyneth Jones, Elizabeth Bear, and Mary Rosenblum (while Melissa Scott is acknowledged in the foreword). Despite these inroads, women's cyberpunk has not been examined in as much detail as its breadth merits. Academia's sometimes tantalizingly brief references to "a 'late' cyberpunk movement ... dominated by women writers" (Moylan 84) or "the feminist/queer cyberpunk that dominated the early 1990s" (Murphy 219) have begged a more thorough exploration, one which accounted for a wide variety of texts and a broader time period. My intent here was to fill this gap.

I began my initial research concerned that cyberpunk was a small and apparently misogynist genre, almost entirely written by men, that might be having a disproportionate influence on the development of Western communications technologies and online cultures. Further reading showed that women's voices could indeed be found within cyberpunk, even if they were reaching a different audience than earlier works. They had never been truly silent. With regard to the first wave, although Cadigan was primarily the only woman included as a writer, feminist critics were vocal in dissecting the genre from the outside — for its sexism, its whiteness, its heteronormativity, or its images of an isolating, morally bankrupt cyberculture (Vint *Bodies* 112). Further, women writing science fiction in the 1990s had taken the genre and turned it to entirely new purposes: they had explored feminist ideas and the promotion of liberal feminist politics, all while using and subverting many of the tropes that defined first-wave cyberpunk. These writers reconfigured cyberpunk's original paradigms and themes in order to explore new meanings and ideas. In broadening the genre's focus, they may have lost a portion of the original audience, but they have also appealed to a diversity of new readers. While early cyberpunk was notable for its impact on a small but influential segment of hacker/programmer society, women's cyberpunk occupies a more complicated and flexible space.

At the beginning of Chapter 2, I cited Andrew Ross. He wrote, "Cyberpunk's idea of a counterpolitics — youthful male heroes with working-class chips on their shoulders and postmodern biochips in their brains — seems to have little to do with the burgeoning power of the great social movements of our day: feminism, ecology, peace, sexual liberation, and civil rights" (152). Thanks to women's cyberpunk of the 1990s, social movement such as feminism, ecological conservationism, and queer rights now have voices within the genre. In some cases, the feminist ideas discovered in the texts may represent unconscious or general attitudes shared by authors from similarly gendered socio-economic settings; in others, judging particularly by my interview with Melissa Scott, they represent very deliberate attempts to express feminist arguments.

Analyzing feminist cyberpunk's treatment of globalization issues has demonstrated that while early cyberpunk focused on the alienation of the individual, women's cyberpunk was more likely to suggest the formation of new community types outside the structures of current patriarchal systems. Examining issues of embodiment, virtual reality and artificial intelligence showed that women authors emphasized the need for corporeality in order to preserve human identity, and moreover, that the feminist wave used robot artificial intelligences to great effect in illustrating fictionalized versions of Donna Haraway's cyborg theory — the idea that cyborgs could be used to break down the gender binaries imposed by society. These chapters emphasized the feminist wave's connection to the first, and the ways in which women had used the same genre trappings — multinational conglomerates, crime, computers, virtual playgrounds, and cyborgs — to create entirely different, even directly contradictory messages. The first wave of cyberpunk, which was predominantly "men's" cyberpunk, was concerned with issues of alienation and the search for identity in the flashing pastiche of the postmodern, postindustrial age. Women's cyberpunk acknowledged those issues while insisting on the importance of embodiment and simultaneously questioning social constructions of community and gender. Women's texts were examined not only as counterpoints to the attitudes and assumptions of early cyberpunk, but also as reflections of larger trends within the feminist movement.

Subsequent chapters explained how women had diverged from the overall cyberpunk paradigm by homing in on smaller background aspects of the genre — ecological destruction and mythological imagery — and altering them in subtle but subversive ways. The first wave's postapocalyptic disinterest gave way to the feminist wave's emphasis on disaster warning and ecological conservationism, with complex arguments that matched up with feminism's tense relationship to ecology. The feminist utopian science fiction of the 1970s, which equated women with nature and situated both against man, likewise gave way to new structures that reconfigured the natural world as a universal human concern while still acknowledging the shared domination of women and the environment. Simultaneously, the mythology that had previously been useful as a tool for explaining the concepts behind newly envisioned technologies became instead a characteristic of the genre through which real religious institutions were critiqued — reflecting, in part, the tensions between feminism and patriarchal religious structures. In changing what had previously been minor but prevalent cyberpunk tenets, women began moving away from the genre's traditional definitions, despite clear links to the first wave's themes and ideas.

Further divergence was evident when examining two themes that women had almost entirely introduced to cyberpunk: reproductive technologies and queer sexuality. These issues had barely been present in the early genre, but were moved front and center in several texts as feminist cyberpunk was altered to accommodate women's more domestic social concerns. These sections not only showed how women's cyberpunk fit into feminist discussions of reproductive technologies, motherhood, and nuclear family structures, they also showed how feminist treatments of family accommodated queer interests and expanded to include definitions of queer marriage—while at the same time, cyborgs and bisexual characters were challenging sexual binaries, and lesbian cyberpunk texts were glorifying the role of the queer outsider in addition to promoting feminist interests.

My analysis of cyberpunk's masculinist and feminist waves is, for the most part, based on themes rather than structures; in a genre filled with markedly disparate texts, political and social subjects are where the two generations most clearly distinguish themselves. The nature of my arguments has caused me to seek congruences between very diverse works; as Jane Donawerth observes, "No individual fiction represents a paradigm in its entirety" (30). Examining feminist participation in cyberpunk has proven to be an excellent exercise for illustrating some of the ways in which fiction can be appropriated as a playground for political ideas—and cyberpunk, previously a male-centered and borderline misogynist genre, became a surprising forum for feminist treatments of postmodern, ecological, religious and socially gendered questions.

I have certainly not said all there is to say on these topics. What remains is to examine each text more fully on its own merits, seeking more in-depth answers to how individual techniques and narrative constructions have been used to create varying effects while still advancing specific messages and ideas beneath the umbrella of a common paradigm. It must also be acknowledged that cyberpunk is not all-inclusive; the fact that it has been expanded to include the voices of women does not mean that the genre has escaped its stigma as a product of white, middle-class beliefs. The 1990s feminist wave widened the pool of cyberpunk writers, but it still lacked a full array of input from authors of different racial or economic backgrounds. Although Thomas Foster has offered an extended racially-based reading of cyberpunk in his *The Souls of Cyberfolk,* more could be done in this area with regard to the analysis of feminist works.

My first purpose in writing this volume was archival—to help shine a light into a neglected vault and provide close readings that may be of value to future researchers. I have centered my study on (very roughly) the first two decades of cyberpunk: the masculinist wave of the 1980s, and feminist writing from the 1990s. This is not to argue that cyberpunk has died in the years since; the genre has been eulogized many times already, and somehow keeps creeping back into our science fictions. Whether we talk about second or third or fourth generations, or attempt to define post-cyberpunk, or suggest that the genre has transitioned into "a more generalized set of practices" (Murphy and Vint xiii), there is no denying that cyberpunk's tropes are still visible in twenty-first-century science fiction works. Some retain their masculinist focus: Paolo Bacigalupi's biopunk *The Windup Girl* (2009), winner of the 2010 Hugo and Nebula awards, focuses a major part of its narrative on the travails of a genetically-engineered sex slave (the titular "wind-up girl") and the men who control her. Ernest Cline's bestselling *Ready Player One* (2011), tinted with 30 years of nostalgia, follows teenaged hacker Wade Watts in a futuristic online treasure hunt laced liberally with 1980s pop culture references. The influences of the first wave remain strong.

But feminist cyberpunk's themes also haunt current writings — *Ready Player One,* for example, ultimately focuses on the male hacker but it is also marked by community, by Watts's friendships with women, and by a moral that attempts to espouse the value of "real life" over online gaming. The influence of feminist ideas seems clear; the line tracing back to *Neuromancer* is not entirely straight. Additionally, some of the women authors whose work I've touched on in this study have produced more recent cyberpunk (or cyberpunk-adjacent) texts; Mary Rosenblum's "Search Engine" (2006) or Lyda Morehouse's *Resurrection Code* (2011) might be included in further examinations of this topic. Other authors, like Justina Robson and Nalo Hopkinson, have added related feminist and post-feminist perspectives to the new millennium's quest for identity; Robson's *Quantum Gravity* series (2006–2011) has adapted cyberpunk tropes to mesh with urban fantasy, while Hopkinson's *Midnight Robber* (2000) melds Afro-Caribbean culture with a far-future, nanotech-dominated society. I hope that I have provided additional background for the analysis of these and other post–1990s science fiction works — in order to help determine what new paradigms have arisen, or what the next generation of "cyberpunk" texts might actually be.

My second purpose in crafting this study was contextual: visibility matters. Women cyberpunk writers need to be heard, and their work acknowledged as part of our larger cultural dialogue about the new digital world in which we are living. A decade into the twenty-first century, Western culture still tells us that technology is for men. Early cyberpunk helped popularize the figure of the computer-savant male, and the vision of his dystopian cyborg techno-future. These stereotypes have continued to loom large in mainstream media. In Chapter 10, I mentioned films including *TRON* (1982), *War Games* (1983), and *The Terminator* (1984); if we continue to use American screens as one measure of such tropes' popularity, then films like *Terminator 2: Judgment Day* (1991), *Sneakers* (1992), *GoldenEye* (1995), *The Matrix* and its sequels (1999, 2003), *Swordfish* (2001), *Terminator Salvation* (2009), or *TRON: Legacy*

(2010) have also propagated variations on these images. The male hacker adept persists in television programs such as *Alias* (2001–2006), *Terminator: The Sarah Connor Chronicles* (2008–2009), *Dollhouse* (2009–2010), *Chuck* (2007–2012), *The Big Bang Theory* (2007–present) or *Nikita* (2010–present). We will have another such icon in Wade Watts, with the coming movie adaptation of *Ready Player One* (Billington). Further, flagship cyberpunk texts continue to attract attention; 2012 rumors persist regarding big-budget film versions of *Neuromancer* (Leiren-Young) and *Snow Crash* (O'Neal).

The repetitiveness of this character archetype is telling. The masculinist techno-tropes alternately supported and created by cyberpunk's first wave continue to mark the way we think about technology and online culture; these stereotypes are in desperate need of challenge. "Men invented the Internet," proclaimed the *New York Times* in June 2012 (Streitfeld)—overlooking contributions from Grace Hopper, Ada Lovelace, Radia Perlman, or other notable women in the history of hardware and software development (Jardin). This invisibility—the assumption that the Internet was designed by and created for men, that men are the sole governors of technological innovation—means that women continue to struggle in IT fields. Only 20 percent of U.S. computer science majors are currently women (compared to 36 percent in 1986), and women hold 27 percent of computer science jobs (down from 30 percent ten years ago) (Goldstein). Those who do pursue IT careers are confronted with continuing signs that their chosen industry is geared toward men: a plethora of "booth babes" (attractive, often scantily-dressed female models) at technology conferences; public tech presentations containing pornography or other sexualized material; companies with slogans like "do IT with me"; or speakers like Mads Christensen, the emcee who opened Dell's May 2012 Copenhagen conference with the line, "All the great inventions are from men; we can thank women for the rolling pin," and continued by encouraging IT workers to practice saying "Shut your fucking face, bitch" (*Geek Feminism*; Wood). On June 4, 2012, someone using the public relations account at computer manufacturer ASUS tweeted a photo focused on the backside of a female model as she displayed the company's new computer at a trade show. The accompanying text read: "The rear looks pretty nice. So does the new Transformer AIO" (Haberman). The pervasive assumption that technology is for men (specifically heterosexual men) colors the entire industry. It is no wonder that science and information technology programs continue to face difficulties in engaging school girls in the classroom; barriers faced by these students include low self-confidence, unhelpful gender-role stereotypes, few female role models, "manuals written by and for males," and the persistent cultural belief that computer careers require social isolation — a life spent in front of a lonely screen (Bean et al.). Surely these stereotypes are cyclical; implicit cultural messages that say computers are "not for girls" discourage girls from participation, which only reinforces the continuing impression that computers are not for girls (or women).

Moreover, the societal convention that says men are the natural leaders in conversations about technology (and that sees men in charge of many online forums) means that men are privileged in setting the tone and content of the web. Cyberpunk imagery may even play an additional role here; Zoë Sofia has argued that "mythic associations" linking cyberspace to "a maternal or feminine body to be penetrated, cut up and manipulated ... present unconscious barriers to women users of computers, whose identification with female bodies makes them/us prone to anxiety about hacking up the matrix" (60). Within these male-dominated online spaces, sites like *Fat, Ugly or Slutty* or the *Geek Feminism* wiki document the harassment that women encounter — on a daily basis — in chatrooms, web forums, games, or comment pages. One recent incident: in June 2012, when *Feminist Frequency* blogger Anita Sarkeesian publicly proposed to create a series of educational videos examining sexism in digital games, her Kickstarter and YouTube pages were flooded with beating, rape and death threats, while her website suffered repeated cyberattacks and her Wikipedia entry was repeatedly defaced with pornography and other defamatory materials (Watercutter). This was before Sarkeesian had even created the videos in question; she had merely promised to voice a future opinion regarding women's experiences with gaming, and game stereotypes. Her example is only a very small case study of a much larger phenomenon — the worst of an online culture fuelled by a much broader misogyny.

This needs to stop — and there are hopeful signs that the tide may turn, like the $158,917 in donations made to Sarkeesian's (original $6000) project, or the fact that immediate public outcries forced apologies from ASUS and Dell. Times are changing — if slowly. Further, while women may be fighting to forge inroads in professional IT and related environments, they already comprise a major market for today's communications technologies: according to Intel researcher Genevieve Bell, women not only control most household purchases of new tech, they are also the leading users of the Internet and the primary adopters of mobile phones and texting, videoconferencing, GPS, ebooks, and social media such as Facebook and Twitter (Madrigal). This contemporary electronic world and its communications webs — the ties that allow us to share our locations and activities, reach friends across vast distances, form massive virtual communities, and mobilize political and social movements — speak far more to the telepresence of 1990s feminist cyberpunk than the disembodied, individualist cyberspace of the 1980s first wave. This user-friendly, accessible online environment is no longer the sole domain of hard-core computer enthusiasts, and it is time to change the tone of the cultural conversation:

> [I]t turns out if you want to find out what the future looks like, you should be asking women. And just before you think that means you should be asking 18-year-old women, it actually turns out the majority of technology users are women in their 40s, 50s and 60s. So if you wanted to know what the future looks like, those turn out to be the heaviest users of the most successful and most popular technologies on the planet as we speak [Bell, qtd. in Madrigal].

We need to acknowledge women's voices, and talk about how the digital age relates to women's issues. Part of this conversation must include the feminist cyberpunk writers who have already spoken, and the feminist science fiction writers who are *still* speaking; just as men alone did not invent the Internet, neither have men alone been involved in considering the implications of this new world.

I have no illusions that my study will suddenly cause *Trouble and Her Friends* or *Archangel Protocol* to become major motion pictures (or otherwise capture our mainstream societal imagination); nor am I arguing that masculinist cyberpunk stereotypes are the sole or even major cause of women's invisibility in Western technological discussions and industries. These issues are part of a historical and ongoing struggle for women's rights, as well as pervasive cultural associations linking men to science and women to nature (Alaimo; Gaard; C. Heller). But cyberpunk is a part of this dialogue (and women's cyberpunk, as detailed in Chapter 6, has already addressed that dubious "nature" link). Our popular fictions, and the myths or archetypes they spawn, have wider-reaching implications; cyberpunk's impact has been particularly notable on the ways we think about technology in the postmodern, digital world. The image of the male hacker endures — but there are other images available. I hope that my work might have a small part in triggering further discussion.

Science fiction's status as a realm where technology meets imagination has made it an ideal battleground for questions of technology's role in postmodern society, as well as questions of human identity and urban alienation. Likewise, the same trappings that made cyberpunk such an excellent exploration of the postmodern condition also allowed women authors the flexibility to produce new and original variants of old themes, expressing feminist concerns about those same questions of human identity, but also about issues such as gender, sexuality and community in a potentially dystopian future. By dissecting women's cyberpunk, I have painted a picture of some of the important issues facing feminism in the 1990s (and, arguably, today), and how those issues were raised within the presumably restrictive settings of a very small subgenre of science fiction — a subgenre that used cyborgs, virtual realities, urban decay, and postmodern, postindustrial visions to ruminate on Western culture at the turn of the twenty-first century. I have also attempted to add to the extensive body of research surrounding cyberpunk itself— its nature, its themes, its impacts and its importance. Such explorations remain relevant; as Vint has argued, "we should not equate cyberpunk's fading from view as a distinct subgenre with a fading from relevance as a literature best suited to help us understand life in information-dominated technoculture" ("Afterword" 230). The world we live in has changed drastically since 1984, and it is changing more drastically still; these are technologically transient times. Today's cutting-edge machine is tomorrow's paperweight; today's online identity is only a profile photo away from reconfiguration. Masculinist cyberpunk, and its approaches to our new cyborg issues, has been thoroughly documented; highlighting feminist cyberpunk may help to ensure that we recognize authors whose work has skirted invisibility, that we broaden the cultural discussion surrounding new technologies, and that we better understand today's science fiction.

Works Cited

Alaimo, Stacy. *Undomesticated Ground: Recasting Nature as a Feminist Space*. Ithaca: Cornell University Press, 2000. Print.

Alkon, Paul. "Deus ex Machina in William Gibson's Cyberpunk Trilogy." *Fiction 2000: Cyberpunk and the Future of Narrative*. Ed. George Slusser and Tom Shippey. Athens: University of Georgia Press, 1992. 75–87. Print.

Allen, Virginia, and Terry Paul. "Science and Fiction: Ways of Theorizing About Women." *Erotic Universe: Sexuality and Fantastic Literature*. Ed. Donald Palumbo. New York: Greenword Press, 1986. 165–83. Print.

Anders, Peter. "Cybrids: Integrating Cognitive and Physical Space in Architecture." *Convergence* 4.1 (1998): 85–105. Print.

Bacigalupi, Paolo. *The Windup Girl*. San Francisco: Night Shade Books, 2009. Print.

Badmington, Neil. "Posthumanist (Com)Promises: Diffracting Donna Haraway's Cyborg Through Marge Piercy's *Body of Glass*." Ed. Neil Badmington. New York: Palgrave, 2000. 85–97. Print.

Baird, Wilhelmina. *Clipjoint*. New York: Ace Books, 1994. Print.

Balliger, Robin. "Sounds of Resistance." *The Global Resistance Reader*. Ed. Louise Amoore. New York: Routledge, 2005. 423–436. Print.

Balsamo, Anne. "Forms of Technological Embodiment: Reading the Body in Contemporary Culture." *Cyberspace/Cyberbodies/Cyberpunk: Cultures of Technological Embodiment*. Ed. Mike Featherstone and Roger Burrows. London: Sage, 1995. 215–237. Print.

_____. *Technologies of the Gendered Body: Reading Cyborg Women*. Durham: Duke University Press, 1996. Print.

Barale, Michèle Aina. "When *Lambs* and *Aliens* Meet: Girl-faggots and Boy-dykes Go to the Movies." *Cross-Purposes: Lesbians, Feminists, and the Limits of Alliance*. Ed. Dana Heller. Bloomington: Indiana University Press, 1997. 95–106.

Barnett, P. Chad. "Reviving Cyberpunk: (Re)Constructing the Subject and Mapping Cyberspace in the Wachowski Brothers' Film *The Matrix*." *Extrapolation* 41.4 (2000): 359–374. Print.

Barr, Marleen S. *Lost in Space: Probing Feminist Science Fiction and Beyond*. Chapel Hill: University of North Carolina Press, 1993. Print.

Bartkowski, Frances. *Feminist Utopias*. Lincoln: University of Nebraska Press, 1991.

Baudrillard, Jean. "Simulacra and Simulations." *Jean Baudrillard: Selected Writings*. Ed. Mark Poster. Cambridge: Polity Press, 2001. 169–187. Print.

Baumgardner, Jennifer, and Amy Richards. *Manifesta: Young Women, Feminism, and the Future*. New York: Farrar, 2000. Print.

Bean, Steve, et al. "The Girls Creating Games Program: Strategies for Engaging Middle-

School Girls in Information Technology." *Frontiers: A Journal of Women's Studies* 26 (2005): 90–98. Print.

Bear, Greg. "Petra." *Mirrorshades: The Cyberpunk Anthology.* Ed. Bruce Sterling. New York: Arbor House, 1986. 105–124. Print.

Billington, Alex. "WB Picks up Ernie Cline's New Novel 'Ready Player One.'" *FirstShowing.net.* 18 June 2010. Web. 24 June 2012. http://www.firstshowing.net/2010/wb-picks-up-ernie-clines-new-geek-novel-ready-player-one/.

Bonner, Frances. "Separate Development: Cyberpunk in Film and TV." *Fiction 2000: Cyberpunk and the Future of Narrative.* Ed. George Slusser and Tom Shippey. Athens: University of Georgia Press, 1992. 191–207. Print.

Braidotti, Rosi. "Cyberfeminism with a Difference." *Feminisms.* Ed. Sandra Kemp and Judith Squires. Oxford: Oxford University Press, 1997. 520–529. Print.

Brodie, Janine. "Globalization, Governance, and Gender Relations: Rethinking the Agenda for the 21st Century." *The Global Resistance Reader.* Ed. Louise Amoore. London: Routledge. 244–256. Print.

Brown, Stephen. "Before the Lights Came On: Observations of a Synergy." *Storming the Reality Studio.* Ed. Larry McCaffery. Durham: Duke University Press, 1991. 173–177. Print.

Bukatman, Scott. "Terminal Penetration." *The Cybercultures Reader.* Ed. David Bell and Barbara M. Kennedy. London: Routledge, 2000. 149–174. Print.

Bull, Emma. *Bone Dance.* New York: Ace Books, 1991. Print.

Butler, Judith. "Critically Queer." *Playing with Fire: Queer Politics, Queer Theories.* New York: Routledge, 1997. 11–30. Print.

Cadigan, Pat. *Dervish Is Digital.* New York: Tor Books, 2001. Print.

_____. "Introduction: Not A Manifesto." *The Ultimate Cyberpunk.* Ed. Pat Cadigan. New York: Simon & Schuster, 2002. vii–xiv. Print.

_____. *Mindplayers.* New York: Bantam Spectra, 1987. Print.

_____. "Pretty Boy Crossover." *Patterns: Stories by Pat Cadigan.* New York: Tor Books, 1999. 127–38. Print.

_____. "Rock On." *Mirrorshades: The Cyberpunk Anthology.* Ed. Bruce Sterling. New York: Arbor House, 1986. 34–42. Print.

_____. *Synners.* New York: Bantam, 1991. Print.

_____. *Tea from an Empty Cup.* New York: Tor Books, 1998. Print.

Cadora, Karen. "Feminist Cyberpunk." *Science Fiction Studies* 22.3 (1995): 357–372. Print.

Calhoun, Cheshire. *Feminism, the Family, and the Politics of the Closet: Lesbian and Gay Displacement.* Oxford: Oxford University Press, 2000. Print.

Camp, Tracy. "Women in Computer Science: Reversing the Trend." *Syllabus* (August 2001): 24–26. Web. 16 June 2012. http://www.cs.cmu.edu/~women/resources/around TheWeb/hostedPapers/Syllabus-Camp.pdf.

Caputi, Jane. "On Psychic Activism: Feminist Mythmaking." *The Feminist Companion to Mythology.* Ed. Carolyne Larrington. London: Pandora Press, 1992. 425–440. Print.

Carter, Raphael. *The Fortunate Fall.* New York: Tor Books, 1996. Print.

Castle, Terry. *The Apparitional Lesbian: Female Homosexuality and Modern Culture.* New York: Columbia University Press, 1993. Print.

Clark, Nigel. "Earthing the Ether: The Alternating Currents of Ecology and Cyberculture." *Cyberfutures.* Ed. Ziauddin Sardar and Jerome R. Ravetz. New York: New York University Press, 1996. 90–110. Print.

_____. "Rear-view Mirrorshades: The Recursive Generation of the Cyberbody." *Cyber-*

space/Cyberbodies/Cyberpunk. Ed. Mike Featherstone and Roger Burrows. Wiltshire: The Cromwell Press, 1995. 113–133.

Cline, Ernest. *Ready Player One*. New York: Crown, 2011. Print.

Csicsery-Ronay Jr., Istvan. "Cyberpunk and Neuromanticism." *Storming the Reality Studio*. Ed. Larry McCaffery. Durham: Duke University Press, 1991. 182–193. Print.

Culpepper, Emily. "The Spiritual, Political Journey of a Feminist Freethinker." *After Patriarchy*. Ed. Paula M. Cooey, et al. New York: Orbis Books, 1991. 146–166. Print.

Dalkey, Kara. "Bouncing Babies." *Not Of Woman Born*. Ed. Constance Ash. New York: Roc, 1999. 190–197. Print.

Davin, Eric Leif. *Partners in Wonder: Women and the Birth of Science Fiction 1926–1965*. Lanham, MD: Lexington Books, 2006. Print.

Deery, June. "The Biopolitics of Cyberspace: Piercy Hacks Gibson." *Future Females: The Next Generation*. Ed. Marleen S. Barr. New York: Rowman & Littlefield, 2000. 87–108. Print.

Delany, Samuel R. "Is Cyberpunk a Good Thing or a Bad Thing?" *Mississippi Review* 16.2 & 3 (1988): 28–35. Print.

_____. "Some *Real* Mothers: ... The *SF Eye* Interview." *Silent Interviews*. Middletown, CT: Wesleyan University Press, 1994. 164–185. Print.

De Lauretis, Teresa. "Fem/Les Scramble." *Cross-Purposes: Lesbians, Feminists, and the Limits of Alliance*. Bloomington: Indiana University Press, 1997. 42–48. Print.

Dery, Mark. *Escape Velocity: Cyberculture at the End of the Century*. New York: Grove Press, 1996. Print.

Dever, Carolyn. "Obstructive Behavior: Dykes in the Mainstream of Feminist Theory." *Cross-Purposes: Lesbians, Feminists, and the Limits of Alliance*. Ed. Dana Heller. Bloomington: Indiana University Press, 1997. 19–41. Print.

Di Filippo, Paul. "Stone Lives." *Mirrorshades: The Cyberpunk Anthology*. Ed. Bruce Sterling. New York: Arbor House, 1986. 178–201. Print.

Doane, Mary Anne. "Technophilia: Technology, Representation, and the Feminine." *Cybersexualities: A Reader on Feminist Theory, Cyborgs, and Cyberspace*. Ed. Jenny Wolmark. Edinburgh: Edinburgh University Press, 1999. 20–33. Print.

Donawerth, Jane. *Frankenstein's Daughters: Women Writing Science Fiction*. Syracuse: Syracuse University Press, 1997. Print.

Easterbrook, Neil. "The Arc of Our Destruction: Reversal and Erasure in Cyberpunk." *Science Fiction Studies* 19.3 (1992): 378–394. Print.

Engler, Steven. "Science Fiction, Religion, and Social Change." *The Influence of Imagination: Essays on Science Fiction and Fantasy as Agents of Social Change*. Ed. Lee Easton and Randy Schroeder. Jefferson, NC: McFarland, 2008. 108–117. Print.

Fat, Ugly or Slutty. 30 June 2012. Web. 30 June 2012. http://fatuglyorslutty.com/.

Firestone, Shulamith. *The Dialectic of Sex*. New York: Bantam, 1971. Print.

Fisher, Mark. "Let Me Tell You About My Mother." *Flatline Constructs: Gothic Materialism and Cybernetic Theory-Fiction*. n.d. Web. 26 May 2006. http://www.cinestatic.com/trans-mat/Fisher/FC3s1.htm.

Forbes, Edith. *Exit to Reality*. Seattle: Seal Press, 1997. Print.

Foster, Thomas. "'The Postproduction of the Human Heart': Desire, Identification, and Virtual Embodiment in Feminist Narratives of Cyberspace." *Reload: Rethinking Women + Cyberculture*. Ed. Mary Flanagan and Austin Booth. Cambridge: MIT Press, 2000. 469–504. Print.

_____. *The Souls of Cyberfolk: Posthumanism as Vernacular Theory*. Minneapolis: University of Minnesota Press, 2005. Print.

Foucault, Michel. *Discipline and Punish: The Birth of the Prison.* New York: Penguin, 1979. Print.

Fouché, Rayvon. "From Black Inventors to One Laptop Per Child: Exploring a Racial Politics of Technology." *Race After the Internet.* Ed. Lisa Nakamura and Peter A. Chow-White. New York: Routledge, 2012. 61–83. Print.

Frankenberry, Nancy. "Feminist Approaches." *Feminist Philosophy of Religion.* Ed. Pamela Sue Anderson and Beverley Clack. New York: Routledge, 2004. 3–27. Print.

Gaard, Greta, and Patrick D. Murphy. "Introduction." *Ecofeminist Literary Criticism: Theory, Interpretation, Pedagogy.* Ed. Greta Gaard and Patrick D. Murphy. Chicago: University of Illinois Press, 1998. 1–14. Print.

Geek Feminism. 29 June 2012. Web. 30 June 2012. http://geekfeminism.wikia.com.

Gibson, William. *Burning Chrome.* New York: Ace Books, 1986. Print.

_____. *Count Zero.* New York: Ace Books, 1987. Print.

_____. *Idoru.* New York: Berkley Press, 1997. Print.

_____. *Mona Lisa Overdrive.* New York: Ace Books, 1988. Print.

_____. *Neuromancer.* New York: Ace Books, 1984. Print.

Goldstein, Dana. "How to Fix the Gender Gap in Technology." *Slate.* 7 June 2012. Web. 16 June 2012. http://www.slate.com/articles/technology/future_tense/2012/06/gender_gap_in_technology_and_silicon_valley_.single.html.

Goonan, Kathleen Ann. *Queen City Jazz.* New York: Tor Books, 1994. Print.

Gordon, Joan. "Yin and Yang Duke It Out." *Storming the Reality Studio.* Ed. Larry McCaffery. Durham: Duke University Press, 1991. 196–202. Print.

Graham, Elaine. "Cyborgs or Goddesses?: Becoming Divine in a Cyberfeminist Age." *Virtual Gender: Technology, Consumption and Identity Matters.* Ed. Alison Adam and Eileen Green. New York: Routledge, 2001. 302–322. Print.

_____. *Representations of the Post/Human: Monsters, Aliens and Others in Popular Culture.* New Brunswick: Rutgers University Press, 2002. Print.

Gubar, Susan. "C.L. Moore and the Conventions of Women's SF." *Science Fiction Studies* 20 (1980): 16–27. Print.

Haberman, Stephanie. "ASUS's Sexist Twitter Gaffe Angers Followers." *Mashable.* 4 June 2012. Web. 29 June 2012. http://mashable.com/2012/06/04/asus-sexist-tweet/.

Haraway, Donna. "A Cyborg Manifesto: Science, Technology and Socialist-Feminism in the Late Twentieth Century." *Simians, Cyborgs and Women: The Reinvention of Nature.* New York: Routledge, 1991. 149–181. Print.

Harding, Sandra. *Whose Science? Whose Knowledge?* Ithaca: Cornell University Press, 1991. Print.

Harper, Mary Catherine. "Incurably Alien Other: A Case for Feminist Cyborg Writers." *Science Fiction Studies* 22.3 (1995): 399–420. Print.

Hawthorne, Susan. *Wild Politics.* North Melbourne: Spinifex Press, 2002. Print.

Hayles, N. Katherine. *How We Became Posthuman: Virtual Bodies in Cybernetics, Literature, and Informatics.* Chicago: University of Chicago Press, 1999. Print.

Heim, Michael. "The Design of Virtual Reality." *Cyberspace/Cyberbodies/Cyberpunk.* Ed. Mike Featherstone and Roger Burrows. Wiltshire: The Cromwell Press, 1995. 65–77. Print.

Heller, Chaia. "For the Love of Nature: Ecology and the Cult of the Romantic." *Ecofeminism: Women, Animals, Nature.* Ed. Greta Gaard. Philadelphia: Temple University Press, 1993. 219–242. Print.

Heller, Dana. "Purposes: An Introduction." *Cross-Purposes: Lesbians, Feminists, and the Limits of Alliance.* Bloomington: Indiana University Press, 1997. 1–18. Print.

Hemmings, Mary. "The Changing Role of Women in Science Fiction: *Weird Tales,* 1925–1940." *The Influence of Imagination: Essays on Science Fiction and Fantasy as Agents of Social Change.* Ed. Lee Easton and Randy Schroeder. Jefferson, NC: McFarland, 2008. 83–91. Print.

Hennessy, Rosemary. *Materialist Feminism and the Politics of Discourse.* New York: Routledge, 1993. Print.

Hoffman, Nina Kiriki. "One Day At Central Convenience Mall." *Not of Woman Born.* Ed. Constance Ash. New York: Roc, 1999. 80–95. Print.

Holland, Samantha. "Descartes Goes to Hollywood: Mind, Body and Gender in Contemporary Cyborg Cinema." *Cyberspace/Cyberbodies/Cyberpunk.* Ed. Mike Featherstone and Roger Burrows. Wiltshire: The Cromwell Press, 1995. 157–174. Print.

Hollinger, Veronica. "Cybernetic Deconstructions." *Storming the Reality Studio.* Ed. Larry McCaffery. Durham: Duke University Press, 1991. 203–218. Print.

_____. "(Re)reading Queerly: Science Fiction, Feminism, and the Defamiliarization of Gender." *Reload: Rethinking Women + Cyberculture.* Ed. Mary Flanagan and Austin Booth. Cambridge: MIT Press, 2002. 301–320. Print.

Hopkins, Patrick D. "Bad Copies: How Popular Media Represent Cloning as an Ethical Problem." *The Hastings Center Report* 28.2 (1998): 6–13. Print.

Hopkinson, Nalo. *Midnight Robber.* New York: Grand Central, 2000. Print.

Howell, Linda. "'Wartime Inventions with Peaceful Intentions': Television and the Media Cyborg in C.L. Moore's *No Woman Born.*" *The Influence of Imagination: Essays on Science Fiction and Fantasy as Agents of Social Change.* Ed. Lee Easton and Randy Schroeder. Jefferson, NC: McFarland, 2008. 139–159.

Huntington, John. "Newness, *Neuromancer,* and the End of Narrative." *Fiction 2000: Cyberpunk and the Future of Narrative.* Ed. George Slusser and Tom Shippey. Athens: University of Georgia Press, 1992. 133–141. Print.

"Interstitial Arts Foundation: Mission Statement." *Interstitial Arts: Artists Without Borders.* 2003. Web. 27 April 2007. http://www.interstitialarts.org/mission.html.

Jameson, Fredric. "Fear and Loathing in Globalization." *New Left Review 23* (2003): 105–114. Print.

_____. "Postmodernism, or, The Cultural Logic of Late Capitalism." *New Left Review* 146 (1984): 53–94. Print.

Jardin, Xeni. "NYT—MEN invented the Internet." *BoingBoing.* 3 June 2012. Web. 16 June 2012. http://boingboing.net/2012/06/03/nyt-men-invented-the-inter.html.

Jenkins, Henry. "Interactive Audiences? The 'Collective Intelligence' of Media Fans." *The New Media Book.* Ed. Dan Harries. London: British Film Institute, 2002. Web. 31 March 2007. http://web.mit.edu/cms/People/henry3/collective%20intelligence.html.

Jones, Gwyneth. *Escape Plans.* New York: Routledge, 1986. Print.

Kakoudaki, Despina. "Pinup and Cyborg: Exaggerated Gender and Artificial Intelligence." *Future Females: The Next Generation.* Ed. Marleen S. Barr. New York: Rowman & Littlefield, 2000. 165–195. Print.

Kaplan, Morris B. "Intimacy and Equality: The Question of Lesbian and Gay Marriage." *Playing with Fire: Queer Politics, Queer Theories.* Ed. Shane Phelan. New York: Routledge, 1997. 201–230. Print.

Kelly, James Patrick. "Solstice." *Mirrorshades: The Cyberpunk Anthology.* Ed. Bruce Sterling. New York: Arbor House, 1986. 66–104. Print.

_____, and John Kessel. "Introduction: Hacking Cyberpunk." *Rewired: The Post-Cyberpunk Anthology.* Ed. James Patrick Kelly and John Kessel. San Francisco: Tachyon, 2007. vii–xvi. Print.

King, Ursula. *Women and Spirituality: Voices of Protest and Promise*. University Park: Pennsylvania State University Press, 1993. Print.

Knapp, Bettina L. *Women, Myth, and the Feminine Principle*. Albany: State University of New York Press, 1998. Print.

Kornfeld, Susan. *Suppression and Transformation of the Mother in Contemporary Women's Science Fiction*. December 2002. Web. 26 May 2006. http://www.perspective.com/susan/WSFSuppressionofMother.html..

Laidlaw, Marc. "400 Boys." *Mirrorshades: The Cyberpunk Anthology*. Ed. Bruce Sterling. New York: Arbor House, 1986. 50–65. Print.

Landon, Brooks. "Not What It Used To Be: The Overloading of Memory in Digital Narrative." *Fiction 2000: Cyberpunk and the Future of Narrative*. Ed. George Slusser and Tom Shippey. Athens: University of Georgia Press, 1992. 153–167. Print.

_____. *Science Fiction After 1900: From the Steam Man to the Stars*. New York: Routledge, 2002. Print.

Larbalestier, Justine. *The Battle of the Sexes in Science Fiction*. Middleton, CT: Wesleyan University Press, 2002. Print.

Leary, Timothy. "The Cyberpunk: The Individual as Reality Pilot." *Storming the Reality Studio*. Ed. Larry McCaffery. Durham: Duke University Press, 1991. 245–258. Print.

Lefanu, Sarah. *In the Chinks of the World Machine: Feminism and Science Fiction*. London: The Women's Press, 1988. Print.

Lehring, Gary. "Essentialism and the Political Articulation of Identity." *Playing with Fire: Queer Politics, Queer Theories*. New York: Routledge, 1997. 173–200. Print.

Leihren-Young, Mark. "Is William Gibson's 'Neuromancer' the Future of Movies?" *The Tyee*. 6 January 2012. Web. 16 June 2012. http://thetyee.ca/ArtsAndCulture/2012/01/06/Neuromancer-Movie/.

Little, Judith A. *Feminist Philosophy and Science Fiction*. Ed. Judith A. Little. New York: Prometheus Books, 2007. Print.

Longenecker, Marlene. "Women, Ecology, and the Environment: An Introduction." *NWSA Journal* 9 (1997): 1–17. Print.

Lorde, Audre. *Sister Outsider*. Freedom, CA: The Crossing Press, 1984. Print.

Luckhurst, Roger. *Science Fiction*. Cambridge: Polity Press, 2005. Print.

Lupton, Deborah. "The Embodied Computer/User." *Cyberspace/Cyberbodies/Cyberpunk*. Ed. Mike Featherstone and Roger Burrows. Wiltshire: The Cromwell Press, 1995. 97–112. Print.

MacAskill, Ewen, and Josh Halliday. "WikiLeaks shutdown calls spark censorship row." *The Guardian*. 3 Dec. 2010. Web. 24 June 2012. http://www.guardian.co.uk/media/2010/dec/03/wikileaks-us-censorship-row.

Madrigal, Alexis. "Sorry, Young Man, You're Not the Most Important Demographic in Tech." *The Atlantic*. 8 June 2012. Web. 16 June 2012. http://www.theatlantic.com/technology/archive/2012/06/sorry-young-white-guy-youre-not-the-most-important-demographic-in-tech/258087/.

Mansbridge, Jane. "Feminism and Democratic Community." *Feminism and Community*. Ed. Penny A. Weiss and Marilyn Friedman. Philadelphia: Temple University Press, 1995. 341–366. Print.

Mason, Lisa. *Arachne*. New York: Avon Books, 1990. Print.

_____. *Cyberweb*. New York: Avon Books, 1995. Print.

May, Timothy. "True Nyms and Crypto Anarchy." *True Names and the Opening of the Cyberspace Frontier*. Ed. James Frenkel. New York: Tor Books, 2001. 33–86. Print.

Works Cited

Mayer, Ruth. *Artificial Africas: Colonial Images in the Times of Globalization.* Hanover, NH: University Press of New England, 2002. Print.

McCaffery, Larry. "Introduction: The Desert of the Real." *Storming the Reality Studio.* Ed. Larry McCaffery. Durham & London: Duke University Press, 1991. 1–16. Print.

_____. "An Interview with William Gibson." *Storming the Reality Studio.* Ed. Larry McCaffery. Durham & London: Duke University Press, 1991. 263–285. Print.

McCallum, E.L. "Mapping the Real in Cyberfiction." *Poetics Today* 21.2 (2000): 349–377. Print.

McCarron, Kevin. "Corpses, Animals, Machines and Mannequins: The Body and Cyberpunk." *Cyberspace/Cyberbodies/Cyberpunk.* Ed. Mike Featherstone and Roger Burrows. Wiltshire: The Cromwell Press, 1995. 261–273. Print.

McGuirk, Carol. "The 'New' Romancers: Science Fiction Innovation from Gernsback to Gibson." *Fiction 2000: Cyberpunk and the Future of Narrative.* Ed. George Slusser and Tom Shippey. Athens: University of Georgia Press, 1992. 109–129. Print.

McHugh, Maureen. *China Mountain Zhang.* New York: Tor Books, 1992. Print.

Merrick, Helen. *The Secret Feminist Cabal: A Cultural History of Science Fiction Feminisms.* Seattle: Aqueduct Press, 2009. Print.

Messerschmidt, James W. *Capitalism, Patriarchy, and Crime.* Lanham, MD: Rowman & Littlefield, 1986. Print.

Milan, Victor. *Cybernetic Samurai.* New York: Arbor House, 1985. Print.

Misha. *Red Spider, White Web.* Scotforth: Morrigan, 1990. Print.

Mittelman, James H., and Christine B. N. Chin. "Conceptualizing resistance to globalization." *The Global Resistance Reader.* Ed. Louise Amoore. New York: Routledge, 2005. 17–27. Print.

Mixon, Laura J. *Proxies.* New York: Tor Books, 1998. Print.

Modleski, Tania. *Feminism Without Women.* New York: Routledge, 1991. Print.

Moody, Nickianne. "Untapped Potential: The Representation of Disability/Special Ability in the Cyberpunk Workforce." *Convergence* 3.3 (1997): 90–105. Print.

Moore, C.L. "No Woman Born." *Reload: Rethinking Women + Cyberculture.* Ed. Mary Flanagan and Austin Booth. Cambridge: MIT Press, 2002. 261–300. Print.

Morehouse, Lyda. *Archangel Protocol.* New York: Penguin, 2001. Print.

_____. *Messiah Node.* New York: Penguin, 2003. Print.

_____. *Resurrection Code.* Des Moines: Mad Norwegian Press, 2011. Print.

Morley, David, and Kevin Robins. *Spaces of Identity: Global Media, Electronic Landscapes and Cultural Boundaries.* London: Routledge, 1995. Print.

Morton, Donald. "Birth of the Cyberqueer." *Cybersexualities: A Reader on Feminist Theory, Cyborgs, and Cyberspace.* Ed. Jenny Wolmark. Edinburgh: Edinburgh University Press, 1999. 295–313. Print.

Moylan, Tom. "Global Economy, Local Texts: Utopian/Dystopian Tension in William Gibson's Cyberpunk Trilogy." *Beyond Cyberpunk: New Critical Perspectives.* Ed. Graham J. Murphy and Sherryl Vint. New York: Routledge, 2010. 81–94. Print.

Murphy, Graham J. "Angel(LINK) of Harlem: Techno-Spirituality in the Cyberpunk Tradition." *Beyond Cyberpunk: New Critical Perspectives.* Ed. Graham J. Murphy and Sherryl Vint. New York: Routledge, 2010. 211–227. Print.

_____, and Sherryl Vint. "Introduction: The Sea Change(s) of Cyberpunk." *Beyond Cyberpunk: New Critical Perspectives.* Ed. Graham J. Murphy and Sherryl Vint. New York: Routledge, 2010. xi–xviii. Print.

Nixon, Nicola. "Cyberpunk: Preparing the Ground for Revolution or Keeping the Boys Satisfied?" *Science Fiction Studies* 19 (1992): 219–235. Print.

O'Neal, Sean. "Paramount will try adapting *Snow Crash* for today's cyberpunks." *AV Club.* 15 June 2012. Web. 16 June 2012. http://www.avclub.com/articles/paramount-will-try-adapting-snow-crash-for-todays,81392/.

Papke, Mary E. "A Space of Her Own: Pamela Zoline's 'The Heat Death of the Universe.'" *Daughters of Earth: Feminist Science Fiction in the Twentieth Century.* Ed. Justine Larbalestier. Middletown, CT: Wesleyan University Press, 2006. 144–159. Print.

Pavic, Miran. "Creator of First Personal Computer Dies." *Wired.* 2 April 2010. Web. 16 June 2012. http://www.wired.com/gadgetlab/2010/04/ed-roberts-altair/.

Pearson, Wendy. "Alien Cryptographies: The View from Queer." *Science Fiction Studies* 26.1 (1999): 1–22. Print.

Peppers, Cathy. "'I've Got You Under My Skin': Cyber(sexed) Bodies in Cyberpunk Fictions." *Bodily Discourses: Genders, Representations, Technologies.* Ed. Deborah S. Wilson and Christine Moneera Laennea. Albany: State University of New York Press, 1997. 163–185. Print.

Pesce, Mark. "Magic Mirror: The Novel as a Software Development Platform." *MIT Communications Forum.* n.d. Web. 31 March 2007. http://web.mit.edu/comm-forum/papers/pesce.html.

_____. *Ritual and the Virtual.* July 1997. Web. 12 January 2006. http://hyperreal.org/~mpesce/caiia.html.

Peterson, V. Spike, and Anne Sisson Runyan. "The Politics of Resistance: Women as Nonstate, Antistate, and Transstate Actors." *The Global Resistance Reader.* Ed. Louise Amoore. New York: Routledge, 2005. 226–243. Print.

Piercy, Marge. *He, She and It.* New York: Ballantine, 1991. Print.

_____. *Woman on the Edge of Time.* New York: Random House, 1976. Print.

Plant, Sadie. "The Future Looms: Weaving Women and Cybernetics." *Cyberspace/Cyberbodies/Cyberpunk.* Ed. Mike Featherstone and Roger Burrows. Wiltshire: The Cromwell Press, 1995. 45–64. Print.

Purkiss, Diane. "Women's Rewriting of Myth." *The Feminist Companion to Mythology.* Ed. Carolyne Larrington. London: Pandora Press, 1992. 441–458. Print.

Reddington, Helen. "Voxpop Puella: A Work in Progress." *Digital Desires: Language, Identity and New Technologies.* Ed. Cutting Edge: The Women's Research Group. New York: I.B. Taurus, 2000. 209–218. Print.

Robedo, Marie Mulvey. "The Male Scientist, Man-Midwife, and Female Monster: Appropriation and Transmutation in *Frankenstein.*" *A Question of Identity: Women, Science and Literature.* Ed. Marina Benjamin. Chapel Hill: Rutgers University Press, 1993. 59–73. Print.

Robins, Kevin. "Cyberspace and the World We Live In." *Cyberspace/Cyberbodies/Cyberpunk.* Ed. Mike Featherstone and Roger Burrows. Wiltshire: The Cromwell Press, 1995. 135–155. Print.

Rodriguez, Francisco Collado. "Fear of the Flesh, Fear of the Borg: Narratives of Bodily Transgression in Contemporary U.S. Culture." *Beyond Borders: Re-defining Generic and Ontological Boundaries.* Ed. Ramón Plo-Alastrué and María Jesús Martínez-Alfaro. Heidelberg: Universitatsverkag C. Winter, 2002. 67–80. Print.

Rosenblum, Mary. *Chimera.* Del Rey, 1993. Print.

_____. "Search Engine." *Rewired: The Post-Cyberpunk Anthology.* Ed. James Patrick Kelly and John Kessel. San Francisco: Tachyon, 2007. 369–388. Print.

Ross, Andrew. *Strange Weather.* New York: Verso, 1991. Print.

Rosser, Sue V. "Using the Lenses of Feminist Theories to Focus on Women and Technology." *Women, Gender, and Technology.* Ed. Mary Frank Fox, Deborah G. Johnson, and Sue V. Rosser. Urbana: University of Illinois, 2006: 13–46. Print.

Rowland, Robyn. *Living Laboratories: Women and Reproductive Technologies.* Bloomington: Indiana University Press, 1992. Print.

Rucker, Rudy. *Software.* New York: EOS, 1982. Print.

Russ, Joanna. *To Write Like a Woman: Essays in Feminism and Science Fiction.* Bloomington: Indiana University Press, 1995. Print.

Satter, Raphael G., and Jill Lawless. "MasterCard DOWN: MasterCard.com, Swiss Bank, Lawyer's Site Hacked by WikiLeaks Supporters With DDOS Attack." *Huffington Post.* 8 Dec. 2010. Web. 24 June 2012. http://www.huffingtonpost.com/2010/12/08/mastercard-down-hacked-wikileaks-ddos_n_793625.html.

Scott, Anne, Lesley Semmers, and Lynette Willoughy. "Women and the Internet: The Natural History of a Research Project." *Virtual Gender: Technology, Consumption and Identity.* Ed. Eileen Green and Alison Adam. New York: Routledge, 2001. 3–27. Print.

Scott, Melissa. *Trouble and Her Friends.* New York: Tor Books, 1994. Print.

Shiner, Lewis. "Inside the Movement: Past, Present and Future." *Fiction 2000: Cyberpunk and the Future of Narrative.* Ed. George Slusser and Tom Shippey. Athens: University of Georgia Press, 1992. 17–25. Print.

Shirley, John. "Freezone." *Mirrorshades: The Cyberpunk Anthology.* Ed. Bruce Sterling. New York: Arbor House, 1986. 139–178. Print.

Smith, Judy, and Ellen Balka. "Chatting on a Feminist Computer Network." *Technology and Women's Voices: Keeping in Touch.* Ed. Cheris Kramarae. London: Routledge & Kegan Paul, 1988. 82–97. Print.

Sofia, Zoë. "Virtual Corporeality: A Feminist View." *Cybersexualities: A Reader on Feminist Theory, Cyborgs, and Cyberspace.* Ed. Jenny Wolmark. Edinburgh: Edinburgh University Press, 1999. 55–68. Print.

Spielmann, Yvonne. "Elastic Cinema: Technological Imagery in Contemporary Science Fiction Films." *Convergence* 9.3 (2003): 56–73. Print.

Springer, Claudia. "Sex, Memories, Angry Women." *Flame Wars: The Discourse of Cyberculture.* Ed. Mark Dery. Durham: Duke University Press, 1994. 157–177. Print.

Sponsler, Claire. "The Geopolitics of Urban Decay and Cybernetic Play." *Science Fiction Studies* 20 (1993): 251–265. Print.

Stanworth, Michelle. "Reproductive Technologies and the Deconstruction of Motherhood." *Reproductive Technologies: Gender, Motherhood and Medicine.* Ed. Michelle Stanworth. Minneapolis: University of Minnesota Press, 1988. 10–35. Print.

Stephenson, Neal. *Snow Crash.* New York: Bantam Spectra, 1992. Print.

Sterling, Bruce. *Heavy Weather.* New York: Bantam, 1994. Print.

_____. *Islands in the Net.* New York: Arbor House, 1988. Print.

_____. "Preface from *Mirrorshades.*" *Storming the Reality Studio.* Ed. Larry McCaffery. Durham: Duke University Press, 1991. 343–348. Print.

Stolba, Christine. "Overcoming Motherhood: Pushing the Limits of Reproductive Choice." *Policy Review* 116 (2002): 31–41. Print.

Stone, Allucquère Rosanne. "Will the Real Body Please Stand Up? Boundary Stories About Virtual Cultures." *The Cybercultures Reader.* Ed. David Bell and Barbara M. Kennedy. London & New York: Routledge, 2000. 504–528. Print.

Strain, Ellen. "Virtual VR." *Convergence* 5.2 (1999): 10–15. Print.

Strathern, Marilyn. "Less Nature, More Technology." *Feminisms: An Oxford Reader.* Oxford: Oxford University Press, 1997. 494–497. Print.

Streitfeld, David. "Lawsuit Shakes Foundation of a Man's World of Tech." *The New York Times.* 2 June 2012. Web. 16 June 2012. http://www.nytimes.com/2012/06/03/technology/lawsuit-against-kleiner-perkins-is-shaking-silicon-valley.html.

Swaine, Jon. "WikiLeaks 'revenge attacks' target MasterCard and Visa." *The Telegraph*. 8 Dec. 2010. Web. 24 June 2012. http://www.telegraph.co.uk/news/worldnews/wiki leaks/8190421/WikiLeaks-revenge-attacks-target-Mastercard-and-Visa.html.

Thomson, Amy. *Virtual Girl*. Ace Books, 1993. Print.

Tiptree Jr., James. "The Girl Who Was Plugged In." *Reload: Rethinking Women + Cyberculture*. Ed. Mary Flanagan and Austin Booth. Cambridge: MIT Press, 2002. 546–577. Print.

Vinge, Verner. "True Names." *True Names and the Opening of the Cyberspace Frontier*. Ed. James Frenkel. New York: Tor Books, 2001. 239–330. Print.

Vint, Sherryl. "Afterword: The World Gibson Made." *Beyond Cyberpunk: New Critical Perspectives*. Ed. Graham J. Murphy and Sherryl Vint. New York: Routledge, 2010. 228–233. Print.

_____. *Bodies of Tomorrow: Technology, Subjectivity, Science Fiction*. Toronto: University of Toronto Press, 2007. Print.

_____. "The Mainstream Finds Its Own Uses For Things: Cyberpunk and Commodification." *Beyond Cyberpunk: New Critical Perspectives*. Ed. Graham J. Murphy and Sherryl Vint. New York: Routledge, 2010. 95–115. Print.

Walker, Sage. *Whiteout*. New York: Tor Books, 1996. Print.

Watercutter, Angela. "Feminist Take on Games Draws Crude Ridicule, Massive Support." *Underwire: The Beat Goes On*. 14 June 2012. Web. 16 June 2012. http://www.wired.com/underwire/2012/06/anita-sarkeesian-feminist-games.

Weed, Elizabeth. "Introduction." *Feminism Meets Queer Theory*. Ed. Elizabeth Weed and Naomi Schor. Providence: Brown University Press, 1997. vii–xiii. Print.

Weiss, Penny A. "Feminism and Communitarianism: Comparing Critiques of Liberalism." *Feminism and Community*. Ed. Penny A. Weiss and Marilyn Friedman. Philadelphia: Temple University Press, 1995. 161–186. Print.

_____. "Feminist Reflections on Community." *Feminism and Community*. Ed. Penny A. Weiss and Marilyn Friedman. Philadelphia: Temple University Press, 1995. 3–20. Print.

Westfahl, Gary. "The Gernsback Continuum: William Gibson in the Context of Science Fiction." *Fiction 2000: Cyberpunk and the Future of Narrative*. Ed. George Slusser and Tom Shippey. Athens: University of Georgia Press, 1992. 88–108. Print.

Whalen, Terence. "The Future of a Commodity: Notes Toward a Critique of Cyberpunk and the Information Age." *Science Fiction Studies* 19 (1992): 75–88. Print.

Williams, Tad. *Otherland: City of Golden Shadow*. London: Orbit, 1998. Print.

Wilson, Robert Rawdon. "Cyber(body)parts: Prosthetic Consciousness." *Cyberspace/Cyberbodies/Cyberpunk*. Ed. Mike Featherstone and Roger Burrows. Wiltshire: The Cromwell Press, 1995. 239–259. Print.

Wolmark, Jenny. *Aliens and Others: Science Fiction, Feminism, and Postmodernism*. Iowa City: University of Iowa Press, 1994. Print.

Wood, Molly. "Why we need to keep talking about women in tech." *CNet News*. 11 May 2012. Web. 30 June 2012. http://news.cnet.com/8301-31322_3-57431869-256/why-we-need-to-keep-talking-about-women-in-tech/.

Woodfield, Ruth. *Women, Work and Computing*. Cambridge: Cambridge University Press, 2000. Print.

Yaszek, Lisa. *Galactic Suburbia: Recovering Women's Science Fiction*. Columbus: Ohio State University Press, 2008. Print.

Yates, Ronald E. "High-flying PC Sellers Veering Toward Wall." *Chicago Tribune*. 19 February 1995. Web. 16 June 2012. http://articles.chicagotribune.com/1995-02-19/business/9502190131_1_pc-industry-marcillac-pc-sales.

Young, Paul. "The Negative Reinvention of Cinema: Late Hollywood in the Early Digital Age." *Convergence* 5. 2 (1999): 24–50. Print.

Young, Stacey. "Dichotomies and Displacement: Bisexuality in Queer Theories and Politics. *Playing With Fire: Queer Politics, Queer Theories.* Ed. Shane Phelan. New York: Routledge, 1997. 51–74. Print.

ZDNet Research. "US Internet Usage 1995–2006." 30 May 2006. Web. 16 June 2012. http://www.zdnet.com/blog/itfacts/us-Internet-usage-1995–2006/10998.

Zoline, Pamela. "The Heat Death of the Universe." *New Worlds.* 1967. Web. 14 April 2012. http://www.crab.rutgers.edu/-barbares/Recent%20American%20Writing/PDFs/Zoline,%20Heat%20Death.pdf.

Index